SHEPHERDING
The Elder Notebook of
Glen Ellyn Bible Church

Edited by,
Dr. Kelly Brady

EQUIP Publishing

SHEPHERDING
The Elder Notebook of Glen Ellyn Bible Church
Copyright @ 2025 by Dr. Kelly Brady, editor

Twelfth Edition. Printed in the U.S.A. Published by EQUIP

All rights reserved. No part of this publication may be reproduced, stored, or transmitted in any form by any means, electronic, mechanical, photocopy, recording, or otherwise, without prior written permission from the author/editor, except as provided by copyright law. However, once written permission is received you are free to reproduce and distribute any portion of this notebook for ministry purposes, provided you do not change the content or charge others for receipt of the content.

All Scripture quotations, unless otherwise indicated, are taken from the HOLY BIBLE, NEW INTERNATIONAL VERSION®. Copyright © 1973, 1978, 1984 by International Bible Society. Used by permission of Zondervan. Rights reserved.

Scripture quotations marked NASB are taken from the New American Standard Bible®, Copyright © 1960, 1962, 1963, 1968, 1971, 1972, 1973, 1975, 1977, 1995 by the Lockman Foundation. Used by permission. (www.Lockman.org)

Scripture quotations marked ESV are from the Holy Bible, English Standard Version, copyright © 2001 by Crossway Bibles, a publishing ministry of Good New Publishers. Used by permission. All rights reserved.

LEGAL DISCLAIMER This book is offered solely as an example of what one congregation has assembled in an effort to address their ongoing needs. We are not offering any legal, accounting, tax, labor, counseling, or any other type of professional advice. We assume no liabilities of any kind with respect to the effectiveness or sufficiency of any material contained in this book. We shall not be held liable or responsible to any person or entity with respect to any loss or incidental or consequential damages caused, or alleged, directly or indirectly, by the material herein.

ISBN 13: 978-0-578-44064-4   ISBN 10: 0-578-44064-4

Also by Dr. Kelly Brady

FOLLOWING JESUS
Defining Discipleship for the 21st Century

WAIT...WHAT?
Biblical Teachings Worth Repeating

DRIVE THRU THEOLOGY
A Guide To The Bible's Teaching
For Those On The Go

RESTORE
Experiencing the Power of a Healing Fellowship

Acknowledgments & Thanks

This notebook is the product of a community effort, as both the Elders and the staff of Glen Ellyn Bible Church have contributed countless hours in research, prayer, and study to provide this record of our theology and philosophy of ministry. It is with the deepest thanks and greatest joy that I want to acknowledge their efforts. It is a tremendous pleasure to serve with each of you.

It is our desire is to strengthen not only the people of GEBC by providing competent and godly leadership, but to share what we've learned with other churches in order to advance God's Kingdom around the world. Toward that end, you are free to reproduce any portion of this notebook for educational purposes, provided you do not change the content or charge others for the content you are distributing.

Finally, in an effort to make this notebook available to as many as possible, we are committed to charging only what is necessary to cover our printing costs, and any proceeds from the sale of this notebook will go to the Benevolence Fund of Glen Ellyn Bible Church, which is dedicated to meeting the needs of the physically and spiritually impoverished.

In Christ,
Dr. Kelly Brady,
Senior Pastor

To the Shepherds
of
Glen Ellyn Bible Church

May we hear the words,
"Well, done!"
Matthew 25:21

Introduction

"Here is a trustworthy saying: If anyone sets his heart on being an overseer, he desires a noble task. 1 Timothy 3:1 (NIV)

  In the verse above, Paul reminds Timothy that serving as an Elder is a noble task, and that having the desire to serve is a good thing. The office of Elder is an important position, and one in which no one should serve under compulsion. Delight, rather than duty, should fuel our service. In fact, having a desire to serve as an Elder is one of the first qualifications for service and an indication that God is calling you to this service.

  Paul appointed Elders in each church he established because they are vital to the effective work of God's people (Acts 14:23), and for that reason this opportunity for service should not be taken lightly. To strengthen the office of Elder at GEBC and equip the men who have a desire for service, we have put together this book. While serving as an Elder, much of the information you will need over the next few years can be found in these pages, and you are encouraged to familiarize yourself with the contents of this book as quickly as possible. It will take some time to process all this information, so don't hesitate to ask if you have questions along the way.

  Sincerely,
  Dr. Kelly Brady
  Senior Pastor

TABLE OF CONTENTS

The Mechanics of Elder Leadership	**19**
Elder Qualifications and Responsibilities	21
Elder Job Description	23
Elder Chairman's Job Description	24
Senior Pastor's Job Description	25
Mechanics of Leadership	28
The Annual Calendar	29
Onboarding for New Elders	30
Annotated Bibliography	44
Membership Process	46
The Membership Class	47
Meeting with Membership Applicants	49
Elder Nomination Timeline	51
Elder Nomination Process	54
Elder Nomination Packet	56
Elder Application Form	62
Elder Service History	68
The Wisdom of Fellow Elders	**71**
Must Be Able To Teach	73
Sheep-like Tendencies, by Kelly Brady	74
Top Ten Charges, by Mark Tucker	76
The Effective Elder, by Scott Brennecke	78
The Call to Equip, Jim Rathbun	80
Servant Leadership, by Mark Macaluso	82
Counting Sheep, by Sue Macaluso	84

Loving One Another, by Bob Neyland	86
Sola Scriptura, by Gary Larson	89
A Privilege to Serve, by Jim Craig	92
My Hope, His Glory, by Joe Schaubroeck	94
Of Sheep and Coins, by Glen Eggert	97
Confession and Compassion, by Alex Dean	99
Inadequacy and Sufficiency, by Bob Thomas	101
The Battle, by Glen Eggert	103
Reflections on Planting, by Glenn Williams	106
Jesus Will Build His Church, by Steve Bult	108
Renewing Presence, by Pam Bult	110
EQ/IQ Balance, by Jeremy Boynton	112
Through, by Bob Neyland	114
Listening and Speaking, by Gary Larson	117
Grace, by Bob Thomas	119
Justice and Unity, by Mark Macaluso	122
Years of Instruction, by Phil Koch	125
Iron Sharpening Iron, by Tim March	127
Abide, by Chuck Martin	130
The Good Shepherd, by Lynnaea Martin	133
After 40 Years at GEBC, by Glen Eggert	135
Be Ignited, by Dan Maas	139
Servant Leadership, by Dave Wiegman	143
For Such a Time as This, by Brenda Dryfhout	146
Leadership Lesson in Loss, by Ken Dryfhout	148
Endure, by Robert Steele	152

The Ministry of Shepherding   **155**
Shepherding is Caregiving   157

Direct and Formal Caregiving	158
Indirect and Formal Caregiving	160
Direct and Informal Caregiving	162
Indirect and Informal Caregiving	164

The Ministry of Prayer	**167**
Elder Led Prayer During Worship	169
Scriptural Basis for Prayer	170
Laying on of Hands	172
Anointing with Oil	174
Intercession	175
Prayer and Fasting FAQ's	177
Prayers of the New Testament Church	184
The Prayer of a Righteous Man	195
Prayer in Jesus' Name	198
Persevering in Prayer	201
Praying in the Spirit	204
Unanswered Prayer	208
Prayer in Tongues	211
Prayer for Healing	214

The Ministry of the Word	**217**
Giving Attention to the Word	218
Position on Racial Equality, Justice and Unity	220
Position on Miraculous Gifts	230
Summary: "Are Miraculous Gifts for Today."	236
Summary: "Four Views on Hell."	239
D.A. Carson on Hell	252

Francis Chan on Hell	253
Sam Storms on Hell	257
Tim Keller on Hell	259
Position on Women in Leadership	261
Position on Church Discipline	278
Position on Hermeneutics	282
R.C. Sproul on Hermeneutics	287
Summary of The Chicago Statement	291
Position on Marriage, Divorce, & Remarriage	297
Position on Fornication and/or Cohabitation	304
Position on Marriage, Gender, and Sexuality	306
Position on Stewardship	308
Encouraging Excellence in Giving	313
Position of Music and Worship	315
Explanation of GEBC's Statement of Faith	317

History and Philosophy of Ministry	**331**
History at GEBC and BBC	332
Multi-Church Ministry Vision	334
History of the Bible Church Movement	336
The Disciplemaking Target of GEBC	338
The Disciplemaking Message	339
The Disciplemaking Methods (4 Activities)	341
Proclaiming the Gospel	342
Restoring the Broken	343
Equipping the Believer	344
Sending Out Disciples	345
The Disciplemaking Mission (8 Attributes)	346
Receive Salvation by Grace	348

Worship in Life Continually	350
Depend on Jesus' Power Fully	352
Connect in Fellowship Deeply	354
Obey Jesus Teaching Wholly	356
Serve with Jesus Passionately	358
Love Others Selflessly	360
Pursue the Lost Intentionally	362
The Disciplemaking Means (10 Actions)	364

The Constitution of GEBC   **365**

THE MECHANICS OF ELDER LEADERSHIP

Elder Qualifications and Responsibilities

There are three different words used in the New Testament to describe the role of Elder, each refers to the same office. The three words are:

> **Elder (presbuteros)** – meaning "old" (1 Timothy 5:1,17), while no specific age is given, this term implies maturity and experience.
>
> **Overseer (episkopos)** – designating those in charge of management. This term emphasizes the exercise of authority (1 Peter 5:2).
>
> **Pastor (poimen)** – meaning "shepherd," this applies to the one who tends, feeds, and guides God's people (Ephesians 4:11, 1 Peter 5:2).

Peter uses all three terms in just a couple of verses.

> "I exhort the Elders (presbutoros)...to shepherd (poimen) the flock of God...exercising oversight (episkopos)..."
> 1 Peter 5:1-2 (NASB)

Scripture details the activities by which these roles are met and they are:

- Equipping, training and ordaining (Acts 14:23, 1 Timothy 4:4, 5:22, Titus 1:5).

- Modeling Christlikeness (1 Peter 5:3).
- Watching over God's people (Acts 20:28, 1 Thessalonians 5:12;1 Peter 5:1-2).
- Teaching Scripture and opposing false doctrine (Acts 20:31, 1 Timothy 5:17, Titus 1:9).
- Praying with/for sick (Acts 6:4, James 5:14).
- Correcting, rebuking and encouraging (2 Timothy 4:2, Titus 1:9, 13, Hebrews 13:17).

The Biblical qualifications of an Elder are:

- Possessing the "desire" to lead and living above reproach (1 Timothy 3:1-2, Titus 1:7-8).
- Not a new convert, demonstrating self-control and integrity, with a good reputation (1 Timothy 3:2,7; Titus 1:7-8).
- Being the husband of one wife and leading his home well, with children who believe and live disciplined lives (1 Timothy 3:1-6; Titus 1:6).
- Prudent, wise, warm, hospitable and submitted to God/others (1 Timothy 3:1-3).
- Free from addiction and not motivated by selfish gain (1 Timothy 3:3, Titus 1:7).
- Able to teach, encouraging the application of Scripture to life (1 Timothy 3:2, Titus 1:9).
- Not intimidating, harsh, or impatient, but gentle, kind and fair (Titus 1:7, 1 Peter 5:2-3).
- Not contentious, picking fights or quarrelling with others (1 Timothy 3:3).

Elder Job Description

A plurality of shepherds working together to provide oversight was God's designed governance for the local church (Acts 14:23). Each individual Elder serves a vital role within a larger team. Meeting on average twice monthly, Elders provide oversight in three areas primarily: discipline, doctrine, and direction.

Providing Disciplinary oversight:
- Pray for the church's disciple-making efforts.
- Equip, teach/preach, model Christlikeness.
- Interview new member applicants.
- Participate in Elder nomination process.

Guarding the Church's Doctrine:
- Read and discuss assigned theological topics.
- Use Scripture to correct, rebuke, and encourage.
- Review the teachers and teaching offered to the church family giving feedback as needed.

Setting the Church's Ministry Direction:
- Attend all Elder and congregational meetings.
- Share in cultivation and casting church vision.
- Review proposed budget annually.
- Monitor monthly cash flow.
- Review and approve staff benefit changes and unbudgeted expenditures.
- Participate in senior pastor's annual review.

Elder Chairman's Job Description

Within the Elder board, the chairman's role is unique. Although the chairman is equal with all other board members, he is charged with working most closely with the senior pastor to set the board and congregational meeting agendas, as well as lead the board and the congregational meetings.

In addition to the responsibilities born by all Elders, the chairman is to:

- Shepherd fellow board members.
- Set board and congregational meeting agendas
- Lead board and congregational meetings.
- Lead the Elder nomination process.
- Lead the annual review for the senior pastor.
- Perform an annual payroll audit each January, comparing the previous year's Compensation Budget Worksheet to copies of the year-end paycheck stubs for each employee to determine that each person was paid according to the authorized budget.

The chairman is nominated by the board during the Elder nomination process. Because of the weight of the responsibility, it has generally been the practice of the board to nominate only Elders who have served a minimum of two years for the position of chairman.

Senior Pastor's Job Description

The Senior Pastor will have primary responsibility for the preaching/teaching ministry of Glen Ellyn Bible Church (GEBC). Additionally, he will cultivate and cast church vision, provide spiritual leadership and guidance for the congregation, as well as perform general oversight of all church ministries and administration. The Senior Pastor will be a standing member of the Elder Board.

Objectives/Purpose:
- Serves as the chief disciple-maker at Glen Ellyn Bible Church, equipping others to make disciples.
- Cultivates and casts the ministry vision, empowering both staff and lay leadership to accomplish the vision.
- Educates and encourages the congregation in godliness during weekly worship services.
- Develops, implements and maintains pastoral care ministries.

Essential Duties / Responsibilities:
Preaching/Teaching
- Serves as primary preacher for Sunday services and selects replacement when not preaching
- Collaborates with the Worship Pastor in planning all aspects of the worship service including; preaching, scripture selection and reading, theme development, order of worship, etc.

- Shares in the planning and leading of special services such as baby dedications, baptisms, weddings and funerals
- Teaches and preaches as able/available in other church programs or services such as small groups, Men's Fraternity, Friday Morning Moms (FMM), etc.

Church Leadership
- Serves as spiritual leader for the church, maintaining an attitude of service and prayer, possessing a passion for Scripture, cultivating personal accountability relationships aimed at strengthening integrity and gaining wisdom
- Works with Elders and staff, developing an ongoing vision and direction for GEBC
- Communicates and leads Elders, staff, lay leadership and church toward vision and values of GEBC
- Shares with Elders, the responsibility of managing the church's budget, as well as encouraging stewardship within the congregation.

Pastoral Care
- Accountable for all pastoral care of the church.
- Works with staff, Elders and other lay members to provide pastoral care, grief and crisis counseling, as well as visitation for people in need.

- Ensures structure and procedures for support and follow up with those needing physical and spiritual care.

Staff and Lay Leadership
- Manages directly or indirectly, all church staff and lay leadership, as well as their respective ministry areas
- Provides supervision, encouragement and accountability to ensure a coordinated approach to ministry
- Supports and encourages individual spiritual growth for staff and lay leaders, as well as professional growth for staff members
- In conjunction with the Elders, recruits and selects new staff members, evaluates performance for direct reports and reviews compensation of all staff members
- Lead 1-2 programs of his choosing based on passion and giftedness

Mechanics of Leadership

Church Keys
Entrance to the GEBC building is coded and a numbered keypad is located beside the Welcome Center doors off the parking lot. Entrance to BBC is keyed. Contact the Facilities Manager, Kurt Wise (kwise@gebible.org) who can provide with either the necessary code or key.

Email
Each Elder is assigned a "gebible.org" email address. This address is made public and is a preferred method of official communication. If you want to link your "gebible.org" email account with another email account, contact Grant Armstrong, Executive Pastor (garmstrong@gebible.org), and he will have your email forwarded to the address of your choosing.

Annual Calendar
The Elder board meets twice per month. Currently we meet the 1st and 3rd Wednesdays from 7:00-9:00 p.m. It is our goal to have everyone at the meetings, but it is our habit to meet even when some cannot make it. Beyond these weekly meetings the Elders also take one retreat annually in January and June. The membership also meets twice annually. The November meeting is used to cast vision and vote on the budget for the upcoming year. The May meeting is used to review the year, cast vision, and elect Elders.

The Annual Calendar

July - Elders begin their one-year term

August - review the Senior Pastor's performance.

September - Elders begin budget process.

October - New Membership Interviews and finalize proposed budget.

November - Fall Gathering

December - Staff bonuses discussed

January - Elder Nomination Process begins.

Payroll Audit by Elder Chairman.

Elder Winter Retreat

April - New Members Interviews

May - Spring Gathering & Onboard new Elders

June - Elder Summer Retreat

Onboarding for New Elders

Joining the Elder board can feel like jumping onto a moving train. The onboarding process aims at getting new Elders up to speed as quickly as possible. We will discuss each of the following critical topics, and the summary is offered as a helpful organizing reference.

- **Overseers, Not Managers** - Elders cultivate and cast vision. Staff implement vision.
- **Hands "On!" and Hands "Off!"** - Elders govern. Staff manage.
- **Board Planning and Process** – Meetings are agenda driven and planned in advance.
- **Making Meetings Count** - Requires keen verbal focus and self-discipline.
- **Healthy Communication** - Is of vital importance for congregation.
- **Maintaining Confidentiality** - Creates safety and strength within the board and church.
- **Staff Oversight** – Elders are cheerleaders, not coaches.
- **Shepherding vs. Representation** - Elders represent God to the people, not the people.
- **Commitment to Service** - Your "yes" is yes.
- **Making Decisions Together** - The goal is consensus in decision making.
- **Guidelines for Meeting** - Come to meetings prepared to share in leadership.

- **Take Ownership** - Shepherding ourselves is the first step in shepherding others.
- **Shepherding Friends** - Shepherding friends can be uniquely challenging.
- **Church and/or Business** - Churches have business elements.

Overseers, Not Managers

Elders are "overseers" (1 Peter 5:2), but what that involves can vary depending upon the size of a congregation. Even the Apostles wrestled with the appropriate division of labor, not wanting to get bogged down in administrative details (Acts 6:1-7). Generally speaking, Elders cultivate and cast vision, while staff implement the vision. In that the Elders oversee two churches with approximately 1100 people and 20 staff, oversight includes being familiar with the staff and ministries of the church but excludes administrative and management activities. It is the role of staff to equip the congregants for works of ministry (Ephesians 4:12), implementing the vision and managing the day-to-day activities of the church.

It can be difficult for board members to limit their leadership to oversight, in that Elders also often serve in various ministries of the church. This places Elders in a position of having dual roles, both as an overseer and implementer of ministry. For that reason, it can be confusing to know how to respond in particular situations, whether as overseer or an implementer. As a general rule, wear the hat with greater authority. For example, if you have concerns about a particular program, express those concerns to the staff in charge, but avoid the temptation to begin managing the program. If congregants express concerns to you about a ministry, encourage the congregant to speak directly to the staff member in charge of that program. If your concerns continue to grow, share them with the Senior Pastor, who is charged with staff management.

Hands "ON!" and Hands "OFF!"
If leadership were described as a dance, then Elders and staff are partners, holding hands in the work of ministry. In the leadership dance, Elders provide the vision, while staff provide the implementation, and it is important we do not step on one another's toes.

Again, one of the most confusing elements of leadership for Elders is what we put our hands "on" and keep our hands "off." Generally speaking, the board is to be hands "on" when it comes to setting direction for the church, approving operational policies and procedures, setting budgetary limits and reviewing organizational achievement. These are strategically important as no other team has the authority or responsibility to do these things. While it is tempting for the board to be involved in implementation and management, it is best that the board remain hands "off" when it comes to day-to-day leadership activities such as running programs, assessing and developing staff, or managing budgets.

While most Elders understand the difference between governing and managing, the difficulty arises when Elders serve at some level in the programming of the church. While it is certainly appropriate for Elders to express their thoughts on specific programs, staff and budgetary issues, it is important not to lapse into actively exercising management influence. We must have a posture of empowering staff to do their jobs.

Board Planning and Process
The Elder meetings are "agenda" driven. Planning in this way allows Elders to better prepare for meetings. Agendas are set by the chairman and the senior pastor working together several weeks in advance. If you have a topic that you would like the board to discuss, let the chairman and/or senior pastor know. While we are constantly in process as a church and always eager to improve, bear in mind that as a relatively large church with almost 80 years of history, there are some matters (e.g., theology and philosophy of ministry) that have been "settled" for some time and may or may not be a priority to revisit.

In this respect, it is important for each individual Elder to understand that their personal ministry passions cannot trump or drive the ministry agenda of the board as a whole. While it is important and expected that

Elders have ministry passion, it is vital that the board collectively identify and affirm the priorities for discussion. In short, the board agenda will not serve the individual priorities of a single member, but rather the collective priorities of the board.

Making Meetings Count
We only have about five hours a month together, which means we need to make the most of every moment. To do so it is vital that we are careful with our words and not distract the group from the focus, whether that is prayer, Scripture study or strategic planning. Because the primary work of the board is discussion, it is most often our words that get us off topic. This can happen through casual joking, sports banter, or the interjecting with an important issue that rightly should be discussed. Remember, if an issue is important to discuss, then it is important to prepare for the discussion so that it can be thoroughly considered. Raising an important, but unplanned, topic for discussion does not serve the church well, as the Elders are unprepared to discuss it thoroughly and the topic only receives superficial consideration. Important topics must make their way onto the agenda. Speak to the chairman in advance, between meetings about platforming a topic for discussion.

Healthy Communication
Unity among board members is not synonymous with uniformity in thought or actions, so we can expect

passionate disagreement on topics from time to time. For this reason, working to maintain healthy communication between board members is vital. Maintaining healthy communication includes treating one another with gentleness and respect, being patient with one another, and being quick to listen, slow to speak and slow to become angry. It is important that we assume the best of one another and speak well of each other, and that we work diligently to resolve matters quickly. As a practice, if we are unwilling to say something to the entire board, then we shouldn't be talking about it with individual Elders. This means when Elders are discussing an issue outside meetings, those discussions need to be shared with the board as a whole as soon as possible. This will help avoid triangulation between board members, as well as help cultivate intimacy and trust within the team. Good communication habits strengthen the team.

Communication with the congregation is an essential component of the Elder role as well. Each conversation requires wisdom to respond with grace, discernment, and integrity. The goal is always to edify. Caution should be exercised to speak in harmony with all board decisions. Differences of opinion on Elder discussions should be addressed among the Elders rather than openly discussed with congregants. On some crucial matters, it will be best to defer to the Elder Chairman or Senior Pastor to speak on behalf of the board as a whole. Paul's exhortation in Ephesians

4:1-3 is relevant. He wrote, "I therefore, a prisoner for the Lord, urge you to walk in a manner worthy of the calling to which you have been called, with all humility and gentleness, with patience, bearing with one another in love, eager to maintain the unity of the Spirit in the bond of peace."

Maintaining Confidentiality
For the Elder team to work well, maintaining confidentiality is important. Board members must feel free to make themselves vulnerable in meetings and to be transparent on all topics, without fear that what is shared will be disclosed to the congregation. This means Elders must be careful not to share the content of boardroom discussions with congregants. Sharing, surveying, or soliciting input from congregants inappropriately undermines confidentiality, and burdens congregants. At the same time, Elders have historically recognized a value in discussing some board issues with their spouse. If an Elder shares with their spouse what the board is discussing it is important that the spouse understands the importance of maintaining confidentiality, and that they be willing and able to bear that burden.

Staff Oversight
Elder oversight of both staff and programs is a part of shepherding. Elders are encouraged to meet with staff and get to know them personally, as well as their areas of ministry. As you meet with staff, bear in mind that

all staff members have a job description, direct supervisor, and annual goals that they are focused on achieving. Please work hard to keep these interactions as positive as possible and avoid acting as a ministry coach. Be a cheerleader in these instances, not a coach. If elders begin coaching staff, lines of communication quickly grow confused. If you have concerns about staff, it is best to address those concerns with the senior pastor.

Shepherding vs. Representation
The office of Elder was not designed to function like the United States Congress. In selecting Elders, we are not selecting someone to represent our preferences. The church is not a representative democracy, with constituents vying for influence or lobbying for a particular agenda. While shepherding certainly includes being sympathetic to the desires of congregants, the function of Elders is not to represent the opinions or preferences of the people. The purpose of Elders is to represent the priorities of God. Elders serve as God's ambassadors to his people. This means that keeping the people of the church happy is not the priority of Elders. The priority of Elders is to support and encourage faithfulness within the lives of the people.

Commitment To the Board
Jesus said that our "Yes." should mean yes (Matthew 5:37). Elders are able to serve for as many as four, one-year consecutive terms. Terms of service run from July

1 - June 30. While it is understood that availability for service changes from time to time, Elders are asked to complete their terms of service each year, rather than resigning in the middle of a year. If an Elder feels unable to continue serving and wants to step down in the middle of a year, they are to make the chairman aware as early as possible, so that a replacement can be found.

Making Decisions Together
Leadership involves decision-making and GEBC uses a shared leadership model for decision making, employing a group decision-making process. Alexander Strauch, in his book *Biblical Eldership* (pp.40-44), identifies three benefits of shared leadership in a group decision-making construct.

1. Balances people's weaknesses. Each member brings expertise and experience. Some people are risk takers, others are more cautious. Together, "our collective strengths outweigh our individual weaknesses."
2. Lightens the load. Some decisions are difficult and complex requiring research, investigation, analysis, and synthesis. Working together, the Elders can lighten the workload.
3. Provides accountability. As much as we may desire to be impartial, personal hurts may cloud our judgment and biases may influence our thinking. Proverbs 11:14 says, "Where no

counsel is, the people fall: but in the multitude of counselors there is wisdom."

Group decision-making also encourages personal growth. Observing others in managing challenging issues provides an opportunity to gain the skills and wisdom associated with leadership. The role of an Elder is a labor of love, and group decision making fosters love within the group and the church (1 Corinthians 13:1-7).

God's plan is to utilize a plurality of Christ-like leaders working together to discover and pursue His will. Decision-making can be frustrating because no Elder is perfect. At times issues do not have simple clear answers. The pursuit of godly attitudes will create a healthy decision-making environment. The Elders will draw closer to each other and most of all, closer to Jesus.

Guidelines for Meetings
God's design is a plurality of Elders, which takes effort and has huge benefits. It can be difficult to maintain a conversational rhythm when we only meet twice monthly but below are some helpful tips in preserving a strong dialogue among fellow elders.
- Come to the meeting prayed up and ready to participate.
- Make listening a priority. Make it a goal to ask good questions of others and invite quieter

members to share. Explore minority opinions and encourage discussion of differing views.
- When it is time to speak, share your heart and avoid holding court. Get to the point, no speeches, or long stories. Make sure to say it in the meeting, not in the hall after the meeting.
- Pick your passion points. Not everything can be urgent. Focus on important points and do not nit-pick.
- Support the decisions of the board…move on when the group moves on.
- Relax, decisions need not be rushed. We have time to pray, study, question, and research.
- Stay out of the weeds and details of operations.

Take Ownership

We will shepherd the church best, as we shepherd ourselves. A healthy board and healthy board members take ownership for themselves and recognize their role in the board functionality overall. In short, we need to be the sheep that we want to shepherd. We need to be committed to giving and serving and sacrificing and growing in faith for the sake of the church. Christ came to serve, rather than be served (Mark 10:45) and we must have the same attitude that Christ has (Philippians 2:5-11). This includes things as basic as making it a priority to attend each board meeting, and being on time to meetings, and coming prepared to fully participate in meetings, having done the pre-meeting work. This also includes things as vital as maintaining a civil discourse during discussions, assuming the best of the other board members, and keeping short accounts with other board members. For the board experience to be a joy, it takes real investment, and that's when it is most rewarding.

Shepherding Friends

When serving on a secular non-profit or para-church board one's family may never be involved. Serving on an Elder Board is categorically unique in that you and your whole family attend worship weekly at the place you are leading. This means your friendships will change. There will be an enriched level of blessing and burden. After all, it's a blessing to shepherd those we love, but it can also be a burden. Most notably, it can be a burden leading your friends. While it is true that as Christian, we are all responsible for one another to a degree, joining the board gives you a formal and official responsibility in the effort of caring for and leading your friends. This can be awkward at times, in that your friends may expect that you represent their views to the board on a particular topic. However, representative democracy is not the model of Elder board leadership. Elders are not charged with representing the desires and/or preferences of a particular constituency. Rather, Elders are charged to represent God's priorities to the church. While we certainly listen to and sensitively weigh the input of congregants, it is important that we remain individually focused on the board's objectives and priorities. This can create friction at times with friends who disagree with a decision the board has made, and requires sacrifice on the part of Elders. It is not uncommon for Elders to feel their friendships are strained.

Church and/or Business

Churches have business aspects (e.g., payroll), but they are motivated by spiritual goals. For this reason, Elders often face the tension in decision making about which to adopt, a church or business perspective. For example, when considering employee sabbaticals, Elders face the dilemma about whether to approach the policy from a business perspective (i.e., considering primarily financial constraints) or from a church perspective (i.e., considering primary relational issues). Fundraising practices raise a similar tension, as Elders are often vexed about whether the senior pastor should know the amounts given by parishioners, as most business owners would certainly know their customers' habits. At the same time, a church perspective might argue that shepherds should not know how much people give. To make matters even more complex, a board may vary from issue to issue on which approach they embrace. In one case, adopting a business approach and then in the next moment adopting a church approach. Here are a couple of common examples:

- While we rely on faith-based offerings, we also often put significant energy into creating financial projections based on previous "revenue" patterns.
- While some spiritualize being debt-free, others see no problem in taking out a loan or carrying a line of credit.
- While we may be generous in staff compensation, some wrestle with "profit sharing" when there is a budget surplus.

Admittedly, while one approach might not fully exclude elements of the other, the tension is hard to escape. Is the church operating on faith, or are we adopting business models of financial management?

Annotated Bibliography

Elders do not have to be professional theologians, but we do have to study. Beyond Scripture, below are some important books with which to familiarize yourself.

Following Jesus: Defining Discipleship for the 21st Century, by Kelly Brady – explains GEBC's philosophy of ministry.

Biblical Eldership: An Urgent Call to Restore Biblical Church Leadership, by Alexander Strauch – details the beauty of a plurality of Elders serving the Church.

Systematic Theology: An Introduction to Biblical Doctrine, by Wayne Grudem – this textbook has served as GEBC's primary theological reference for over 30 years.

Organic Outreach for Churches: Infusing Evangelistic Passion in Your Local Congregation, by Kevin G. Harney - the staff and Elders discussed this book together in 2014 to strengthen evangelism.

Better Together: Making Church Mergers Work, by Jim Tomberlin and Warren Bird - Elders discussed this book in 2020 in preparation for a second campus.

Healing the Sick: Biblical and Practical Wisdom for Healing the Sick in Naturally Supernatural Ways, by Alex and Hannah Absalom – the staff and Elders discussed this book in the summer of 2021.

Be the Bridge: Pursuing God's Heart for Racial Reconciliation, by Latasha Morrison - the congregation discussed this book in 2022. Provides a reflection on black experience within the white church.

The Color of Compromise: The Truth About the American Church's Complicity in Racism, by Jemar Tisby – offers a detailed description of racism in American churches.

Messy Grace: How a Pastor with Gay Parents Learned to Love Others Without Sacrificing Conviction, by Caleb Kaltenbach – Elders and staff read this book in 2022, maintains the historic conservative sexual ethic, while calling the Church to love the LGBTQ community.

Space At The Table: Conversations Between An Evangelical Theologian and His Gay Son, by Brad and Drew Harper – excellent book, maintains a conservative sexual ethic and calls us to love the LGBTQ community.

The Other Half of the Church: Christian Community, Brain Science and Overcoming Spiritual Stagnation, by Jim Wilder and Michael Hendricks – excellent book on discipleship that appeals to the whole person. Staff discussed this book in 2022.

Your Not Crazy: Gospel Sanity for Weary Churches, by Ray Ortlund & Sam Alberry – staff and Elders read this in 2023, a call for churches to not simply offer Gospel Doctrine but to also cultivate Gospel Culture.

Membership Process

Participating in the membership process is a great opportunity to shepherd the flock, as the heart of the membership curriculum is aimed at presenting the gospel and explaining the nature of the church, as well as teaching GEBC's vision for disciple-making. The process for membership includes:

- Attending Class on Spiritual Gifts and Wiring.

- Attending Membership Class: All potential members are to attend the class.

- Completing a Membership Application: Applications are completed electronically and are then distribute to the Elders

- Meeting with Elders: Each applicant meets with an Elder. Married applicants meet as a couple. During the meeting applicants are encouraged to ask questions they may have about GEBC. These interviews are Sunday morning.

- Being Presented to the Congregation: Upon approval for membership by the Elder Board, new members are introduced to the congregation electronically.

The Membership Class

Staff teach the membership class, and the content is guided by a Membership Notebook that each participant receives electronically. Below is an outline of the content in the Membership Notebook.

- The Gospel and the Church
- The Philosophy and Ministry of GEBC
- The Theology of GEBC
- The Elders, Staff and Missionaries
- The Finances of GEBC
- The Constitution of GEBC
- The Membership Application

When teaching the class our goal is to be:

Relaxed and warm: This is a great opportunity to shepherd. Remember that the class is less about communicating content and more loving those attending and sharing your passion for Christ and his church. If you are asked a question to which you feel you do not know the answer, let them know that you will get back to them, either by email or phone.

Prayerful: Open the class in prayer and close the class in prayer. If someone shares something that is weighty, do not hesitate to pray for that person/issue immediately.

Thorough: Go through the material slowly. Do not assume people understand the content. Ask at the end of each page, whether there are questions.

Intentional: Do not assume everyone in the class is born again. The first section of the membership booklet is titled "The Gospel and the Church." Go slowly through this material and invite them to ask questions. Share your story of conversion. Invite anyone who wants to talk about salvation to speak with you, either before/after class or by phone or email.

Direct: Make sure to explain that there are times when we feel some are not ready. Invite anyone who has questions about their readiness to speak with you outside of class. Those who are not ready often have a sense this is this case. Here are some examples of those we might ask to wait on membership.

- Those who cannot explain the Gospel or express their conversion
- Those who can't affirm the statement of faith.
- Those unwilling to support the church financially or serve regularly.
- Those whose lifestyles are inconsistent with expectations for membership (see GEBC's Constitution, Article V, section 4, Responsibilities of Membership)

Meeting with Membership Applicants

Elders meet with all applicants. These meetings take place on Sunday mornings. Married couples meet together with an Elder. After all the interviews have been completed, Elders confer with one another and if there are no concerns, applicants are extended an invitation to membership. If there are concerns, Elders will meet again with applicants to ask further questions, or even ask applicants to wait on membership. When meeting with applicants, it is important to:

- **Begin and end with prayer.** And if you sense an opportunity to pray for a particular issue during the meeting, then pause and do so.
- **Share your story of conversion.** Sharing your story will give you a platform later to ask clarifying questions about their story of conversion.
- **Ask questions.** Come with some standard questions to ask, but also formulate some questions specific to the applicant based upon what you glean from their application. Here are some potential questions:

    1. How did you come to GEBC?
    2. What have you most enjoyed at GEBC?
    3. What do you believe are some of the strengths and weaknesses of GEBC?

4. How are you currently growing in faith?
5. What might help you to grow in your faith?
6. Who has been influential in your faith development?

- **Ask them to share their story of conversion.** Bearing in mind that it is hard for many to describe the gospel clearly, it is important to discern their understanding of salvation. For reference, the gospel is clearly defined in the front part of the Membership Notebook. If you discover that they have never prayed to ask God's forgiveness of their sin and placed their trust in Jesus' death for salvation, then ask to lead them through the prayer of salvation. While we are not looking for people to parrot certain evangelical phrases (e.g. sin, repentance, salvation), words do carry meaning. Do not hesitate to ask them for clarification along the way.

- **Let them know that we will follow up with them quickly.** While it is tempting to promise them membership at the close of the interview, the Elders discuss applicants before extending an offer of membership. Avoiding the promise of membership will also give you some space/time to consider their answers and whether you need to follow up with them on any issues/topics.

Elder Nomination Timeline

Only members can serve on the Nominating Committee, nominate potential Elders, or serve as Elders.

January 15 - Elders nominate five members from the congregation to sit on the Nominating Committee (NC). Two Elders make up the remainder of the committee, including the Chairman of the Elder Board, who acts as Chair of the Nominating Committee. Those nominate are invited by the board chair to serve on the NC. NOTE: It is wisest to identify two dates between March 15 and April 15 for the Nominating Committee to meet and interviewing each potential nominee. If subsequent meetings are needed, then they must complete their meetings before April 30.

January 26 - The Elder Nomination Packet is emailed to the congregation, which is asked to submit names of Elder nominees using the Elder Nomination Form by February 9. Staff and their spouses are excluded from consideration, as well as those who have been members for less than a year. A person cannot nominate themselves.

February 19 – All potential nominees must be submitted prior to the Elder meeting. While the chairman will know who nominates whom, potential nominees are submitted to the board for consideration without noting who submitted their names. The goal is that potential nominees are considered on their merit, rather than on the merit of those who recommended them. The Elder board reviews the list of potential Nominees removing any not currently qualified biblically, or those who clearly and opening demonstrate a posture of being out of step with GEBC's vision/mission and philosophy of ministry. Those approved for consideration are contacted by the Chair of the Nominating Committee and asked to complete an Elder Application by March 15. At this meeting, the Elder Board also designates who will be the next Chairman of the Board.

March 19 - Elder Applications are reviewed and submitted to the Nominating Committee for prayerful consideration before the first meeting, which will be scheduled on or before April 15.

April 16 - The Nominating Committee convenes before April 15 and interviews each potential nominee. The committee ranks the candidates in order of nomination. If subsequent meetings need to take place, then they must complete their meetings before April 30. The goal is to create a shortlist of nominees, prioritizing those approved for nomination (1st, 2nd, 3rd and 4th nominees). The Chairman will contact the approved nominees to offer them positions of nomination in the order agreed upon by the NC. The Chairman shall instruct the NC that all discussions during the meeting are strictly confidential. Open discussion is essential for the best assessment of nominees, but all assessments must be kept in strict confidence. The NC is informed who will be the next Chairman of the Board.

May 4 – Spring Gathering is announced, and Elder nominees are presented electronically (pic and bio) to the congregation.

May 18 – Elder Nominees are voted on at the Spring Gathering.

Elder Nomination Process

January - Below is an example of the email that is sent to the potential Nominating Committee members.

> Dear Sir/Madam,
> As you may know, each year there is a rotation of two Elders off the Elder Board and therefore there is a need for the congregation to elect two new Elders to replace them. The first step in the process is to select a Nominating Committee. The Nominating Committee is composed of two Elders (one being the Chairman of the Elder Board who will serve as Chairman of the Nominating Committee) and five people selected from the congregation. The purpose of the Nominating Committee is to review, evaluate and prioritize the Elder Application Forms submitted by those that have been nominated from the congregation and have a desire to serve.
>
> The Elders believe that you would be a valuable member of the Nominating Committee and would like to ask you to serve. The time commitment is not substantial but would involve reviewing several applications and then attending at least two meeting to discuss the applications, interview the applicants, as well as prioritize the

candidates. We would conduct as much business by email as possible but, as stated previously, there would be at least two face to face meeting in March.

Please let me know if you would be willing to serve by February 19. If you have any questions, please do not hesitate to contact me either by email or by phone.

Sincerely,
Chairman of the Elder Board

January - The Elder Nomination Packet is emailed to the congregation, which is asked to submit names of Elder nominees using the Elder Nomination Form. Below is the Elder Nomination Packet.

Elder Nomination Packet

Therefore, I exhort the Elders among you... shepherd the flock of God. 1 Peter 5:1, 2

Dear GEBC Family:

What do you think of when you hear the word "Elder"? Peter wrote that Elders are the shepherds of God's flock, which includes overseeing the ministries of the church, guarding the church's doctrine, teaching and equipping the congregation for lives of godliness, cultivating and casting the church's vision, caring for the staff, sharing in pastoral care, and overseeing the church's budget. With such weighty responsibilities, filling the Elder positions with capable men is of the utmost importance for the church's effectiveness, and you are invited to recommend for consideration the names of those you believe to be qualified to serve as an Elder at GEBC.

Attached you will find the Qualifications and Responsibilities of an Elder, which includes the Elder Nomination Form. Please look these materials over closely and submit the names of those you have prayerfully considered as soon as possible.

We realize that the Elder Nomination Form assumes congregants know those they are nominating well. However, if you do not know potential nominees well enough to answer all the questions on the nomination form, please do not let that keep you from nominating someone. The Elder board is happy to consider all nominated.

Sincerely,
Kelly Brady, Senior Pastor
Glen Ellyn Bible Church

Elder Qualifications and Responsibilities

Elders care for God's people (1 Peter 5:1-2). While there are three different words used in the New Testament to describe this role, each refers to the same office. The three words are:

> **Elder (presbuteros)** – this term means "old" (1 Timothy 5:1), and possesses a sense of title (1 Timothy 5:17). While no specific age is given, this term implies maturity and experience.
>
> **Overseer (episkopos)** – commonly used to designate those in charge of management. This term emphasizes the function of an Elder in exercising authority (1 Peter 5:2).
>
> **Pastor (poimen)** – this word means "shepherd" and applies to the one who tends, feeds, and guides God's people (Ephesians 4:11, 1 Peter 5:2).

Here are all three concepts together in two verses:

> "I exhort the Elders (presbutoros)…to shepherd (poimen) the flock of God…exercising oversight (episkopos)…"
> 1 Peter 5:1-2 (NASB)

Scripture details how these roles are met:

- Equipping, training, and ordaining (Acts 14:23, 1 Timothy 4:4, 5:22, Titus 1:5).
- Modeling Christ likeness (1 Peter 5:3).
- Watching over God's people (Acts 20:28, 1 Thessalonians 5:12;1 Peter 5:1-2).
- Teaching Scripture and opposing false doctrine (Acts 20:31, 1 Timothy 5:17, Titus 1:9).
- Praying for the sick (Acts 6:4, James 5:14).
- Correcting, rebuking, and encouraging (2 Timothy 4:2, Titus 1:9, 13, Hebrews 13:17).

Considering the weighty responsibilities of Elders, the Biblical qualifications of an Elder are:

- Possessing the "desire" to lead and living above reproach (1 Timothy 3:1-2, Titus 1:7-8).
- Not a new convert, demonstrating self-control and integrity, with a good reputation (1 Timothy 3:2,7; Titus 1:7-8).
- Being the husband of one wife and leading his home well, with children who believe and live

disciplined lives (1 Timothy 3:1-6; Titus 1:6).
- Prudent, wise, warm, hospitable and submitted to God/others (1 Timothy 3:1-3).
- Free from addiction and not motivated by selfish gain (1 Timothy 3:3, Titus 1:7).
- Able to teach, encouraging the application of Scripture to life (1 Timothy 3:2, Titus 1:9).
- Not intimidating, harsh, or impatient, but gentle, kind and fair (Titus 1:7, 1 Peter 5:2-3).
- Not contentious, picking fights or quarrelling with others (1 Timothy 3:3).

Elder Nomination Form

Thank you for taking the time to complete an Elder Nomination Form. Please note that you must be a member to nominate someone for consideration and only men who have been members for over a year may serve as an Elder. Please complete the form as thoroughly as possible, adding as much detail as possible. Incomplete forms will not be considered.

Full name

Email address and phone number

Are you a member of GEBC? (Yes/No)

Full name of the nominee

Have you alerted the man you are nominating that you are nominating him? (Yes/No)

Has the man you are nominating expressed interest in serving as an Elder (Yes/No)

Please answer "yes," "no," or "I don't know" to the following questions about the man you are putting forward as a nominee:

Has he been a member of GEBC for at least one year?

Is he spiritually mature, and able to make wise decisions?

Is he above reproach, without known immoral conduct?

Is his marriage and family a model of godliness?

Does he offer spiritual leadership in his home?

Is he sincere, reasonable, self-controlled, and disciplined?

Is he able to teach, possessing sound doctrine, able to encourage those who do not understand the Scripture?

Is he humble and teachable?

Is he approachable, welcoming and hospitable?

Please answer the following questions with short answers.

How has he been involved in the ministries of GEBC?

When/where have you seen the man exercise spiritual leadership?

Why do you feel this man will make a good Elder?

How will serving as an Elder most likely stretch and/or challenge this man?

Elder Application Form

I exhort the Elders among you...
shepherd the flock of God. 1 Peter 5:1, 2

Dear Sir:

You have been nominated to serve as an Elder at GEBC. To help the nominating committee consider your qualifications for and interests in serving, please fill out the attached Elder Application Form and return it by email.

This office of Elder is an important position within the church. As such, we would suggest that before beginning this application that you take time to meditate upon the following passages of Scripture: 1 Timothy 3:1-11, Titus 1:5-9, 1 Peter 5:1-3.

Your answers to the questions in this application will be read by the members of the nominating committee and the Elder board. Thank you for taking the time to complete this application.

Sincerely,
Mark Tucker
Elder Board and Nominating Committee Chairman

2025 Elder Application

Name:
Address:
Cell Phone Number:

Family Section:
Name of Wife and names of children. Please give ages of the children.

If you or your wife have been divorced, describe the circumstances of your divorce and the process of restoration that you went through.

Church Membership Section:
List the churches at which you were previously a member and your areas of service.

For how long have you been a member of GEBC and how have you served in ministry here?

Spiritual Information Section
When and how did you receive Christ as savior?

Describe the current health of your faith on a scale of 1 to 5, (1=unhealthy and 5=healthy). Explain the key elements that have contributed to that condition.

Describe the most recent experience you have had sharing your faith with a non-Christian.

Describe your prayer life and your habits of Scripture study.

Describe your history of giving financially to GEBC.

Describe any other giving to Christian ministries and your passion for those ministries.

How have you grown in the "grace of giving" (2 Cor. 8:7) over the last few years?

What is your practice and posture toward activities such as tobacco use, drinking alcohol, and viewing movies that contain graphic violence and/or sexual situations? How do you manage these responsibly?

What practice of confession and/or types of accountability do you have in your life? On what specific issues do you seek accountability, and with whom?

Is there any scriptural qualification for the office of Elder that you feel/know you fail to meet?

Is there anything in your life that causes you to be concerned about your ability/readiness to carry the responsibilities of the office of Elder faithfully?
Is there anything in your lifestyle that could potentially bring reproach to yourself, your family, or Christ?

List some specific ways in which you lead your family spiritually.

How would you describe the relational and spiritual health of your marriage?

What are some of your spiritual gifts and how have you exercised them in ministry?

Whom have you shepherded in the past? How do you believe you will be used by God to shepherd in the future?

Describe an instance in which you successfully resolved a conflict with someone outside of your family, or an instance in which you mediated a dispute between two parties.

Doctrinal Information
Can you wholeheartedly affirm GEBC's statement of faith? If not, what points are you unable to support?

How would you describe the truthfulness of Scripture and its authority in our lives?

When studying the Bible, how do you determine the meaning of a passage and identify its application to our 21st century situation?

What is your personal theological position on the following topics?
- Exclusivity of the Gospel
- Abortion
- Miraculous Gifts
- Women in Leadership
- Racism

Leadership Information
Why are you eager to serve as an Elder at GEBC?

How much time and energy do you have to commit to exercising the office of Elder?

How does your wife feel about the possibility of your serving as an Elder?

Ask your wife to write a brief statement of her conversion experience.

Have you ever been in conflict with any of the current Staff or Elders of GEBC? If so, how did you address (or how are you continuing to address) the conflict?

In your mind, what is the difference in role between the Elders and Staff?

What are your passions outside of church, family, and work?

Describe an occasion on which your faith was tested and how you responded to that. How are you different now?

Mission and Philosophy of Ministry
Using GEBC's Discipleship Target, describe your involvement in the church's mission and methods.

What most excites you about the direction and ministries of GEBC?

What most concerns you about the direction and ministries of GEBC?

How would you describe your personal vision for GEBC's future ministry?

What do you see as some of the biggest challenges facing the American church in general?

What do you see as some of the biggest challenges facing GEBC specifically?

ELDER SERVICE HISTORY

2000-2001	2001-2002	2002-20003
Howard Grimberg (1)	Howard Grimberg (2)	Howard Grimberg (3)
Steve Cevaal (1)	Steve Cevaal (2)	Steve Cevaal, Chr. (3)
Chuck Martin, Chr. (3)	Gary Larson (1)	Gary Larson (2)
Tom Ennis (3)	Mark Tucker (1)	Mark Tucker (2)
Tom Howard (2)	Tom Howard (3)	Phil Koch (1)
Dave Wiegman (2)	Dave Wiegman, Chr. (3)	Rich Zimmerman (1)

2003-2004	2004-2005	2005-2006
Gary Larson (3)	Mike Hendriksen (1)	Mike Hendriksen (2)
Mark Tucker, Chr. (3)	Wes Wetherell (1)	Wes Wetherell (2)
Dave Ochs (1)	Dave Ochs (2)	Dave Ochs (3)
Phil Koch (2)	Phil Koch (3)	Scott Brennecke (1)
Stan Yohe (1)	Dave Wiegman (1)	Dave Wiegman Chr. (2)
Rich Zimmerman (2)	Rich Zimmerman, Chr. (3)	Mark Tucker (1)

2006-2007	2007-2008	2008-2009
Mike Hendriksen (3)	Mike Hendriksen, Chr. (4)	Scott Brennecke (4)
Jim Kraus (1)	Jim Kraus (2)	Jim Kraus (3)
Dave Ochs (4)	Glen Williams (1)	Mark Macaluso (1)
Scott Brennecke (2)	Scott Brennecke (3)	Bob Neyland (1)
Dave Wiegman Chr. (3)	Dave Wiegman (4)	Jim Rathbun (3)
Mark Tucker (2)	Mark Tucker (3)	Mark Tucker, Chr. (4)
Jim Rathbun (1)	Jim Rathbun (2)	Glen Williams (2)
	Rich Zimmermann (1)	Rich Zimmermann (2)

2009-2010	2010-2011	2011-2012
Jim Craig (1)	Jim Craig (2)	Jim Craig (3)
Gary Larson (1)	Gary Larson (2)	Gary Larson (3)
Mark Macaluso (2)	Mark Macaluso (3)	Mark Macaluso (4)
Bob Neyland (2)	Bob Neyland, Chr. (3)	Bob Neyland, Chr. (4)
Jim Rathbun (4)	Glen Eggert (1)	Glen Eggert (2)
Dave Wiegman (3)	Dave Wiegman (4)	Bob Thomas (1)
Glen Williams, Chr. (3)	Joe Schaubroeck (1)	Joe Schaubroeck (2)
Rich Zimmermann (3)	Rich Zimmerman (4)	Mark Tucker (1)

ELDER SERVICE HISTORY

2012-2013	2013-2014	2014-2015
Jim Craig (4)	Alex Dean (1)	Alex Dean (2)
Gary Larson (4)	John Vandervelde (1)	John Vandervelde Chr (2)
Glen Eggert (3)	Glen Eggert (4)	Jeremy Boynton (1)
Joe Schaubroeck (3)	Joe Schaubroeck (4)	Steve Bult (1)
Bob Thomas (2)	Bob Thomas (3)	Bob Thomas (4)
Mark Tucker, Chr. (2)	Mark Tucker, Chr. (3)	Mark Tucker, Chr. (4)
Dave Wiegman (1)	Dave Wiegman (2)	Dave Wiegman (3)
Rich Zimmermann (1)	Rich Zimmermann (2)	Rich Zimmermann (3)

2015-2016	2016-2017	2017-2018
Glen Eggert (3)	Glen Eggert (4)	Tim March (1)
Bob Neyland (1)	Bob Neyland, Chr. (2)	Bob Neyland, Chr. (3)
Jeremy Boynton (2)	Jeremy Boynton (3)	Jeremy Boynton (4)
Steve Bult (2)	Steve Bult (3)	Steve Bult (4)
Gary Larson (1)	Gary Larson (2)	Gary Larson (3)
Bryan Chapman (1)	Bryan Chapman (2)	Bryan Chapman (3)
Dave Wiegman Chr. (4)	Mark Macaluso (1)	Mark Macaluso (3)
Rich Zimmermann (4)	Bob Thomas (1)	Bob Thomas (3)
		Phil Koch (2)

2018-2019	2019-2020	2020-2021
Tim March (2)	Tim March (3)	Tim March Chr. (4)
Bob Neyland, Chr. (4)	Dave Wiegman (1)	Dave Wiegman (2)
Chuck Martin (1)	Chuck Martin (2)	Chuck Martin (3)
Glen Eggert (1)	Glen Eggert (2)	Glen Eggert (3)
Gary Larson (4)	Dan Maas (1)	Dan Maas (2)
Bryan Chapman (4)	Mark Macaluso, Chr. (4)	Ken Dryfhout (1)
Mark Macaluso (3)	Bob Thomas (4)	Robert Steele (1)
Bob Thomas (3)	Phil Koch (3)	Phil Koch (4)
Phil Koch (2)		

ELDER SERVICE HISTORY

2021-2022	2022-2023	2023-2024
Bryan Chapman (1)	Mark Tucker (2)	Mark Tucker (3) Chair
Scott Fedyski (1)	Position not filled	Mark Macaluso (3)
Ken Dryfhout (2)	Ken Dryfhout (3)	Ken Dryfhout (4)
Robert Steele (2)	Robert Steele (3)	Robert Steele (4)
Dan Maas (3)	Dan Maas (4)	Ryan Osterholm (1)
Dave Wiegman (3)	Dave Wiegman (4) Chr.	Ben Wilson (1)
Glen Egger (4)	Steve Bult (1)	Steve Bult (2)
Chuck Martin Chr. (4)	John Greening (1)	John Greening (2)
2024-2025	**2025-2026**	**2026-2027**
Mark Tucker (4) Chair		
Mark Macaluso (4)		
Tim March (1)		
Ryan Osterholm (2)		
Ben Wilson (2)		
Steve Bult (3)		
John Greening (3)		
2027-2028	**2028-2029**	**2029-2030**

THE WISDOM OF FELLOW ELDERS

Must Be Able to Teach

Elders must be able to teach (1 Timothy 3:2), and there is perhaps no better opportunity than to instruct fellow Elders. Toward that end, we have made a habit over the last several years of asking those Elders rotating off the board to share some parting words of wisdom. These letters are then read aloud to the Elder Board during the annual summer retreat, which is the last meeting before Elders, who have served their four-year term, rotate off the Elder Board.

After collecting these letters over the course of a decade some trends have become clearly visible. First, you will notice that the letters reflect the different personalities of the shepherds, each with their own passion for particular elements of leadership. This is to be expected as each man has different ability and gifting. Secondly, you will notice that the men reference both the blessings and the burdens of shepherding. This is also to be expected as churches, just like individuals, go through seasons of ministry that are easier and more fruitful, as well as seasons that are difficult and require endurance.

In the end, hearing these letters of wisdom read aloud each year has become something that I've looked forward to with great anticipation. For me, as the only paid shepherd among the Elders, it is a delight to hear how God has worked in and through the men with whom I partner in the ministry. I thank God for each of these letters.

Sheep-like Tendencies,
by Kelly Brady (2004)

Ever follow your appetites too far? Sheep do it all the time. With their eyes on the ground and completely engrossed in filling their bellies they wander through a pasture eating, until they are separated from the flock. So strong is their appetite that sheep must be *made* to lie down (Psalm 23:2).

They are also discontented animals. With easy access to a pasture full of grass, they reach for grass among thorns and get hung up. Ever make poor relational decisions, reaching for something off limits, only to get entangled in sin, and unable to fully enjoy what was easily within reach?

Physical weakness is also a problem for sheep. For example, because of their short legs and heavy wool, they can easily roll to their side and wind up unable to get back on their feet. It's called being "cast." Thrashing about on their side, they soon find themselves upside down, completely on their backs. In this position, the blood leaves their legs, which then grow numb, and they then become immobile. If the weather is hot, they last only a couple of hours. Ever find yourself helpless and in need of rescue?

Perhaps the greatest threat to sheep though is fear. Sheep are easily spooked, and when that happens, they make poor decisions. Ever allow fear to drive you into self-sabotaging behavior? There are countless tales of sheep plunging off steep cliffs, *together* no less, an entire herd running to their death out of fear. So fearful are sheep that they will not drink from rushing water. Can you imagine? Fear of rushing water can prevent them from getting the hydration they need in order to survive. For sheep to drink from water it must be calm, quiet waters.

With all these sheep-like tendencies in mind, Jesus said of himself, "I am the good shepherd" (John 10:11-16), and all the benefits listed in Psalm 23 (i.e., the green pastures, the quiet waters, the paths of righteousness, and the experience of peace even in the place of darkest fear) become ours when we admit our sheep-like tendencies. Still, many are tempted to pretend that they don't have sheep-like tendencies. But the only animal humanity is compared with in Scripture is sheep. I'd like to have been compared to a cheetah or a bear. But the truth is that my appetites lead me into trouble. My discontentedness gets me entangled in sin. In my weaknesses I find myself "cast." And I've made many self-sabotaging decisions out of fear.

Psalm 23 is one of the best-known passages in all of Scripture, but how often have we missed one of the most obvious points in this famous song? King David sang, "The Lord is my shepherd." In other words, he sang "I am a sheep!"

We are at our best as Elders—as the shepherds of God's flock—only as we admit our sheep-like tendencies and experience the care of the Good Shepherd. Then, and only then, are we ready to shepherd others.

Top Ten Charge
by Mark Tucker (2004)

Be Men of Prayer – The ministry of shepherding starts, continues, and ends with prayer. If you do only one thing as an Elder, make it prayer. Pray regularly for the other Elders, the staff, and the effectiveness of the ministries of the church, as well as the families within the church. Remember, it was prayer, which the first Apostles made sure was a priority in their shepherding efforts (Acts 6:4).

Think Big and Be Bold – It is important to set the right pace, but we also need to take risks. We need to dare to dream, step out in faith, and try new things. People want to be led by leaders who believe that God is doing great things in and through us. Remember, Jesus said that his followers will do even "greater things" than he did (John 14:12).

Be Truthful and Open – Wearing the "belt of truth" in life is an indispensable part of leading effectively (Ephesians 6:14). Tell the truth in all circumstances, with each other, with the staff and with the congregation. There can be no hidden agendas.

Seek Outside Counsel – Plans fail for lack of counsel (Proverbs 15:22). Individuals and teams have limits, blind spots. We can't possibly know everything. For this reason, it is vital that we talk to other church leaders and seek outside counsel, particularly on difficult issues.

Start with "Yes" – Elders are gatekeepers, but we are also cheerleaders. If possible, let your first reaction to the ideas of the staff and the congregation be "yes." It is deflating to be met with a "no" each time you approach a leader. While not every idea must be approved, every person can be encouraged.

Be generous – We are servant leaders, called to pour ourselves in the care of others. Just as Jesus came to serve, rather than be served, we are to serve others, sacrificially and generously (John 13:15).

Pursue, Encourage and Support the Staff – Elders are the team leaders of the entire congregation. It's our job to pursue, encourage and support the staff, so that they can do the same for the congregation. This is as simple as talking to them, rather than about them. To serve well, staff must feel safe with us, be careful not to violate their trust.

Challenge the Staff – The role of the staff is to execute the vision. But as vocational ministers it is easy for staff to grow frustrated with volunteer leadership. Challenge them to dream, but also to be patient in the process, to trust the leadership and appreciate the congregation.

Utilize the Congregation – The role of the congregation is to serve (Ephesians 4:12). Don't hesitate to call them to service.

Be Unified – Unity is not uniformity or unanimity. Unity is loving partnership for a greater goal. Christ prayed that we would be completely unified (John 17:23).

The Effective Elder,
by Scott Brennecke (2009)

As a new Elder, I found myself gazing around the table at the others, quietly identifying their spiritual gifts: wisdom, leadership, giving, discernment, et cetera. It seemed that all the gifts were spoken for. I prayed that God would reveal his purpose for my being an Elder and he is faithful!

Seven days later he brought a fellow into my life in an astounding manner whose marriage was in crisis. Shortly thereafter was a woman from church with marital problems who literally fell into my arms sobbing—in a hardware store. Next was a man who had bankrupted his business, and then there was a small group with relational issues. God brought these people into my life to illustrate for me that my spiritual gifts are mercy and encouragement. As I employed these gifts my spiritual growth increased dramatically.

Scripture seems to pluck the spiritual gift of shepherding from the list and gives it unique emphasis as it pertains to the office of Elder. First Peter 5:2 directs Elders to, "shepherd the flock of God..." The voice of the verb is active, not passive. It is written as a directive. One aspect of shepherding takes place at elders' meetings. Equally important, however, is providing spiritual care and guidance to the congregation on a more personal level. Both are halves of the singular Biblical role.

Consider a shepherd in the field and his sheep. They are under his care, and he alone is responsible for them. He directs them and nurtures them. He guards them. He tends to the injured in order that they may be restored. He is actively engaged with his flock on many levels because they are his very livelihood. In short, a shepherd has many tasks but only one goal - the welfare of the flock. This is the very model that scripture cites for Elders to mimic. A congregation counts on its Elders to care for them just as a flock of sheep depends upon their shepherd.

This will mean taking the initiative. Seek out individuals in the congregation. Know their names, not just their faces. Ask how the church is doing for them and their family. In turn, ask how they serve the local church. Listen and pray with them. Above all do not wait for them to come to you; go to them.

Being available. Spend time with them and establish relationship. Then, if difficult times come, you have already connected with them. When you show up during their time of need you will be expected because they already know you. Simply put, an effective Elder is intentional. Each month you should be able to note those whom you have extended care; at the end of each year there ought to be many with whom you have connected. Whether meeting for coffee or picking up the phone, all Elders can make a tangible difference in the lives of those under their care. Most importantly, by Elders fully embracing their role, the Father will receive more glory.

The Call to Equip,
by Jim Rathbun (2010)

It has been a great privilege to serve these past four years. It is not a responsibility I have taken lightly. Scripture sets a high bar for this "noble task" (1 Timothy 3:1), as those who must be above reproach (1 Timothy 3:2). Having reflected on the name of this body (the "Elder Board"), I would encourage us to increasingly seek to function as a plurality of Biblical Elders rather than a corporate "board."

During my Elder term, I have been blessed to see abundant fruit in the GEBC body as we have focused on the Sending quadrant of the *Disciplemaking Target*. God has enabled us to send out our own to plant a church in Downers Grove. God has raised up and sent out scores of short-term workers who have been exposed to His work among the nations. God has raised up and sent out from our congregation several long-term missionaries. I am convinced that the raising up and sending out of long-term missionaries in increasing numbers hinges on effectiveness in the area of equipping. Let me encourage you to be proactive in this. Do not be "hands off" as a board regarding global outreach and church planting globally any more than we were hands off regarding the church plant in Downers Grove.

It is appropriate that we focus now on the Equipping quadrant of the Disciplemaking Target. Casting and cultivating vision for the congregation was the role of the Elders in the area of Sending and will continue to be so as we direct our emphasis on Equipping. Biblical teaching is foundational to Equipping. It is Scripture ("all Scripture") that is the means (2 Timothy 3:15-16) by which believers are "thoroughly equipped for every good work" (2 Timothy 3:17). Keep the Bible in "Glen Ellyn Bible Church." Increasingly, Americans are biblically illiterate, and the church in North America is following the culture. Read scripture in the corporate service, encourage the congregation to bring their Bibles and open the text. Provide Sunday morning and weekday Bible study opportunities. In keeping with the Elders' requirements (1 Timothy 3) of being "able to teach," increasingly engage in teaching ministries of the church.

Do not let pastors, or even staff, "do the work." Instead, hold them accountable to do the hard work of equipping the saints (NASB) or preparing God's people (NIV) for the works of service (Ephesians 4:12). Equipping is "building up." Consider yourselves members of the "building committee" and overseers of this important process. Devote yourselves to the public reading of Scripture, to preaching and to teaching." (1 Timothy 4:13) Give your attention first to prayer and the ministry of the word (Acts 6:4). Finally, I exhort all of you with Paul's words to Timothy: "Watch your life and doctrine closely. Persevere in them, because if you do, you will save both yourself and your hearers" (1 Timothy 4:16).

Servant Leadership,
by Mark Macaluso (2012)

Growing up as a Pastor's kid, I always looked up to the generation of older men that were the bedrock of our congregation, even as my Dad was much younger than they were. They felt like the Mount Rushmore of our little Baptist church. They were a compelling mixture of serious and manly, yet warm, congenial, and funny, and displayed love for the LORD, their families, and the church. I remember wanting to be like them because they did so much for a place and community that I loved. They took the youth on canoeing trips, they led the family camp, they sang in the choir and they practically built the church (at least that's how it felt every church work day). Maybe I am being too nostalgic, but I thank God for the great examples of Christian men and servant leaders they were to me and probably to my Dad, a young pastor.

So, what does that have to do with Glen Ellyn Bible Church? Let me encourage and challenge the Elders to always be involved in the lives of those in our body. I feel deeply that we should be a visible encouragement as we live out the example of Jesus Christ. Let us do so by being present at as many church functions as we can, being involved in small groups with those in the pews, leading worship, serving in many capacities. As I think of all the ways we can be involved, I am almost hesitant to make such a bold challenge as I recall how so many within our group are doing exactly these things. This is without a doubt a case of "preaching to the choir."

However, there have been times when the board has missed opportunities to be in the lives of the community. Five or six years ago, before I was on the board, I wrote a letter to the Elders about my disappointment from having returned from a very good Men's Retreat but realizing there was only one elder in attendance. It felt like a miss. This was probably because the one Elder who was there gave me a no-holds-barred challenge to "get off the sidelines and get in the game" of leading within the church. That put me on a track to start a small group, get serious about inviting accountability in my life, and putting to use the gifts God had entrusted to me. What a blessing that was and continues to be to me, my wife and kids.

So, let this be a simple reminder of how our visibility in doing these things can be a good example and a way to lead the flock that Christ has given us. This should not be a show for our own exaltation and pride, like the Pharisees, but as Christ's example of washing the disciples' feet.

You all have been a shining example to me of how well leadership can be done. Do not hide your light inside a board room; let it shine for all to see. Thank you, my brothers, for your leadership to this rookie elder and all you mean to me as humble, passionate leaders and examples of Christ's love and grace.

Counting Sheep,
by Sue Macaluso (2012)

When my husband, Mark, was asked to consider being an Elder, I immediately questioned God's timing, His care over our family, and what compromises we would have to make in serving this way. It was flattering that my husband was asked, but I was hesitant to think that God would want Mark to take time away from our children and me, as well as break the steady flow of service opportunities we were neatly engaged in at church. I was quick to respond to the elder nomination and even the acceptance of being an elder's wife with a multitude of prayers. But deep down in my heart, it became a surrendering of trust, obedience, and eternal investment.

I would have wanted Mark to delay accepting the responsibility until it was the "perfect time," but I learned to trust that God knew what he was doing with our time. A lengthy, cryptic phone conversation in the car as we headed out of town on our family vacation, Wednesday evenings of going to bed without saying good-night, time consumed by three-inch thick books or theology via emails, this was time well spent as it grew Mark's skillfulness as a shepherd not only at church, but also within our home. The children and I reaped huge benefits of spiritual leadership as Mark modeled how to care Biblically for others. By trusting God with time for Mark to shepherd, our flock of four at home was abundantly blessed. God is not obligated to supply our needs when we do our own thing. He calls us into obedience and asks that our plans be his plans.

Mark was the one being selected for eldership, and I thought that I could stay on the sidelines, passively showing my support while doing my own thing. When the call for duty would come, Mark eagerly answered. I, on the other hand, would be quick to fill the void with my own activities. I did not recognize my responsibility to the flock. I came to learn God was also calling me to serve alongside him. Each time another lamb approached Mark at church, by phone, or e-mail, (or his fellow shepherds beckoned), not knowing the situations, I would pray for both lambs and shepherds. This spilled into engaging the kids in prayer for their dad every time he was serving. Lifting the elders and our congregation up in prayer regularly became an act of obedience as we developed a healthy appreciation and respect for the elder position.

When Mark completed his tenure, the children and I reflected on how quickly the years had passed and how powerful the journey had been in both our family and the GEBC family. Many sheep were tended to, redirected, loved, and rescued. God used Mark's elder role to open my heart and eyes to celebrate the assurance of dwelling in green pastures. My prayer for all who serve as Elder's wives is that we would demonstrate trust, and obedience, that releases God's power, provision, and blessing upon their family.

Loving One Another,
by Bob Neyland (2012)

I feel inadequate to give "words of wisdom" to you. It has no doubt been the most humbling and challenging leadership experience in my life but also the most rewarding. That God actually called me to this role is kind of unbelievable given some of the past misdeeds of my life. But are we not all sinners saved by grace? All I can do that could possibly be of some worth to you would be for me to share what I have learned and express some words of encouragement.

First, I have learned that handling the tough issues that come before us is made a lot easier when we love those with whom we serve. Maybe I have been overly fortunate to have served where there has been good chemistry, but I have experienced a camaraderie and friendship like no other with you. It is amazing what kinship in Christ can do for a friendship. In the heat of battle and sometimes even in disagreements among ourselves it is so wonderful to know that at the end of the day, we will be brothers, unified, supporting one another and standing accountable together before God. My encouragement, if you have not done so already, spend time with one another and build relationships that evolve into keen friendships. That will make your service even more joyful!

Secondly, I have learned that my greatest joy is being able to give care to hurting individuals, whether it be visiting the dying and their family members, caring for the sick, or giving financial advice. I confess I have not done enough of this. Whether by email or phone call, we must get to know the people of the church so that we can provide care. My encouragement is to make it a priority to figure out people's needs. A small investment of time goes a lot further than you might think. Especially pay attention to the older ones that might begin to feel disconnected.

Thirdly, I have learned to submit to God's brand of leadership. I have always heard the phrase in business that "dual leaders, means no leaders." But God has a different view. God makes something work that cannot or will not work in business. Major decisions benefit from the meshing of our individual ideas. It does not have to be in your "wheelhouse" for you to have a valuable opinion on a particular subject. When we have fully discussed and hashed out a major decision and are unified as a group, we come to a better, more God honoring result. It takes longer, but God wants it that way. My encouragement is to always speak what God has placed your mind on all issues even if it is not in your area of "giftedness."

Fourthly, I have learned that while not all of us will be biblical scholars, each is to be committed first to Scripture and prayer and then to meeting individual feelings. As I have stated previously, the caregiving aspect of shepherding is vital but most problems in a church stem from leadership straying from the Word of God and straying from a commitment to being prayerful prior to acting.

We have come under a lot of scrutiny and criticism by some because of the discipline we have implemented. Although we may never get the implementation exactly right, we must never veer from what Scripture tells us to do. The most important aspect about our disciplinary process is that we have been true to Scripture even when it has been very hard to do, and we have bathed our decisions in thoughtful prayer. My encouragement is to base every decision on Scripture and allow enough time to pray corporately and individually about the steps we are about to take before we take them.

Fifthly, I have been reminded that we are in our positions because of the divine call of God. We are not appointed based on business acumen, intellectual capacity or even our "giftedness," but are appointed because God has called and equipped us for leadership in such a way that the work we do will be a joy and not a burden. Therefore, we need to remain holy in all aspects of our lives. If we begin to lack discipline and self-control in our personal lives, we open ourselves up to attack from the devil, and he will surely attack us! But we, like all believers, are provided an escape from the temptations of the devil. No temptation is unbearable. We have the power in Christ to resist it. This is, in my opinion, even more applicable to us as leaders as the devil relishes in bringing leaders down because of sin. My encouragement is to see yourself as divinely called and treat your role with the awe and reverence that it deserves.

Sola Scriptura,
by Gary Larson (2013)

It has been a tremendous honor to have the opportunity to serve as an elder during many different chapters of GEBC's history. During that time, we have seen remarkable blessings and also some severe challenges. But the one constant of which we always must remind ourselves is the principal message with which I want to leave you. This is not our church. It is Christ's church. We succeed best when we remind ourselves before, during and after every decision that we are representing Christ. Scripture uses a variety of metaphors to remind us that it is His church rather than ours.

- We are the Bride of Christ (Ephesians 5:25-27; 2 Corinthians 11:12; Revelation 19:7-9, 21:1-2)
- We are the Body of Christ (1 Corinthians 12:27; Ephesians 4:12)
- We are Ambassadors of Christ (2 Corinthians 5:20)

And ultimately these metaphors point to the reality that he is the head of the Church. Colossians 1:18 reminds us, "And he is the head of the body, the church. He is the beginning, the firstborn from the dead, that in everything he might be preeminent."

(ESV) There is always a strong temptation to believe that the buck stops with us. It never does—or at least we should never fool ourselves into acting as if it does.

But in serving as Christ's ambassadors, He provides the opportunity and even the mandate to make decisions on His behalf to advance His Kingdom. So, the second issue that churches need to face and that Elders need to face is, "Who or what has the authority to direct the decisions that impact the Church?" Over the centuries, that authority has been vested in councils, popes, tradition, the Magisterium, denominational governance, etc. Some Evangelicals appoint their own popes, whether it be best-selling authors or highly respected scholars. Even at independent non-denominational churches like GEBC we end up asking who has the authority to decide. Who gets to make the final call? Is it the congregational membership, is it the senior pastor, is it the staff or is it the Elders? We typically answer the question by affirming that it is the elders who have the ultimate authority to make the church's decisions. But our Statement of Faith embedded firmly in the Reformation is unambiguous. The real source of authority is Scripture (sola Scriptura). We are tasked with always putting our wills, individually and collectively, under the explicit authority of Scripture.

So how does all of this become practical? I think we all agree that Christ needs to have preeminence and that Scripture is our sole and final authority. But that still needs to get translated into practical guidance as to what Scripture says and how we as a Church can best fulfill its mandate and serve as Christ's ambassadors. I have been pleased that we have done the challenging work of discussing and clarifying our doctrinal statement. We have probably not always been as good at finding Christ's wisdom as to what we all need to do about it, as individuals and as a church. So my encouragement to each of you that continue in service to Christ and His word through service to GEBC is that you commit to learning how corporate decisions can best advance the Kingdom. I do not pretend that it is easy or that I have a formula that accomplishes it. I have been thankful that everyone on the Board is together committed to learning. From my own perspective, based not on my success but rather my frequent failure, my final advice comes from James.

> My dear brothers and sisters, take note of this: Everyone should be quick to listen, slow to speak and slow to become angry… Do not merely listen to the word, and so deceive yourselves. Do what it says. James 1:19-22 (ESV)

A Privilege to Serve,
by Jim Craig (2013)

It has been a privilege to serve on the board these past four years. During my term, I have come to appreciate the unique gifts of each board member and how the Lord uses those gifts to complement each other and to serve His purposes. Before presenting a "charge" to you, allow me to pause briefly and share specific highlights for me that stand out during our last four years of ministry together. There are many memories, but these are most notable:

- Witnessing the Lord's amazing work of forgiveness and restoration in a staff member's life following his public confession of sin.
- Experiencing God's wisdom and unity that He poured out on the board while decisions were made for his restoration, and the care giving for our congregation.
- Growing together as a board in the disciplines of fasting and prayer.
- Developing a deeper passion for doctrine as a result of our Statement of Faith exercise.
- Sharing the burdens of our congregation by listening and joining them in prayer.

Before officially rolling off the board, I give you this "charge." Continue to guard and teach sound,

Biblical doctrine to both adults and children in our church. As our world moves further away from Christian values, understanding what and why we believe will become even more important.

Look for opportunities to share your faith with people you meet. Plenty of opportunities exist, but they usually go unnoticed because our lives are busy and we do not look for them. The signs can be subtle: a death in the family, illness, fear of losing a job or just restlessness in a person's life. I borrowed an idea from Kelly and created a short handout of "My Story." Initially, it felt awkward handing it out to certain people. But it has helped create dialog and it no longer feels awkward. If we are asking our congregation to be more intentional in reaching the lost, I am convinced the leaders need to help set the pace.

Finally, take time to meet the needs of our congregation. Spend quality time with a few people rather than trying to take care of everyone's needs. Pray with individuals when you can, follow up with a phone call, or write a note. People appreciate a follow-up contact because few take the time to do it and it shows a genuine interest in others.

Men, it has been a privilege serving with each of you. Kelly, thank you for providing sound preaching of God's word each week. Mark, I appreciate your gifted leadership of the board and the countless hours you spend shepherding.

My Hope, His Glory,
by Joe Schaubroeck (2014)

Looking back over the last four years, I have often wondered why God did not choose someone more qualified to serve as an Elder. When I compare myself to others within the congregation, I see how inadequate I am and how much I still need to grow. Like Moses initially feeling inadequate to God's calling but being obedient, my hope is that my serving was obedient, that it brought glory to him, and that it furthered his kingdom, and I thank you for putting up with my weaknesses!

I want to take this opportunity to thank Mark Tucker and Bob Neyland for their leadership as chairmen of the board of Elders. I also want to thank all of those that served as fellow Elders. I have been amazed how often I see a parallel to the parable of the body (i.e. many parts, all needed) in the varied personalities, spiritual gifts, backgrounds, training, etc. we bring individually to the Elder board. Bob Neyland commented on this in his letter as "plurality of leadership." I concur and would add a "variation with unity." In any case it is a strength of God's design in allowing for prayerful consideration of many viewpoints but without a splintering of leadership.

As we have talked about many times, God has provided the right people to be Elders at the right time and for this I praise him. I also want to thank Pastor Kelly. While there are so many things I could write, I want to note your insatiable appetite for: new ideas, moving forward, and not being intimidated by change. These have been a personal inspiration for me.

I also praise God for our staff. I want to thank them and their families for their dedication, sacrifices, and service. While there were many staff events outside of our control during my tenure, I would encourage the Elders to continue to invest time and effort in our staff, as well as in the processes to select and develop the staff for the positions God has entrusted to them.

As I look back on my personal experience as a leader, our study of theology and the discipline of writing explanatory comments for our statement of faith were fantastic learning and growth experiences for me. My desire is that the entire congregation could have the opportunity to study theology in this manner. I recommend and encourage this becomes a focus for every new elder.

While I am a supporter of traditions, I am even a stronger advocate of change to achieve differing results. I feel honored to have been on the board for both the celebration of Kelly's 20 years of service, as well as the 70th anniversary of GEBC. I celebrate God's faithfulness to us as a church. However, I am equally delighted to see the many new programs launched this year. I hope GEBC continues to celebrate the traditions while transforming itself to be able to better reach the least and the lost. There are no failures in trying something new only learning steps in the process for success!

I am excited for the future. I see a tremendous opportunity in the vision and strategy efforts currently in process. Whereas we seemed to struggle over the initial years of my term in how to approach, define, organize, etc. around vision and next steps, it seems that Knute Larson's visit helped to spark efforts in bringing clarity while Kelly's and John Vandervelde's recent structural approach has added organization to the process. I believe we have a better understanding now of ourselves as a residential church, rather than a regional church, as well as our history in disciple-making and how we can leverage our strengths to bear fruit in the future. I will continue to pray for your wisdom and hearing God's will for GEBC's future path.

I have heard many of you say, "once an elder, always an elder." I do not take this lightly and will be praying not only for you on the current board going forward but all those who have served previously as well. Among other things I will pray for: protection from the devil for you and your family, wisdom, strength, and perseverance. Through God, I am sure you will continue to love and shepherd the flock well and stay true to his word. I will miss you and our frequent interactions. May God continue to bless you and GEBC to bring glory to himself.

Of Sheep and Coins,
by Glen Eggert (2014)

As I reach the end of my term, I would like to leave you with two primary thoughts. The first is this: do not forget about the lost. It may seem like a little bit of an odd thing to say to those serving as Elders, but the truth is that we, or maybe just I, spend far less time remembering the lost than forgetting about them. There can be so many other good things that we easily get caught up in doing so many of these other good things that we forget about the lost.

I am excited that conversion growth is rising to priority status as we set some vision and goals. I would like to caution you, however, that even the task of outreach can become something that causes us to look right past the lost. The widow's missing coins and the shepherd's missing sheep are not simply statistics or measurable goals. Every single lost coin and every single lost sheep is a real person headed toward an eternity without Christ. Some of these people have no doubt about how lost they are and others have no idea that they are lost at all. All of them, however, are equally in need of hearing that Jesus is the only way to peace with God. If we forget that "The Lost" all have faces, names and hearts, we will never think of them as being as valuable to God. Unless our hearts break as Jesus' does for those who do not know Him, we will never experience the joy of being able to say, "I found one of the lost ones!"

My second thought is this: do not forget what it means to be found. We who have been found by Christ forget all too easily what being found is all about. As products of our comfort-obsessed culture, we find it far too easy to settle securely into the bowl on the dresser with all the other found coins and find cuddling up with all the other found sheep far more desirable than going out looking for the lost ones. We can even reach the point where we do not want the mess and bother of dusty coins or burr-covered sheep, so we push them out to the edges of the bowl or fold where that type "belong."

Remember, the value of coins and sheep are not simply collecting them. Just as coins are meant to be spent and sheep are meant to be sheared for wool, so too our value to Christ's Kingdom is not measured simply in the collection of our souls but in how we are spent for God's glory. Sitting in the bowl or lounging in the comfort of the fold with the sheep we like is not a sign of maturity, but rather is a sign that we have forgotten what being found is all about. We must always remember that when we were found it was not just about saving us from our sin, but saving us to a life of bringing God glory. To fully experience the joy of our salvation we must daily ask ourselves how we can be spent for God's glory. As, with God's help, you are able to keep these two thoughts near the front of your mind, you will find that your heart beats more nearly to that of Christ and will find a sharper focus in your service as an elder.

Confession and Compassion, by Alex Dean (2015)

When I came on to the board, I began with some trepidation. The verse that was continually on my mind was Hebrews 13:17. "Obey your leaders... for they are keeping watch over your souls, as those who will have to give an account." Keeping watch over the souls of the body of Christ is a weighty task, but I have been encouraged to see the second half of this verse fulfilled in the men on this board. "Let them do this with joy and not with groaning..." Thank you for serving with such joy.

Before I present a challenge, allow me to share just a few highlights from my time on the board

- The board's willingness to host Koinonia House/Radical Time Out, the subsequent growth in the ministry and seeing attendees of RTO begin to attend GEBC.
- Growth of Celebrate Recovery and the incredible impact it is having on the church.
- Cultivation of a compelling vision and implementation strategy.
- Seeing Ken grow as a leader and become more comfortable in his role as worship pastor
- Being a part of a sending church and participating in a mission trip to El Salvador.

As for the challenge, let me remind you that God delights in broken and contrite hearts (Psalm 51:17), and Scripture encourages us to confess our sins to one another (James 5:16). While confession is prevalent within the Celebrate Recovery ministry and is occasionally practiced within other contexts, it is an area in which GEBC could grow. That growth should be led by the board. As leaders confess their own sinfulness, visitors and members alike will realize that the perceived façade of the suburban church (that we "have it together") is not real, and Christ will be glorified in His work to redeem and sanctify broken hearts.

Accelerate the work of caring for orphans and widows (James 1:27, Romans 8:15). I am thrilled to see the number of families that are either interested in, or actively participating in, caring for orphans. The adult education class on orphan care was well attended, and although there were many impactful moments, the people who most impacted me were Stan and Melodee Yohe. They were there not because they had any intention to adopt, but because they wanted to know how they could help younger couples interested in Safe Families or Adoption.

I will be excited to hear how God works at GEBC in the coming months and years. It was a privilege to serve with you.

Inadequacy and Sufficiency, by Bob Thomas (2015)

In the story of the Rich Young Man we learn of someone who is uncovered by Jesus for his covetousness (Mark 10:21). Before Jesus exposes him, however, we learn of a man who falls on his knees before Jesus, acknowledges Jesus as good, keeps the commandments and shows interest in knowing the secret of eternal life.

The suburban church's pews are filled with such men and women. Idolatry may take forms other than riches but it exists nonetheless. Jesus teaches us that entering His kingdom requires more than assent to His attributes in a hope of gaining His affirmation. There is a tendency in people that makes us long to gaze into the eyes of a Jesus so that we feel better about ourselves. But this is a Christianity of our own making.

> "At this the man's face fell. He went away sad."
> Mark 10:22

The evangelism on which we must initially focus must occur within these walls. The outward manifestation of seeking the lost and caring for the least will be a natural outgrowth of people being radically saved.

> "Only when <u>He</u> gives us a new heart to abandon everything for Christ will we be free

from our personal form of idolatry and yield to the principles of the divine kingdom." Sinclair Ferguson

As we embark upon an effort to see external works of evangelism and compassion, we must remember that all change is initially internal and subject to no less than the sovereign work of God.

> "Who can be saved?" With man this is impossible, but not with God; all things are possible with God." Mark 10:26, 27

I feel the same sense of inadequacy after four years of service as I did before agreeing to serve. As humbling as that feeling is, it serves as a reminder of God's grace. Salvation is all about our inadequacy giving way to His sufficiency. We have been corporately humbled in years past. The Lord has pruned our membership and leadership. The Lord has proved sufficient throughout. I pray with expectant faith that the Lord will make us a people that, like Isaiah, stand in awe of His holiness and glorify Him with our lives (Isaiah 6:5).

It has been a pleasure and honor to serve with a group of men that have truly exemplified Christ to me. May the Lord bless you.

The Battle,
by Glen Eggert (2017)

If you are not approaching this task with some measure of reluctance, then you have probably far underestimated the battle that you are entering. The job of an Elder is not simply a management task (Ephesians 6:12). One of my favorite boyhood books, "The Boy's King Arthur," tells tales of battles so fierce that the combatants "Hewed one another into cantels." Simply put, the battles were so violent that they cut great chunks of flesh and armor from each other. The enemy is formidable and there are times that the ground around you is going to be littered with spiritual cantles. If you dare to fully engage in this battle, your personhood, your marriage, your family, your possessions, and every other aspect of who you are will be targeted by the enemy (1 Corinthians 10:12).

If you are generous, be wary of your greed. If you are merciful, be wary lest you become judgmental. If you are wise be wary lest you become arrogant. If your marriage is strong, watch out for your lust. If you speak the gospel easily, be wary lest you never listen to people's pain. If the attack begins to wear you down confess your weaknesses to each other before your armor is gone and your wound is mortal.

Though the battle is real, we are not without resource. Our strength for the battle comes from none other than the God who says, "My strength is perfected in your weakness." Through His Holy Spirit we are "more than conquerors in all these things" (Romans 8:37). Fight the battle on your own, and you will surely go down. Fight in the power of the Holy Spirit and even your "cantels" will fight for Christ. Drink deeply from the vine of Christ and the wounds that you will surely suffer will be no more than the pruning that leads to the joy of great fruit in every aspect of your life.

Remember, we have each been given at least one gift. If God gave you intellect, then tear down the intellectual strongholds of the enemy or build a tower of truth. If God gave you a heart for the lost, go find them and lead them to Jesus. If God filled you with compassion for humanity, then feed the starving and house the homeless. If God has broken your heart for those unjustly treated, then do whatever it takes to set the captives free and bring justice. If God gave you the weapon of generosity, then give till you see the enemy bleed. If God has given you the heart of a servant, then find those who need to be served and give yourself up for them. If God has given you the wisdom and discernment to prophesy, then speak the truth unashamedly. If God built you to pray, then get some calluses on your knees. Recognize that God didn't give the "best" weapons to some of you and stick others of you with a broomstick. Whatever weapon God gave you, He gave it to you because in your hands, through His Spirit, it is the weapon that will turn the tide of the spiritual battles you face.

The beauty of being called as an Elder is the fact that we were called together. None are called as solitary heroes, but as part of a band of brothers. Not only do you have someone at your back in every spiritual battle, but we also have collectively every gift needed for what our church will face. You have been called as part of the right group of men, with the right weapons, to fight for God. As you fight together, don't lose sight of the end game. The weapons you wield are ultimately to be used to cut a path through the enemy so that people can look up and see Jesus. If you feed the hungry man, but never point him to Jesus, he will just be a fat man walking in darkness. If you free the captive and never point her to Jesus, she will just become the slave of a different shade of evil. If you house the homeless, and never shown them the way to Jesus, they will just be a bit more comfortable on their way toward their ultimate home in Hell. If you give, if you pray, if you teach, if you prophesy, and it is not done to point people to Jesus, then the little bit of ground you may think you are winning will be overtaken by the darkness as soon as you are gone.

You men have been called to be a part of God's story in this place at this time. Dare to run to the darkest part of that battle. Fight together, in the power of God's Spirit and you will kick in the gates of Hell. If you dare to lead by going in first, the people who are looking to you, infused with the hope of Christ's resurrection power, will rally to your side and the darkness will be pushed back.

Reflections on Planting,
by Glenn Williams (2018)

I continually thank God for the ongoing impact GEBC has on my life and family. When we moved from Grand Rapids in 2005, I had no notion of the pathway God would lead us down. My kiddos grew as Christ-followers through the Children's and Youth Ministry at GEBC. We found community and a sense of purpose in our roles of service at GEBC. So, to start, I extend my personal heartfelt gratitude to each of you for your leadership. It has made a difference!

When Four Corners Community Church (FCCC) was planted in January 2010, as the mother church GEBC was generous. First and foremost, in the decision to send out two of its "A" team leaders. Sending both Brian From and Dave Schubert was sacrificial. GEBC also gave FCCC the gift of financial freedom through the startup money ($400,000) and through a monthly gift of $10,000 to our operating budget for the first eleven months. What blessings.

Cultivating and casting the vision to plant a church was hard, involving many debates about the wisdom of church planting specifically, as well as the timeliness of planting for GEBC generally. There were many meetings required for cultivating the vision and working to cast the vision in soil that sometimes was not fertile to the notion of a church plant. I know that Kelly paid a price during that season and continue to thank God for how he used Kelly.

These blessings notwithstanding, if I were to plant a church again, here's what I'd do differently.

- Collaborate earlier and more often with GEBC. (e.g., pulpit exchange, worship team exchange, and sharing of youth events, etc.
- Clearly identify vision prior to launch. FCCC did not settle on a church vision or mission prior to launch. As a result, we focused on the activities rather than vision/mission. Activities are a great way to build community, but without a clear vision we lacked clarity for why we were doing what we were doing.
- Develop a leadership team covenant. Above all else, unity in the Spirit through the bond of peace matters most (Eph. 4). Entering into a covenantal agreement with God and with each other to uphold these precepts should be a part of any planting process.

As a church leader, there is nothing in my life I'd trade for the season of leadership transitioning from GEBC to FCCC. Serving seven years in a row (4 at GEBC and 3 at FCCC) was not a burden. It was a gift as I watched God grow his church. I will start and continue to pray that the next church plant out of GEBC has an even greater impact on the sending community and the Kingdom of Jesus Christ here on earth.

Jesus Will Build His Church,
by Steve Bult (2018)

A lot has transpired in the life of Glen Ellyn Bible Church over the past four years. It has been a difficult season, and a verse that frequently comes to mind is Galatians 6:9 which reads, "Let us not become weary in doing good, for at the proper time we will reap a harvest if we do not give up." I think I can speak for some of us and say that there were times when we have become weary of doing good. However, God gave us the strength and wisdom to persist, and as a church, we seem to be reaping a harvest now.

As I think about the four years that I have served, the thing that comes to mind most often is the importance of having the right people in place and equipping them to do their work. The hiring of John Vandervelde, as Executive Pastor, is one of the best examples of this. John has no doubt been the right person at the right time for GEBC. He has allowed Kelly to focus on the areas in which he is most skilled. Having John take over as Executive Pastor allowed us to deal with other challenging situations which ultimately resulted in getting more of the right people in place in Matt, Mark, Grant, Sarah, and several others. I applaud Kelly, John, and the Elder Board for the way they went about bringing these people on board.

As I think of the people who make up our staff, I cannot imagine Engage 2020 without John or the

Caregiving Center without Sarah, or the hospitality efforts made without Grant. So, now that we have the right people in the right positions, my charge to you is to continue to provide each of our staff members the best possible leadership training. God has given us great leaders in each position, and it is imperative that we steward their gifts and grow them in their bandwidth as leaders. God has given us the five talents, and it's crucial that we invest and maximize those talents.

As I leave the Board, there is one other verse that I have come back to often that it is so important for us as Elders to remember. That verse is Matthew 16:18 which reads, "...I will build my church, and the gates of hell will not prevail against it." This was a verse that some of us came back to frequently about three years ago when times were quite challenging. It's in the tough times that this verse is so important to remember—no matter what happens, Jesus is building His church, and nothing stands a chance against it. However, in our current season of growth and expansion, it is also important to remember this verse. We must remember that God is the one who builds His church and not us. As much as we humans like to take credit, God is clear that *He* is the one doing the building. To Him be the glory!

Renewing Presence,
by Pam Bult, (2018)

Glen Ellyn Bible Church is God's most abundant provision for me and my family. Standing amongst friends and family on a Sunday morning to worship together, being rooted and encouraged in God's Word each week are truly the life-giving activities that restore, renew and refocus me. Because my work as a psychotherapist ushers me into difficult places in others' lives, I often tell my children, "I could not do my work without the weekly blessing of worship at GEBC." Some weeks I can literally feel my mind shift back toward God's sovereignty, away from the stresses and back toward God's promises. In addition, GEBC welcomes me, calls me "sister" and friend. I can feel with clarity my need for community, and it is often through relationships at our church that I find God meets that need-not only for myself but also for my family.

And so, when Steve was invited to be an elder, we were excited for him to be part of leadership, to contribute in a new way to the care and building of our church community. Four years later, as he has completed his time in this role, we pause with gratitude yet again, for our church, and for this rich opportunity he has enjoyed. My encouragement to elders and to wives is to stay clear on the importance of this invitation to lead. When Scripture invites us to see the church as the Bride of Christ, it brings to mind strong words such as "beloved" "precious" "invaluable." Our church changes lives. It welcomes, disciples, heals, feeds, clothes – all in Jesus' name.

This summer, more than ever, because of some difficult circumstances in our extended family, we are reminded every day of the darkness in our world. Sometimes, as we climb the steps of GEBC on a Sunday morning, that darkness presses in, but then the sounds of worship, the greetings of friends, the warm welcome, and ultimately the presence of God stand in stark contrast. Darkness fades in the presence of light. We are bathed again in the goodness of our God, His truth that saves and restores.

Leadership relies on day-to-day realities of meetings, phone calls, emails, challenges, decisions. As you partake in these tasks, know that your work is life changing. Glen Ellyn Bible Church, because we are rooted in Christ and His Word, is light in the darkness. This summer, my family is reminding each other, "The light always wins." You serve on the winning team. As you serve, remember that every interaction matters, that what you do is life-giving, and light-generating.

I hope that you will regularly feel the value of your work and service in leading our church. Be prayerful and thoughtful in every decision. Being Christ's light in the world is no small task, and yet what joy to also know that Christ loves GEBC even more than we do and promises to guide us! Thank you, in advance, for your time, contribution, and great care of our church. We are grateful to our leaders!

EQ/IQ Balance,
by Jeremy Boynton (2018)

Hardly seems possible that four years have come and gone and that I am writing this letter. In many ways, I am very proud of the body of work we have created together as a Board. In other ways though, I feel barely qualified to be in this leadership position and am simply thankful that I haven't contributed to blowing up the church or myself while leading with you!

I have always considered myself a good leader. That is until I joined this Board. I have discovered that leading with a group of peers can be quite a bit more difficult than leading alone and is probably the highest level of leadership that exists. Pretty much all other leadership is really management—that is leading because I am "in charge." In fact, I came to the Board unaware of how poor of a leader I was. And dragged the Board thru my learning experience likely in somewhat painful ways at times. I am very thankful to come out the other side of that, and I want you to know that I truly love you guys!

So, regarding a "charge" to the Board, I would simply share a few of my personal passion points. From day one as an elder, I have prayed a simple prayer most mornings for three specific things:

1) That God would grant us clarity of vision.

2) That God would enable us to love well Kelly and John.
3) That God would raise the EQ (emotional quotient) of each Board member

If we seek God's vision, and we love our frontline leaders, and we push our intellect toward living the expressions of our hearts (EQ), we will create something contagious, a powerful and magnetic leadership that will shape culture profoundly. This EQ/IQ balance is important. It is certainly the point of Boathouse Party outreach. At Boathouse Party there is no programmatic IQ needed, meaning no sermon or lesson is given. But there are very intentional EQ ingredients: food, wine, and conversation. At Boathouse Party, we are simply using EQ magnetism to point people to Jesus, by loving them thoroughly. EQ is also the point of our involvement with International Justice Mission and the Lily House in the Dominican Republic. After all, it's one thing for our IQ to comprehend that the sex trafficking trade is evil. It's another thing altogether to provide our people an opportunity to personally engage in helping fight the war! It's all about engaging their EQ.

So, I guess I do have a request for you after all. My heart's cry is that the Elder Board would continue to seek out EQ moments and adventures, to reach both those in the Church and those outside of it. For the single grand purpose of spreading the fame of Jesus!

Through
by Bob Neyland (2019)

As I complete my term as Elder, one word seems to be impressed upon my mind, "*through.*" Being from Texas, I was raised with a "getter done" mentality in which you rarely asked for help and if you did you were considered weak. Although our founding fathers proclaimed a belief in and reliance on God as evidenced in our Constitution and our coinage states "in God We Trust," they also believed in what might be called "rugged individualism." This is the virtuous ideal in which an individual is totally self-reliant and independent from outside assistance. The thought is that given opportunity and hard work, a person could accomplish almost anything. While this seems good and admirable on the surface, it has resulted in an independence from God and an elevation of self. Our culture screams "It's all about me!"

We have become a society of egotists. I was once counseled by a Senior Partner that I needed to promote myself more if I wanted to make partner in the firm where I worked. I was told I needed to be more vocal about my accomplishments. While maybe there is some truth and practicality to this type of "it's all about me" philosophy in the corporate workplace, we need to never let it permeate the church and especially its leadership.

As an Elder, I want to always substitute the word "*through*" in place of "*about.*" If I think anything is about me then I am not only prideful—and the point opposed by God—but I am also stupid. Pride makes me take on God, and that is one contest I will lose. So, if it's not about you, me or us; it is *through* you, me and us that God accomplishes his work for his glory.

As leaders we are called to make disciples. But who is really making the disciples? We are the means by which God accomplishes his work. We are much like a writing instrument. A pen may be beautiful and valuable, but it has no writing power. It causes nothing. It can be very instrumental when the author picks it up for use. If a pen I want to use is not clean, filled or available, I simply go to one that is! A particular pen might be necessary but not indispensable. Similarly, we must be continually on our knees seeking the Holy Spirit's direction lest God move on to someone who is. We need to be filled and available, clean, and useable. In other words, we need to be the pipe through which God's will is done on earth as it is in heaven. We are His instruments. We are powerless to accomplish our leadership responsibilities on our own. We need to take our visions, our desires, and our preferences as leaders to the throne of the Lord and ask for his confirmation and direction.

My friend and GEBC missionary Mboligihe came to me several years ago and said that his community desperately needed dental care and asked if I could make that happen. I was at first clueless! What I initially thought was an impossible task (I didn't know ANYTHING about dentistry) turned into an incredible Godly adventure. The Lord worked through me and others to accomplish what I could never have accomplished. God opened the opportunity to not just provide a dental service but to provide trainers to train lay people which could provide the service long after we had gone – a much better solution than anyone envisioned. We didn't just bring fish, we taught people how to fish! Availability and prayer is all I brought to the table.

Scripture describes how King Asa, had been blessed with decades of peace and spiritual success because he sought after the Lord with all his heart. But after 35 years of serving the Lord, King Asa made a fateful error in judgment. When the king of Israel set up a blockade around Judah, Asa appealed to the king of Aram for help. The core problem was not the political alliance he developed but that Asa had neglected to seek spiritual guidance from the Lord first. A prolonged time of war resulted. In an earlier time, scripture describes how The Lord reduced Gideon's army to such low levels that it was only by God's power working *through* Gideon that the Israelites defeated the Midianites. The Bible is full of accounts where the Lord acted *through* His servants to accomplish His will.

I mentioned earlier that we are powerless by ourselves as instruments. Here's amazing news regarding our responsibilities and responsiveness from the Apostle Paul: "I can do all things *through* the One who strengthens me." Remember, it's not *about* you. It's *through* you!

Listening and Speaking
by Gary Larson (2019)

In offering a charge and advice to the elders, I would identify two places in my life where at least some growth has occurred that serves as a valuable lesson to all present and future elders. The first is to genuinely cultivate the discipline of listening well and speaking less. James 1:19 says, "But everyone must be quick to hear, slow to speak and slow to anger." For most of my life, I've mastered the "slow to anger" part but failed at the "quick to hear" and "slow to speak" parts. I'm in either my sixth or seventh term as an elder (my exact memory is foggy) and I've had the reputation during some of those terms as the elder who can single-handedly make meetings last late into the night. I still on occasion fall into that trap and when I listen to myself say all of the words I was dying to say, I recognize that more often than not they could have or even should have been left unsaid. An old proverb suggests that God gave us two ears and one mouth so that we would get the ratio of listening to speaking correct. But on an elder board with as many members as we have, two to one should become more like ten to one. And every voice I listen to has value. Every once in a while, what I say might also have value but less often than I'm tempted to think. I'm thankful that I've been genuinely learning this lesson in my life as I get older, and it serves me well not only as an elder but in every setting of life.

The second lesson that I've learned more slowly than I should have is the lesson of receiving spiritual advice and wisdom from my wife. For theological reasons that we've tried to study carefully, we don't have women as elders or as teaching pastors at GEBC. But that doesn't mean that women aren't the source of tremendous spiritual wisdom and insight. Each of us would identify our wives as strong spiritual partners. In my case, I've discovered that my wife has rare gifts of spiritual discernment and a practice of spiritual disciplines that exceeds my own. When we were first married, we attempted to have devotions together as a couple, but it rapidly became a case of Gary acting as a graduate school trained theologian or "Bible answer man," a role that I've too often tried to take as an elder or Sunday School teacher as well. In more recent years, we end every single night reading the Bible out loud to each other with very little commentary. It's a very important discipline and one to which my wife holds us accountable. It is still important for us as elders to serve as spiritual leaders in our homes as we do in the church. But it is equally important to recognize that spiritual leadership involves partnership and that the most important partner we have is our wives.

As I rotate off the Board, you all won't have to listen to me regale you with presumed insight (or just plain opinion). But I trust that those who take my place will be quick to hear and slow to speak and that all of us would listen to God's Spirit most of all.

Grace
by Bob Thomas (2020)

"Look, these many years I have served you and I never disobeyed your command, yet you never gave me a young goat, that I may celebrate with my friends." Luke 15:29

Twenty-five years ago, a friend told me about revival breaking out at Wheaton College. I got off the couch and headed to College Church, where students and faculty were meeting, to see for myself. The night had already begun, I entered the church to worship music playing and was stunned to see a packed house with arms raised. Seats were at a premium and I found mine in the third row next to a student on his knees weeping. Someone took the stage and said, "we don't know what is happening here, all we know is that the spirit of the Lord is moving, we are learning as we go." Having been in pockets of revival in the past I felt that perhaps I might have something to share on the subject. But I found myself driven to my knees, next to that student, as this time, it was I who wept, as I heard the voice of God speak to my heart: "Bob this isn't about you it's about me."

This completes my second four-year term on the elder board. I have served alongside men of character and spiritual depth that have challenged and furthered my walk with the Lord. My most cherished memories are of times that were outside of our scheduled elder meetings. I have had the opportunity to pray for the various needs of fellow elders expressed in an atmosphere of transparency and love that is rarely found in the world in which we live.

Forgive me, but the thought did come to mind, why wouldn't those prayers be answered? The men petitioning have honored you with their lives and Lord you are a God that honors those who honor you. I have been a staunch proponent of clinging to the doctrine of grace since coming out of the Catholic Church but when these thoughts surface I am forced to grapple with the reality that there remains a nugget in my belief system that we are deserving of His love.

Timothy Keller in his book, The Prodigal God writes: "Careful obedience to God's law may serve as a strategy for rebelling against God." What a sobering thought, especially for elders, men who find themselves in a position that calls for obedience and have scriptural mandates of conduct to qualify for the office. I have not only prayed for but have also received prayer by the men of faith gathered here tonight. On one such occasion I found myself in a situation that many of you share to this day, a child that walked away from the faith he or she knew at an early age. Nothing (I will say it again), nothing was as devastating as the thought of my son turning his back on the Lord of the universe and dabbling in false religion. I shared with, prayed with, and shed tears with some of you seated here tonight. Where was God in those prayers? How would my faith and the faithfulness of the elders with whom I prayed enter into the equation? My son came back to the Lord, and I am delighted to report that he has been the priestly head of his home in the aftermath of his prodigal journey.

Where was God? He was at the center of not only my son's restoration but also mine as he retaught me that His word is true. Jesus will not lose one that the Father gives Him. He really is faithful to complete the work that He started. And my faithfulness and the faithfulness of the elders with whom I prayed—well it is not about us it's about Him.

In my eight years on the board, we have expressed regret that we are not seeing more converts. The Great Commission is at the forefront of what it means to be a follower of Christ. My prayer is that we will love because He first loved us and love as He loves, all the while knowing it is all about Him. Oh, that the Lord will touch us and allow our hearts to mourn the prospect of a relative, friend, neighbor or co-worker relegated to a life without Jesus as I mourned for my son, as you mourn for your sons and daughters.

In writing this charge I feel somewhat presumptuous. There have been times in listening to my fellow elders that I wondered if the same Holy Spirit lives in me that obviously dwells in you. Your Godly wisdom has left an indelible mark on my soul. Perhaps it is more of a reflection than a charge. I leave it to future boards to contemplate its purpose. I have learned it is not about what we do even in doing the work of the church but rather what He did.

Justice and Unity
by Mark Macaluso (2020)

Note: At this time (June 2020), waves of protests against racial injustice and police brutality sweep across our nation, and we are in the first months of the Covid-19 global pandemic.

The last year has been something. After finishing the Welcome Center build, we found ourselves with a budget deficit and a capital campaign to finish, but God was good and people responded and gave, and we finished the year just above budget and the building paid off, no debt. God is Good!

Then we started hearing about a virus and before long we had to close our doors – no services for the first time in over 75 years. But God has sustained us, teaching us that the Church exists regardless of the building it meets in, and our congregation has rallied watching services via online video, prayer meetings and Small Groups gathering via Zoom. The previous season of growth in the grace of giving and being rooted in His Word kept us strong. God is Good!

After the horrific death of George Floyd, we have seen a national swell of protests. Sadly, this is not the first unjustified death of a black person by a white police officer or of protests thereafter, but it feels unique. At least, it feels unique to me. Maybe the virus's impact on my daily routine has caused more reflection, but the Holy Spirit has taken a hold of me to awaken compassions in me that were pitifully dormant.

I have never been wired as a very emotional person, but my daughter Emiko is gifted with an off the charts compassionate heart. God brought her home during this pandemic and stirred conversations that brought me to my knees in sorrow over how people of color have been treated in this country, but more importantly to my own sinful indifference, selfish attitudes, and ignorance. Once I began earnestly considering what the lives of African Americans around me are like every day (my boss, several direct reports, Robert S, Caleb & Izzy V, Maya & Joel M, even our mailman that I see every day now out my window as I work at home), it got way more real to me, and our Lord Jesus started cutting away at the calcification around my heart. I continue to learn more and will stay engaged in how I can help our community do better and heal, starting with myself. I care and love more than I ever have. God is good!

I hope and pray that we all will keep the discussions about racial equality and justice going and use it as momentum toward changing the activities and attitudes of our predominantly white, suburban church. I would like to see our church connect with another church and organizations locally to partner with people of color to get to know one another, worship together, work together and change all our understanding and empathy for each other. We praise and serve the same God that created us all in His image. Our Care Center is wonderful in this respect, and I hope we can extend that work. In the past, we partnered with a church in Lawndale, traveling together, sharing rooms with and attending Promise Keepers in Indianapolis as an entire group. Those were great weekends, but relationships were short lived. We have partnered with *Outreach Community Center* and *RTO/Koinonia House* and *By The Hand*, but let's take it up a notch and do more altogether. Maybe we get to know more folks at Second Baptist Church of Wheaton. I'm not sure how, but I'm motivated and about to have free time on my hands, so let's do this!

Lastly, as we endeavor to spread these wings and exercise these atrophied muscles, I trust the board will lead in unity. I think it is God's wonderful timing to finally have an Elder of color, but this cannot just fall on Robert. It must be led by our entire board. Robert, I am grateful for God's choosing you to join our Elder board at this time. We have much to learn as a church and I'm grateful for your voice to expand our understanding and perspective. You and Ken are both great additions to the leadership of our church. I thank God for his wisdom and guidance to bring the right leaders together in every season.

I leave you with Romans 12:12 "Be joyful in hope, patient in affliction, faithful in prayer." May God be glorified and may our body grow in God's teaching, even in times of trial and sorrow. Again, I say - God is Good! Praise be to Him! Thank you, my brothers, for your encouragement and brotherhood in Christ. You all mean so much to me as humble, passionate leaders and examples of Jesus' love and grace.

Years of Instruction
by Phil Koch (2021)

What a joy it has been to serve with you. I have now been involved in some form of church leadership for 45 years, and I'd like to share 5 points of Godly learning as if I were addressing a twenty-five-year-old Phil. These 5 points have been areas of great joy and challenge for me personally and I hope you can take some encouragement from them.

First, never unplug from your power source. It is so important to stay connected to our Lord regardless of all the busyness that life throws your way. A commitment to daily scripture study and prayer is required to keep you focused on the important work that He has for you. Just like "brushing your teeth," if you don't do it, you know something is missing. Without a daily grounding in God's word, unplugging from the believer's power source is sure to happen.

Second, make space in your life for the stranger, immigrant, and nonbeliever. The Pharisees criticized Jesus for spending time with tax collectors and sinners (Matthew 9:12). Jesus' response was, "It is not the healthy that need a doctor but the sick. But go and learn what this means: I desire mercy, not sacrifice. For I have not come to call the righteous, but sinners." Equally important throughout the scripture are references to welcoming strangers and immigrants (Leviticus 19:34). I know in my own life it is very easy to want to spend time with those who are fun to be with, have all the same beliefs and build me up at the expense of being used more fully for eternal purposes.

Third, be all in on your marriage. As the years on my odometer keep spinning forward, I am reminded of what a great Godly gift I have in my wife. She has played a critical role in my church leadership roles and provided a perspective that I needed but just didn't know it. I would encourage all to invite your spouse into conversations around spiritual leadership of the church and thus create a sounding board who will provide honest God inspired feedback. Be prepared for some intense but valuable instructions and opinions.

Fourth, don't forget that you are a survey of one, which means you need to lean on each other. There were 12 disciples for a reason. I can't help but think the disciples were an incredible support to each other. Despite human weaknesses they served together well. You are in service together and your personal thoughts and opinions need to be tested against other believer's thoughts and opinions. Always be willing to listen to other lines of thinking no matter how far you are from embracing a different point of view.

Fifth, declutter your life and focus on eternity. I am convinced that we all are partly hoarders and junk collectors. We have filled our time and lives with STUFF. Slowly STUFF takes over and crowds out our true church mission of making disciples. Managing all the clutter takes away from Godly service and none of the clutter matters in the least.

Iron Sharpening Iron
by Tim March (2021)

    I will admit, writing a "charge" to the Elders proved much more difficult than I had imagined. Kelly gave us plenty of prep time, but I struggled with the message I wanted to convey. In fact, it has been something on my mind since I first received the Elder Notebook and read the wise, wise, words of the men who have gone before me – what a blessing to have those archived for future elders to read.

    My four years on the Elder Board were a sweet time both personally and, it seems, for the church. We had many highs and just a few lows. God was, is, and will continue to be faithful to GEBC. When people ask if I was ready to rotate off the board I respond enthusiastically, "Yes". Not because I was unhappy with my time or the stress of it all but because it bookends a period of my life with which I look back on with happiness. I leave with excitement for the church and where you men will lead it. I will cheer on, and pray "from the sidelines." Within that context, I still struggled to join my two overarching thoughts, that the board should lead courageously and embrace Christian brotherhood. I was having a hard time until Kelly preached on Revelation 2:1-3:22 and asked the pointed questions, "Who do you trust to carry the words of Jesus to you?" and "Are you that person to someone?"

Over the summer, since rotating off, it seems a lot has happened. Kelly went on sabbatical, you all have continued your work on a position paper and there is an ongoing discussion of a multisite ministry. Not to mention the COVID reality. This all is happening while we read, hear, or talk about the podcast "The Rise and Fall of Mars Hill." This podcast highlights the struggles created in an unhealthy church leadership culture. How can we, as Elders, avoid the pitfalls which so quickly entangle us as individuals or lead us astray as a body of believers? I find the answer is clear – intentional community.

We have heard this before and quite honestly, some (maybe most) on the board have this down quite well. But I do believe the board, collectively, can work on community. The easy stuff, as Macaluso charged us, like being involved in the lives of those in our body (i.e. present at church functions, involved in small groups, serving, choosing to start with "yes" when asked) many of you are doing well at. Maybe not so easy, is being well prepared for board meetings through prayer and dedicated time to know the topics to be discussed so that when the meeting occurs, we can lead well and communicate our positions clearly to Kelly, John, and other staff. Our job is not to multiply kisses as our enemy does but to be iron to one another. Thoughtful introspection, honest conversations, and meaningful pushback makes a board better.

I am not talking about arguing for the sport of it – something I probably could be accused of at times.

That is not what I mean, nor do I think it is something with which the board often struggles. However, when discussing the weighty issues there should be some heat produced, some sparks flying, and iron sharpened. We all have our individual communities, our spheres of influence, but the men on the board of Glen Ellyn Bible Church should be the men who carry the Word of Jesus to one another. Christian brotherhood amongst the board is imperative.

If I may, some practical applications: seek out your fellow board members outside of Wednesday night – I found our time from eight o'clock until prayer ended to be so life-giving as we checked-in. Extend that to a morning coffee or a dinner together. Engage with Kelly or John regularly to understand the pressure points of the church so that you can pray for or provide a way forward. When you feel the Spirit prompt you in a meeting whether affirming or challenging the topic at hand don't let the moment pass you by – be men of action. Leading is difficult but thank God you men get to do it together. Cherish your time together and work to strengthen the bonds. Authenticity, in my experience, provides a way forward to engage in meaningful conversations about how the Lord is leading you, this board, and His Church. It is in this context I believe God will bless your times together, as iron sharpens irons you will lead us well into the post "Engage 2020" mission.

Abide
by Chuck Martin (2022)

I'm grateful to be a part of this now longstanding tradition of outgoing elders writing a charge to current and future board members. It's an opportunity to reflect on serving the church the last four years and remember God's faithfulness to his people and our leadership team through many unique seasons. A quick list includes the completion of Engage 2020, the COVID outbreak, locking down the church due to state mandates, reviewing endless Covid protocols, parking lot services, remote services, live streamed services, masked services, masks for worship time and no masks for preaching time. We followed that up with a racial justice paper, launching a REACH vision, and beginning a journey to consider adopting Poplar Creek Church as our second campus. And then most recently, we experienced the unexpected leadership transition of two elders stepping off the board, and the intense shepherding work which followed.

In all these circumstances, God has been faithful. He has been our rock and our provider; our comforter and our protector, our guide to lead us through darkness, and the one who has delivered us through all the storms we faced. Just remembering all that has taken place the last four years, I feel like I should be more tired and worn out from all that we've experienced. But Jesus tells us in Matthew 11 that His yoke is easy, and His burden is light. Walking this journey with Christ has not only made it possible, but there has been great joy and peace knowing that we're not alone and he doesn't expect us to go through any of it without his help. Working alongside each other in a yoke requires the two parties to not only share the burden but to actually pull at the same pace or the work will be more difficult. God has grown me in learning to wait on Him and work with him at his speed – it's only then that I get to experience the fruits of the light burden.

Speaking of fruit, I want to encourage all of you with another verse that has been transformative in my walk the Lord. In Matthew 15:5, Jesus tells us that he is the vine, and we are the branches and that if we remain in him and he in us, we will bear much fruit, but apart from him we can do nothing. I've meditated on this verse and the verses after it and have been struck by the decisiveness that Jesus communicates in that the result of not abiding in Him is that we can do NOTHING - not even a little bit fruit but NO FRUIT. So, if we want to be fruit bearers of his work in us, what does it mean to abide in him? The words that have come to mind as I've meditated and prayed over these verses are humility, submission, and rooted. Humble myself before the Lord in prayer, submit myself to the authority of Christ, and root myself in the living Word of God.

The fruit Jesus is talking about are the things that can only be attributed to God's good work in and through us. He's not talking about a good work that we accomplish in our flesh. He wants his Father to be glorified through the fruit that he bears in us and that can only happen if we abide in Him. I've been greatly encouraged to see us growing as a church in abiding more deeply and depending on Christ to be the one to do the work. The more we continue to grow in this abiding nature, the more we will experience His good work in the ministries of Glen Ellyn Bible Church.

So, my charge to you all is to abide more deeply in the Vine of Christ so that you can help shepherd our church to become greater fruit bearers for God's Kingdom work at GEBC. Jesus goes on to say in verse 8 that it is to his Father's glory that we bear much fruit and that we then show ourselves to be his disciples. May the people of Glen Ellyn Bible Church be known as disciples of Jesus Christ as they bear more and more fruit for the Glory of the Father.

As hard as these last few months have been with all that has been on my plate, it has been a joy to walk the journey trusting the Lord to do the hard work and help us navigate the path forward. It has also been a joy to walk alongside Kelly as we've prayed together, wept together, and encouraged one another. Even in difficult circumstances, there is a unique gift in sharing true fellowship in our mutual love for Christ and his church. I pray God's blessing over all of you as you serve GEBC diligently in the coming ministry year.

The Good Shepherd
by Lynnaea Martin (2022)

To the men who have, are, or will serve GEBC:

Thank you for giving your time and service to the Lord by leading GEBC. I have been the beneficiary of three decades of service by faithful men such as yourselves. I've felt cared for, seen, heard, protected, and challenged by the Elders. My ever-growing love for Jesus, his Word and his church has been fostered in great part by your diligence. The elders of this church have set this trajectory in me, and I praise God for it.

After having a few terms of service as wife of an elder, I know this calling comes at a cost. It takes time away from your family. It requires you to diligently practice what is being preached. It exposes you to spiritual attack. It places you in the middle of difficult decisions. It reveals to you the various trials and temptations congregants face. It demands stamina.

But the role comes with blessings as well. You are some of the first to sense where the Holy Spirit is leading GEBC. You have the privilege of praying over the sick in anticipation of the Lord's healing. Elders get to work together as a microcosm of the Body of Christ, benefiting from each other's gifts and wisdom. You are irst in line to hear testimonies of the great things God is doing. And, most importantly, you are personally cared for and led by Jesus, THE Good Shepherd.

He is your example. He is your ever-present help. He is the abundant source of all you need to fulfill your duties. Jesus embodies all the character traits that I long for in my elders such as: love for God, humility, faithfulness and courage. Jesus loved God with all his heart, soul, mind and strength. This love spilled over into his sacrificial love of God's people. May Jesus help you grow your love for God and our church.

Jesus was gentle and humble in heart. He did not elevate himself but, instead, brought himself low to serve others. God raised him up in due time. May Jesus help you to humbly serve others.

Jesus was faithful to do the Word of God. He taught God's commands to all who would listen. He obeyed all that God required. May Jesus help you to uphold God's Word and to respond to the Holy Spirit.

Jesus was courageous in trials, defending himself and his flock with the Word of the Lord and through constant communion with his Father in prayer. Opposition did not deter him. May Jesus impart to you his courage to do battle in the spiritual realms.

It is because of the Gospel that you are serving. It is a high holy calling and I personally want to thank you for entering into it. My ongoing prayer for you is from Col. 1:9-11: I "continually ask God to fill you with the knowledge of his will through all the wisdom and understanding that the Spirit gives, so that you may live a life worthy of the Lord and please him in every way: bearing fruit in every good work, growing in the knowledge of God, being strengthened with all power according to his glorious might so that you may have great endurance and patience."

After 40 Years at GEBC
by Glen Eggert (2022)

The end of this term not only marks the end of a term of service, but coincides with the end of 40 years at GEBC. Knowing that God's new course for Janille and myself means that this is the last charge I will give to GEBC elders, I have chosen to share a few of the many lessons that God has taught me in this place hoping they may be an encouragement to you.

First, God's goodness is often seen in moments, but His faithfulness is seen over time. Psalm 46:10 says, "Be still, and know that I am God." Knowing that He is God is not just a second command paired with the command to be still. It is the result of being still, a discipline that requires waiting. Put your feet on the path that God has called you to and stay there. No matter how rough the trail becomes, don't give up. Somewhere ahead lies the beautiful vista of God's faithfulness. Perhaps it may take years, or even a lifetime, but if you persist you will see beyond doubt the faithfulness of God.

Second, God is good even when it doesn't feel that way. One of the advantages of growing older is the fact that you suddenly discover your present is built on a foundation of experience. For me that experience has demonstrated time after time that God's goodness is greater than and more enduring than the times of trouble. Romans 8:28 is no longer a theological theory for me, it is a demonstrated fact. While I haven't seen the end of every story I am part of, God has shown me enough endings to prove that He is unfolding His good plan even when I can't see it. Hold on to the promise of God's goodness. He will not let you down.

Third, stop trying to please God and put your efforts into learning to love Him. If you spend your life trying to please God, all you will experience is slavery. How are Romans 6:18 (which says that we have "become slaves to righteousness") and John 8:36 (which says, "if the Son sets you free, you will be free indeed") both true? The answer is love. Any slavery, even the slavery to righteousness, is simply a crushing bondage. Don't pick up the wrong yoke. Growing up in the twilight of the Jesus people years there was a little chorus that somehow wormed its way into my life. It goes like this:

> I keep falling in love with Him over and over and over and over again. I keep falling in love with Him over and over and over and over again. He grows sweeter and sweeter as the days go by, Oh what a love between my Lord and I, just keep falling in love with Him over and over and over again.

Fourth, live as if God lives inside you. Why? Because He does. Too often we live like there is still a chasm between us and God. We pray as if we are mailing letters to a distant relative. We tell Him we love Him as if we're sending Him a postcard from a foreign country. The reality, however, is that when God closed the chasm of our sin He didn't go back to the other side. He stayed and took up residence inside of us. He has chosen to contain all of His character and attributes in our heart. If this is indeed the case, how might our lives change if we actually expect God to answer when we speak to Him? How might our prayers change when they are empowered by the very presence of God? What difference would it make if we stopped thinking of God as our absent Father and started to know Him as "Daddy?" What would the impact be if we changed our long-distance love relationship with God into a marriage?

Fifth, embrace the gift that God has given you. From my very first spiritual gifts inventory, I spent a lot of time disappointed. Of all the cool gifts that I could have received, I got stuck with encouragement. I felt like the kid who desperately wants a video game system only to tear open a box of socks. Instead of getting to be on the field, I was left cheering in the stands. When God gives you a gift, however, it will begin to leak out even if you don't want it. By His grace I began to see the effects of these leaks and gradually began to release my resistance and gift envy. As I submitted to Him and began to try my gift out, I discovered that there is no such thing as a "dud" gift. Every gift He gives is infused with His power. My gift of encouragement wasn't a second-hand invitation to watch the big boys play. It was an invitation onto the spiritual battlefield. Did you know that there is a prophetic side to encouragement? Did you know that

God performs miracles through the gift of encouragement? Did you know that the gift of encouragement can be used to lead people from the kingdom of darkness into the kingdom of light? Guess what. Every one of these benefits is present in whatever gift God gave you. If you remain stuck in jealousy for the gifts you didn't receive, all you'll have are socks in a drawer. Dare to put the socks on and you'll discover that you've actually been given a superhero costume and an invitation to see the power of God at work in and through you.

Sixth, ask God to change the desires of your heart to match the desires of His. We struggle to resist sin, but the reality of scripture is that just as we are unable to save ourselves so too we are unable to make ourselves more Christlike. Instead of continuing to ram our heads against the wall harder, doesn't it make sense to simply ask Him to do the changing of our hearts? Think of the implications of God changing our desires. We can't be tempted by something we don't want. James 2:4 says, "You do not have, because you do not ask." It really is that simple. Start asking God to do the work and watch Him change your heart.

Each of these lessons has fundamentally changed me. Despite my trust in God's good plan for my life, there are moments when I wish that I had learned these things sooner. It is my prayer that, by sharing them with you now, you too will get to experience the joy that each of these has brought to me. All Glory to God.

Be Ignited
by Dan Maas (2023)

Mary Oliver's poem "What I Have Learned So Far" addresses the beauty of quiet reflection, but also charges the reader to commit to active and passionate labor in the cause of what we believe; what she refers to as the "just" and the "holy."

> *"What I Have Learned So Far"*
> *Meditation is old and honorable, so why should I not sit, every morning of my life, on the hillside, looking into the shining world? Because, properly attended to, delight, as well as havoc, is suggestion. Can one be passionate about the just, the ideal, the sublime, and the holy, and yet commit to no labor in its cause? I don't think so.*
>
> *All summations have a beginning, all effect has a story, all kindness begins with the sown seed. Thought buds toward radiance. The gospel of light is the crossroads of — indolence, or action. Be ignited, or be gone.*

"Be ignited, or be gone." There is a plain brevity to that charge that leaves me both challenged and inspired. Are we on fire as followers of Jesus? It is clear to me that each one of you brings unique giftings and perspective to the table. I trust what has been said before: God has placed you on the board at the right time and for the right purpose. I have learned more from you and admire each of you more than you probably know. What I am suggesting is that you stay on the board, and you do so with a renewed commitment to serve with all you have. Be ignited, or be gone.

The question I pose is this: Are you *ignited* to serve in your current role of leadership? We know that ignition of an engine requires a spark. Without that it is an inoperable hunk of metal. As we consider how God would have us lead his people, it is critical that we examine what is sparking the fire inside us. It is not lost on me that it may be easier to "sit on the hillside" (or rather 501 Hillside) waiting for God to move. Let's not neglect to remember the importance of waiting on God as a worthy discipline. But let's not confuse waiting on God with complacency, laziness, or fear-driven inactivity. Make no mistake. If you have accepted the position of elder there is *work* to be done. The good news is that it is not work that must be done by our own merits, but rather the work of Jesus in our lives that moves us to faithfully give, serve, and lay our lives down for others.

Let's acknowledge something every one of us knows to be true but cannot be stated often enough. We cannot work hard enough to earn our salvation in Christ. 2 Timothy 1 states, "He has saved us and called us to a holy life—not because of anything we have done but because of his own purpose and grace." It is a gift (we have often said free but not cheap) that will never be matched. But men, it should move us to action! It should ignite us…move us away from a complacent, lukewarm faith and spark a desire to rise to the calling. My charge to you is to pause, and to take a transparent and honest look at what is sparking your fire right now. Is it Jesus?

Allow me to share three brief action points to consider. Each of these has helped ignite my faith in recent years:

1. **Acknowledge your imperfection and sinfulness.** Do this out loud and in front of each other. Confess to each other and pray over each other (James 5:16). Some of the most powerful and moving moments for me personally on the board have been when we have paused the "business" of the evening's agenda and engaged in the business of approaching the throne together.
2. **Remind yourself regularly how God has gifted you, then put that talent to work.** Be relentless in your pursuit of service in this way. Consider writing a personal mission statement that captures how you believe God wants to use you. I recognized early on that one of my best ways to serve the congregation was to pursue other men one-on-one, encouraging them in the truth and promises of God. This became one of the most fulfilling and joyful parts of my experience at GEBC.

3. **Be ready for battle.** We have seen God unfold the multi-church vision into a tangible reality for the first time and we are making overt moves to reach more with the gospel…expect warfare. Put on the full armor of God. Stand back-to-back as brothers ready to defend the Kingdom and the congregation from attack. I'm convinced one of the best ways you can do this is to continue to be in the Word together. The Sword of the Spirit, the Word of God, is your weapon. Wield it.

Men, whether you are stepping onto the board for the very first time or you are a veteran, the next season of service is upon you. Be ignited! God has proved over and over again in each of our own lives and in the life of GEBC that He is up to something. It won't always be easy and quite frankly we can be assured it will require sacrifice. It will require that we pick up our cross and follow Him (Matthew 16:24). But we can also be assured that what He is up to will be GOOD (Psalm 27:13), it will be more than we can ask or ever imagine (Ephesians 3:20), and it will bring Him glory. We know that something as small as a spark can lead to something as spectacular as an explosion. It is my prayer that each of you finds your spark in Christ, that you would find His grace in your life blindingly beautiful, and that his work in you in this next season would move you to be men of action.

Servant Leadership
by Dave Wiegman (2023)

The saying is trustworthy: If anyone aspires to the office of overseer, he desires a noble task. (1 Tim 3:1)

  A description of an elder that I have always struggled with, and at times have even rejected, is that of being a leader. I have always felt that what I was doing was serving the church. Don't get me wrong, we have all been given gifts for the benefit of the church, but being an elder is more than just serving. Not separating out these two roles, leadership and service, is where I think I was going wrong. These are not two competing roles, but roles that work well together. We serve Christ, but our leadership is for the flock. That all said, I would encourage all elders to lead in a few specific ways.

  I recently heard a quote from Kenny Smith, the basketball analyst – "Champions do daily what everybody else does occasionally. They aren't extra ordinary - they just do the ordinary extra." I'd like to change that a little and say "Elders do daily what others may do occasionally." I am reminded of Hebrews 2:1 – "Therefore we must pay much closer attention to what we have heard, lest we drift away from it." Following Christ, setting an example, being a leader in the church is as much about consistency as anything else, about not drifting. There is a high responsibility in the role we have been given.

I just wanted to remind us all of the things that we can be doing to make sure we don't drift away. The first thing that comes to my mind is to pray. It is easy to come up with ideas when a problem is presented. I know that I default to looking for solutions before someone finishes telling me what they have a question about. God has given us minds to process and gifts that lead us to provide direction, yet we can't forget what James says – "if any of you lacks wisdom, let him ask God, who gives generously to all without reproach.' Our heavenly Father wants us to seek him out. I know that spending time in prayer before a meeting, or any other situation, gives me a sense of peace going into the conversation. God has provided us with the means to communicate with him and praying is admitting that we need more than what we have to offer. Prayer as elders should be done privately, as a group, and also demonstrated to the flock we are leading. They need to see us depend on Him, not ourselves. If we don't encourage people to seek God, we could be setting up people to drift away, and maybe ourselves as well.

Another thing that comes to mind is using God's Word when giving advice or counseling someone. I'm sure I have some good things to say, but I can't add much to what God has said in the Bible. When people come and ask for help in a certain situation, or ask for prayer, or seek guidance for a decision, do we point them to God's Word? Once upon a time a friend of mine and I started memorizing the book of James. I can't tell you how many times I used verses from that book to provide direction to folks. Our spending time in God's Word and then using it as we talk with people about the issues in their lives will encourage them to start doing the same. It is in this way that we provide leadership to the people in our congregation.

The last thing that I think we need to be reminded of, and to remind others of, is the gospel. The gospel is the truth of Christ's death and resurrection, but we need to remember each day what was accomplished for us so that we live our lives differently. I don't know about you, but I need to think daily of how much I was forgiven, how much grace I was shown, how much mercy was extended, how much I am loved just as I am. In doing so I will forgive others, I will show them grace, I will offer mercy, and will accept people, and love people, for who they are. We should be so grateful for God accepting us for who we are each and every day that the same attitude overflows to the people we come in contact with daily.

These are just three things that come to mind when I think of leading as an elder, I'm sure there are many more you can think of. If we will lead in these (and other) ways we can shepherd the flock God has given us towards wanting to do these things daily, and not leave them for only occasionally. This will grow the kingdom and we'll see more people come to follow Jesus and deepen their relationship with him.

For Such A Time As This
Brenda Dryfhout (2024)

With the lives of the Jews hanging in the balance, Mordecai sends a message to his cousin Esther, a young woman who had been brought into the palace of the king. Mordecai, distraught and weeping at the thought of what might happen to him and his people, knows she is in a position to help. When Esther expresses concern about visiting the king without being summoned, Mordecai responds: "Don't think you are safe just because you're in the palace. And if you are quiet, God will save His people from another place. And who knows but that you have come to your royal position for such a time as this?"

If the past four years have taught me anything, it is that I cannot predict the situations you will face, the people you will encounter, the heads that will cry on your shoulders, the problems that will trip you up, or the bonds you will form as a group. Starting this journey as a family, we could not have anticipated a global pandemic. We didn't foresee the pain and confusion that fractured relationships from people leaving the church would bring. We didn't know God would call a former teacher and mentor to serve on the board with Ken, bringing new life to that mentorship role. Nor were we prepared to walk the journey of sickness, loss, and grief.

But what I know without a doubt and with great conviction is that each of you men has been called for such a time as this. It is a time to be humble, faithful to your wife, self-controlled, hospitable, and respectable. It is a time to lead your families, to preach and to teach, to shepherd the flock, and to watch over them. It is a time to pray over the sick and confess your sins to one another. This group of men has been brought together from many different places and experiences to do the work of God for this church.

My prayer for this group is that when troubles arise, you are quick to gather and even quicker to join in prayer. When the hurting and the broken come, may you offer safe spaces of comfort and care. May your eyes be on the lookout for the widows, orphans, and foreigners, offering this church as a refuge. Be there for each other in the ups and downs of everyday life and spend time laughing together. Lead confidently, knowing that this group of men is not an accident or a random occurrence, and that you are all here for such a time as this.

Leadership Lessons in Loss
Ken Dryfhout (2024)

Re-reading the experiences and collective wisdom of past elders and their wives in preparation for writing my own charge led me to agree with Solomon who writes in Ecclesiastes 1, "What has been will be again, what has been done will be done again; there is nothing new under the sun. It was here already, long ago; it was here before our time."

So much was "here before my time". However, I know that God created us individually and designed us for life collectively so I hope the reflections I contribute can be an encouragement and blessing for those who follow, despite the dour title of my charge "Leadership Lessons in Loss".

It should be said at the start that my tenure on the elder board has been a privilege and full of significant blessing. The opportunity to have a front row seat to experience all that God is going through this community of faith, serving alongside these men and getting to sit under their influence - all of this has been an incredible honor.

However, I have not felt led to focus my charge on the fruitful aspects. Rather, the time I've spent with God processing my experience has led me to understand more clearly the way in which the Lord uses the difficult aspects of leadership to refine us for future fruit bearing. And the last 4 years have brought their fair share of challenges - in my case both in service as an elder and in my personal life.

Just in case we needed a recap, we began in the throes of COVID and worked through everything that followed: political polarization, engaging the church body on the topic of racial equality, justice and unity, the resignation of two elders who were also close friends, the departure of several long-time families as a result of one or more of these factors, and a general decline in church attendance nationwide. Add to that the complete turnover of the student ministries team, the adoption of a struggling church, and the hiring of a number of staff positions in building back a new team poised for ministry growth. On a personal level, several close friends and family members have moved out of state and my father passed away this spring after a struggle with cancer and stroke. In short - it's been a lot and I'm sure I'm missing a few things.

Now, of course God is good - he always has been and always will be - and while I could skip to the part where we talk about how all of this has given way to new fruit, I don't want to move too quickly past the important work He does in the difficult moments.

In John 15, Jesus is meeting with his disciples shortly before his death and says to them, "I am the true vine, and my Father is the gardener. He cuts off every branch in me that bears no fruit, while every branch that does bear fruit, he prunes so that it will be even more fruitful."

This imagery of a vine, or perhaps in our midwestern context, a tree being pruned was helpful to me in processing my elder tenure. At several times, I felt as if God was removing things - relationships, self-confidence, independence, pride. And so it shouldn't surprise me that some of the same benefits a tree realizes from being pruned are applicable to the way in which he has cared for my soul.

For example, pruning can help keep the people around the tree safe. A dead branch can fall from a tree at any time, endangering nearby people, buildings or power lines. The pruning God does in our lives serves to do the same - cleansing us in a way that can remove elements that can be damaging in our relationships.

Pruning a tree can influence in what way the tree grows. With proper pruning, a tree can be made to grow in a certain configuration of limbs and branches that is more ideal for the structural integrity of the tree. We easily head off in a certain direction thinking we have all the right information only to realize that we needed redirection or reconstruction.

The desired effects of pruning take time to be revealed. It makes the tree vulnerable, even looking somewhat naked. In the cases of severe pruning, it can be downright ugly. The changes God works in us aren't instant either. They take time to be worked out and the reasons aren't always clear. When we're being pruned, it can make us feel vulnerable, afraid and uncertain of the next step to take. It strips away the things not of God that we use to prop ourselves up.

Finally, a tree can't prune itself. It must be acted on by an arborist that knows what the tree needs and the right cuts to make. God's word and the work of his Holy Spirit come together to do this work. We can't do it on our own.

So, what's the takeaway? What's the charge?

1. Pruning comes after the fruit. It's a part of God's work in your life to continually conform you to his likeness. Take heart - don't be discouraged.
2. It's revealing. Loss reveals where your trust has been placed and whether you care more about your comfort and reputation or the advancement of the Kingdom of God. Keep focused on obedience.
3. Rely on each other to know if you're being cut off or pruned. Plurality of leadership is a beautiful thing - for leadership can be a lonely place. Check one another in truth and love.
4. Know that he's doing this work to bear more fruit in you. It may not always feel that way in the moment, but he is faithful and good to carry out the work he's begun in you.
5. Remain in the vine. There's a strong temptation to jump ship during the pruning process - to take what seems to be the easy way out in the moment. Don't miss out on the blessings he has in store for you - remain connected to him and to one another.

Endure
Robert Steele (2024)

While limping through a trial ten years ago, I met with Kelly for encouragement and guidance. At that time, I had freshly failed the bar exam, and the Lord was mercifully confronting sin and pain in my life as if to draw out venom from a wound. During our meeting, Kelly immediately opened God's word and shared scriptures from the book of James:

> Consider it a great joy, my brothers and sisters, whenever you experience various trials, because you know that the testing of your faith produces endurance. And let endurance have its full effect, so that you may be mature and complete, lacking nothing. James 1: 2-4 (CSB).

Never could I have imagined the depth of healing, restoration, and faith refining that the Scripture would ignite over the next decade. The Greatest Shephard drove away despair, pride, selfish-ambition, and shame that all would have devoured me. He called me into humble submission, to turn over my purposes for His, teaching my heart how to truly love God and love others.

It was from a posture of prayer and submission that God called me to service. And although many words came to mind to describe this season as an Elder, "endurance" is the word that rang clearest in my soul. At the beginning of my eldership, Brittney and I celebrated our oldest daughter, Victoria's, birth; toward the middle we deeply wept as our second child, Jodi, went home to be with our Father in Heaven; and at the end of my four years, we rejoiced at the birth of our third child, our youngest daughter Emelia.

My fellow elders have witnessed my tears and borne my burdens, for the heart of a father longs to know his children. And still, our souls sing praises to the greatest Father whose heart longs for a wandering world to know His love so much so that He sent His one and only son to endure death on a cross.

Although I am tempted to say my time on the board felt unique, I am gently reminded that there is nothing new under the sun. I was wounded by a friend yet fortified by many brothers. As a black man, I deeply felt the pain of racial unrest as our nation continues to struggle with a legacy of sin that has by no means left the Church unscathed; but Christ's victory over sin binds us together with the blood of the lamb. By God's grace we saw Bartlett Bible Church's debt retired, weathered storms of strife during periods of transition, living out Paul's call to "be completely humble and gentle; be patient, bearing with one another in love" and making "every effort to keep the unity of the Spirit through the bond of peace." Ephesians 4:2-3 (NIV).

Through these things, we continuously learn what it means to love others, for "love bears all things, believes all things, hopes all things, endures all things." 1 Corinthians 13:7 (ESV). And so, I've learned that to endure (among many things) is to *live out* the love our Father has shown us, to pray for those who may have wounded you, and to be "peacemakers who sow in peace." James 3:18 (NIV). So, as we love God and others, while praying unceasingly, I encourage you all with the words from the Book of Hebrews:

> Let us lay aside every hindrance and the sin that so easily ensnares us. Let us run with endurance the race that lies before us, fixing our eyes on Jesus, the pioneer and perfecter of faith. For the joy set before him he endured the cross, scorning its shame, and sat down at the right hand of the throne of God. Hebrews 12:1-2 (CSB).

Grace and peace be with you!

THE MINISTRY OF SHEPHERDING

Shepherding is Caregiving

The Apostle Peter charged the Elders to shepherd God's flock (1 Peter 5:1-2), which happens directly (i.e. through personal contact) and indirectly (i.e. by caring for caregivers or overseeing caregiving structures). Elders also have formal (programmed) responsibilities and informal (non-programmed) responsibilities in their shepherding ministry. Below is a grid that outlines the various roles of the Elders in the caregiving effort.

Elder Caregiving	Direct Care (personal contact)	Indirect Care (leadership oversight)
Formal Care (Programmed)	Leading prayer in worship Leading annual meetings Membership interviews Teaching/Preaching	Overseeing Staff, finances and programs Leading the Elder Nomination Process
Informal Care (Unprogrammed)	Counseling and Mentoring Participation in Groups Hospital Visitation Funeral Attendance	Modeling Christlikeness Praying for Parishioners Praying for Staff Praying for Ministries

In serving as a shepherd, we are not going to be perfect, but we are to be diligent. Carrying out our responsibilities is complicated in that elders are both shepherds and sheep. Elders are both following the Good Shepherd, as well as responsible for helping others follow after him. Humility is essential.

Direct and Formal Caregiving

Elders provide direct and formal care in four ways. Below is a description of each.

Leading Prayer in Worship

A time of Elder led prayer is a part of worship quarterly. Leading prayer in congregational worship services helps:

- Fulfill our calling as Elders (Act 6:2-4)
- Raise the prominence of prayer (Acts 2:42)
- Strengthen our shepherding (1 Peter 5:2)

As you prepare to lead in prayer, make sure to read over the Scripture passage that is being preached that day so that the content of the prayer is integrated into the theme of the morning. We asked that each prayer offered be fully typed and no longer than one page, single spaced, size 14, Times New Roman font.

Leading Annual Meetings

The membership meets twice annually. The November meeting is to vote on the budget for the upcoming year. The May meeting is used to review the year and elect Elders.

Leading Membership Interviews

Participating in the membership class and hosting the interviews is a key part of the ongoing shepherding effort for the Elders, as the heart of the membership curriculum is aimed at presenting the gospel and explaining the nature of the church, as well as teaching about GEBC's vision for making disciples. "The Mechanics of Elder Leadership" section describes in detail the membership process.

Teaching / Preaching

Elder's must be able to teach (1 Timothy 3:2; Titus 1:9). Opportunities to teach range from weekly small group meetings and Sunday school classes to Men's Ministry events to preaching. Teaching and preaching are an important function of Elders because we know that the Apostles gave their "attention to prayer and the ministry of the word" (Acts 6:4), and Paul wrote to Timothy, "Do your best to present yourself to God as one approved, a workman who does not need to be ashamed and who correctly handles the word of truth" (2 Timothy 2:15). The goal is that every Elder is ready, willing, and able to teach or preach.

Indirect and Formal Caregiving

Elders provide indirect and formal care in four ways. Below is a description of each.

Overseeing Staff

Inasmuch as the Elders directly oversee the senior pastor, they indirectly oversee all staff. It can be confusing to identify the differences in the roles of staff and Elders, but GEBC is best described as a congregationally ruled, Elder led, and staff driven church. Congregationally ruled means the congregation annually approves by vote the Elders nominated and the budget proposed. Elder led and staff driven means that the Elder board is responsible for the church as a whole, overseeing the doctrine, discipline and direction, while the staff is responsible for the implementation of vision. To better understand the various responsibilities within the church we have identified four types of leadership.

- Elders – oversee the whole church by guarding the doctrine, disciplining those needing correction, and setting the church's direction.
- Pastors – implement the vision by overseeing ministries as whole and day-to-day operations.
- Directors – oversee specific programs, which involves leading and managing volunteers.
- Coordinators – lead an individual event or program, which involves empowering laity.

Elder Leadership	Staff Leadership
Cultivate and cast vision	Implement vision
Pray and dream	Pray and design
Vision and mission	Strategy and tactics
Answer "why" and "what"	Answer "how"
General direction	Specific details
Align staff	Align laity

Overseeing Programs

Inasmuch as Elders indirectly oversee the staff of the church, they also indirectly oversee all the programs of the church. This oversight is formally accomplished as the Elders monitor the congregation's attendance and giving.

Overseeing the Church's Finances

Along with the staff, the Elders work each year to develop a budget for a vote at the November business meeting. Ongoing, the Elders work closely with the Senior and Executive Pastors to monitor cash flow, as well as raise funds to accomplish the vision.

Leading the Elder Nomination Process

The Elders nominate five members from the congregation to sit on the Nominating Committee (NC), whose primary purpose is to work together to select elder nominees. Two Elders make up the remainder of the committee, including the Chairman of the Elder Board, who acts as Chair of the Nominating Committee.

Direct and Informal Caregiving

Elders provide direct and informal care in three primary ways. Below is a description of each of these areas. These are informal in that they are not required, but often accompany the role of serving as Elder.

Counseling and Mentoring

Shepherding involves pastoral counseling. When you meet with someone make sure to:
- Share God's word.
- Pray together. Pray at the beginning and end, as well as to be sensitive in the meeting to opportunities to invite the Holy Spirit to care for those we are meeting with.
- Provide resources. It takes a team with varied gifts to bring restoration. Ask staff with help to identify needed resources.

Participation in Various Groups

The primary means for shepherding at GEBC is groups. All groups at GEBC are:
- "leader-led" - all groups are led by leaders.
- "inviting" - groups are open to newcomers.
- "multi-generational" - include all stages.

It is impossible in a church our size (1000+) for the staff and Elders to disciple everyone, but group leaders help shepherd the flock. In many respects, these small groups are miniature churches.

Hospital Visitation

A distinguishing mark of Christian ministry is visiting the sick (Matthew 25:36). A favorite passage to read to the sick is Romans 8:18-39. Here is an outline:

- 8:18: the glory of heaven will make the sufferings of earth seem inconsequential.
- 8:19: all creation awaits God's glory.
- 8:20-21: sin brought suffering and death.
- 8:22-25: all creation is groaning, and we wait patiently for God's redemption
- 8:26-27: God's Spirit is made available to his people to help us while we wait.
- 8:28-30: we can be confident that in all things God works for our good.
- 8:31-39: illness can't separates us from God

Funeral Attendance

Offer more than platitudes. First, express your sorrow. If one member suffers, we all suffer (1 Cor. 12:26). Second, remind them that death was not what God intended for us to experience. God desire was that we would live forever (Gen. 2:9). The sinfulness of man brought death (Rom. 5:12). The good news is Jesus overcame death (Rev. 2:8). Those who trust in his death for the forgiveness of sin will share in his resurrection (Jn. 11:25). Through his resurrection, we will live forever. We are to comfort those facing death with the certainty of being reunited with those who have gone to heaven (1 Thess. 4:13-18).

Indirect and Informal Caregiving

Elders provide indirect and informal care in three ways primarily: 1) modeling Christlikeness, 2) praying for parishioners, and 3) prayer for ministries. Below is a description of each of these areas.

Modeling Christlikeness

The ministry of caring begins with caring for yourself and your family. While it is often assumed that Elders are caring for themselves and their families, the importance of this ministry should not be taken for granted. Caring for one's family is one of the qualifications for serving as an Elder (1 Timothy 3:4-6), and by caring for ourselves and our family we offer a godly model for others to emulate (1 Peter 5:3). Remember, the leader is the message in many respects. Paul urged the Corinthians to "imitate" him (1 Cor. 4:16). We can't communicate beyond our character. This seems to be part of the message in Jesus' response to Martha about her frustration with Mary not helping in the ministry (Luke 10:38-42). What are you doing weekly to abide in the vine (John 15:1-4)?

The truth is that our public ministry is only as solid as our private lives are godly, and for this reason we need to be ready to explain our personal decisions. While we may be tempted to think that what we do with our own time, talent and treasure is our business and not a matter for public scrutiny, the truth is that every area of our lives is open for critique, as those we lead will have questions about our personal habits of godliness. Of course, this is true for every believer to a certain degree, but it is true to a much larger degree for leaders. Leaders are expected to "set an example" (1 Timothy 4:12), which means we do not have the luxury of living the unexamined life. When questioned on our personal habits, we need to be able to give a reasoned response for our behavior.

For example, I was recently asked why I drink alcohol when so many struggle with addiction to the substance. Someone even suggested that if I wanted to drink that I should do it in the privacy of my own home, implying that who I am in private can be different from who I am in public.

My response is that I enjoy the taste of some alcohol but work to avoid any and all self-medicating (i.e. buzz or drunkenness). I reminded them that all things were created by God to be enjoyed (1 Timothy 4:1-6), as long as we receive them with thanksgiving and prayer. In other words, we can enjoy all that God has given us if what is created is submitted to his lordship in our lives. My goal in life is to avoid license (living in a manner worthy of someone in hell merely because heaven is a certainty) and legalism (believing that I have merited heaven). We are to be mastered by nothing (1 Corinthians 6:12-20), but neither are we to believe that we are saved through our self-discipline (Galatians 2:16). In other words, abstaining from beer is not required by the gospel and could be misconstrued by some as trying to earn one's way to heaven. Being able to offer this type of reasoned response for personal habits is an important part of setting an example. It can be tiresome to do this type of work, but the ability to discern between right and wrong behavior is a mark of spiritual maturity (Hebrews 5:14).

Praying for Parishioners and Ministries

Just as the Apostles allowed nothing to distract them from the responsibility of prayer, we wholeheartedly embrace this role as one of the primary functions of an Elder's call to ministry (Acts 6:4). Caring for widows is certainly important work, but the Apostles realized the appropriateness of delegation in ministry and the necessity that Elder leadership focus heavily on prayer. We see this clearly as James directs the sick within congregations to call for the Elders of the church to pray for them (James 5:14). In an effort to cultivate a posture of prayerfulness, the Elders have begun to set aside certain seasons for prayer and fasting. These seasons can include:

- At the beginning of the calendar year.
- Each Wednesday During Lent
- Each Day During Holy Week
- At the beginning of the Ministry Year (September)

THE MINISTRY OF PRAYER

Elder Led Prayer During Worship

A time of Elder led prayer is a part of worship quarterly. Leading prayer helps to:

- Fulfill our calling as Elders (Act 6:2-4)
- Raise the prominence of prayer (Acts 2:42)
- Strengthen our shepherding (1 Peter 5:2)

Leading in prayer is far from perfunctory, but rather an indication of our firm commitment to the ministry of prayer. Just as the Apostles allowed nothing to distract them from the responsibility of prayer, we wholeheartedly embrace this role (Acts 6:2). In our contemporary church, that focus is now the responsibility of the Elders. We see this clearly as James directs the sick within congregations to call for the Elders of the church to pray for them (James 5:14).

To cultivate the discipline of prayer, the Elders have begun to set aside certain seasons for prayer and fasting together. Most recently we have prayed and fasted together:

- At the beginning of a calendar year.
- Each Wednesday during the Lent
- Each Day During Holy Week
- At Ministry Year Kick Off (September)

Scriptural Basis for Prayer

Prayer was an activity of Jesus.
Simon, Simon, behold, Satan demanded to have you, that he might sift you like wheat, but I have prayed for you that your faith may not fail. Luke 22:31 (ESV)

But now even more the report about him went abroad, and great crowds gathered to hear him and to be healed of their infirmities. But he would withdraw to desolate places and pray. Luke 5:15-16 (ESV)

Prayer is an activity of the Holy Spirit.
Likewise, the Spirit helps us in our weakness. For we do not know what to pray for as we ought, but the Spirit himself intercedes for us with groaning too deep for words. Romans 8:26 (ESV)

We are told in Scripture to pray.
Jesus told his disciples a parable to show them that they should always pray and not give up. Luke 18:1 (NIV)

One day Jesus was praying in a certain place. When he finished, one of his disciples said to him, "Lord, teach us to pray, just as John taught his disciples." Luke 11:1 (NIV)

Be joyful always; pray continually; give thanks in all circumstances, for this is God's will for you in Christ Jesus. 1 Thessalonians 5:16-18 (NIV)

Prayer is a means to receiving from God.
Whatever you ask for in prayer, believe that you have received it, and it will be yours. Mark 11:24 (NIV)
And I will do whatever you ask in my name, so that the Son may bring glory to the Father. You may ask me for anything in my name, and I will do it. John 14:13-14 (NIV)

Again I say to you, that if two of you agree on Earth about anything that they may ask, it shall be done for them by my Father who is in heaven. For where two or three have gathered together in my name, there am I in their midst. Matthew 18:19-20 (NASB)

The prayer of a righteous man is powerful and effective. Elijah was a man just like us. He prayed earnestly that it would not rain, and it did not rain on the land for three and a half years. Again he prayed, and the heavens gave rain, and the earth produced its crops. James 5:16-18 (NIV)

Laying on of Hands

While the laying on of hands during prayer may appear to be little more than placing a hand on someone else's shoulder, as a biblical and theological practice it is profound, and the Elders are in the habit of doing so as they pray with/for congregants.

Jesus laid his hands on people when healing them.
When the sun was setting, the people brought to Jesus all who had various kinds of sickness, and laying his hands on each one, he healed them. Luke 4:40 (NIV)

Laying on hands accompanied Paul's healing.
Then Ananias went to the house and entered it. Placing his hands on Saul, he said, "Brother Saul, the Lord—Jesus, who appeared to you on the road as you were coming here—has sent me so that you may see again and be filled with the Holy Spirit." Acts 9:17 (NIV)

Paul laid hands on when praying for healing.
His father was sick in bed, suffering from fever and dysentery. Paul went in to see him and, after prayer, placed his hands on him and healed him. Acts 28:8 (NIV)

Laying on of hands accompanied ordination.
They presented these men to the apostles, who prayed and laid their hands on them. Acts 6:6 (NIV)

So after they had fasted and prayed, they placed their hands on them and sent them off. Acts 13:3 (NIV)

Laying on of hands should not be done hastily.
Do not be hasty in the laying on of hands, and do not share in the sins of others. Keep yourself pure. 1 Timothy 5:22 (NIV)

Laying on of hands is an elementary teaching.
Therefore let us leave the elementary doctrine of Christ and go on to maturity, not laying again a foundation of repentance from dead works and of faith toward God, and of instruction about washings, the laying on of hands, the resurrection of the dead, and eternal judgment. Hebrews 6:1-2 (ESV)

Anointing with Oil

Oil was most often used to set something or someone apart for special service to God. Kings, priests, and sacrifices were anointed with oil, as they were set apart for special service (Exodus 29:7-8, 1 Samuel 10:1, Ezra 6:9-10). The term "Christ," or Messiah, means "anointed one," as Jesus was set apart by God for special service in the work of redemption (Matthew 1:16, Mark 8:29).

Christians place a little bit of oil on the forehead of those receiving prayer for healing, and the oil is understood as setting the person apart for the special care of the Holy Spirit. It is important to understand that there is no special power in the oil. Power comes from God who moves as we act in obedience to Scripture. Anointing the sick with oil is not a substitute for medical treatment. We can both receive medical treatment and receive oil during prayer for healing.

The first disciples anointed the sick with oil.
They were casting out many demons and were anointing with oil many sick people and healing them. Mark 6:13 (NASB)

Anointing the sick with oil is commanded.
Is any one of you sick? He should call the elders of the church to pray over him and anoint him with oil in the name of the Lord. James 5:14 (NIV)

Intercession

To intercede is to pray on another's behalf. To intercede is to ask that all that was accomplished by the death of Jesus Christ be applied to another's life. That would include salvation, as it is through Jesus' shed blood that we are saved from our sins. That would include healing, as it is by his wounds that we are healed. That would include deliverance from evil, as it is by his blood we are ransomed from sin. In this way, our prayers of intercession are always and only an extension of Jesus' work on the cross.

In Luke's gospel, we read that Jesus interceded in prayer for his disciples. Jesus pled in prayer for his disciples, and this is what Paul is urging in Timothy's life (1 Timothy 2:1). In fact, we are most like Jesus when we live to do what he lives to do—that is make intercession for the saints (Hebrews 7:25).

Intercession is, in fact, one of the few activities in which we can be assured that we are precisely emulating the character, conduct and concerns of Jesus. Yet too many times we lack confidence in prayer because we think our access to God depends upon our righteousness. In fact, many lack confidence in prayer because they are constantly reminded of their sinfulness during prayer. Their hands come together for a moment of silence and their mind immediately goes to their shortcomings: an angry word, a lustful thought, some piece of gossip that they shared about another person. And they think to themselves "I'm not worthy to talk to God." When that happens, we must respond, "It's true!" We must admit that we are not worthy, nor will we ever be worthy to approach God's throne on our own righteousness.

If you have this problem, then the next time you feel unworthy to pray because of sin, simply begin your prayer with thankfulness. Begin your prayer by celebrating the righteousness of Christ that is offered to all who trust in his death and resurrection. Based upon Christ's righteousness we are urged to come boldly before God's throne of grace (Hebrews 4:16).

There are some however, who make the opposite error in prayer! Some are particularly bold in prayer because they feel they are deserving. If we feel as if God owes us an answer to our prayers, for any reason, then we are misunderstanding Jesus' work as an intercessor. That is why we pray in Jesus' name. We pray in Jesus' name because it is his person and work upon which we depend to get ourselves a hearing before God's throne. We cannot depend upon our own righteousness. We must depend upon Christ's righteousness. Imagine closing your prayers by using your own name. "Father in heaven, I ask these things in my own name. Amen." We cannot be our own mediator. There is only one mediator between God and man, the man Jesus Christ (1 Timothy 1:5). There is only one who truly lives to make intercession—Jesus Christ, and this is good news for both the unrighteous and the righteous, both the moral and the immoral.

Praying and Fasting FAQ's

What is the purpose of fasting?

Fasting is abstinence from food and/or drink. Fasting is self-denial to focus on seeking God. While fasting and in reply to Satan's temptation Jesus said, "Man does not live on bread alone, but on every word that comes from the mouth of God" (Matthew 4:4). In fasting, we acknowledge that we have a need greater than food, a need satisfied only by God. Fasting helps us to put our relationship with God in its proper place—first, and we are promised that all who seek him will find him (Jeremiah 29:13,14, Matthew 7:8).

What are some of the outcomes of fasting?

Focus us in prayer. Every example of fasting in the Bible is joined with prayer. To fast without praying is to diet. Ezra declared a fast while petitioning God for safety (Ezra 8:23). Nehemiah and Daniel fasted while asking God to act on behalf of the Israelites (Nehemiah 1:4, Daniel 9:3). Believers in Antioch fasted while commissioning of Saul and Barnabas (Acts 13:3).

However, fasting is not a hunger strike, aimed at coercing God. In fact, God refused to listen to the Israelites when they fasted during Jeremiah's day (Jeremiah 14:12). David fasted while his son was dying, but God did not spare the boy's life (2 Samuel 12:16). We fast because we long for his presence, not because God is unwilling to care for us. God is eager to answer our prayers (James 1:5, Matthew 7:11).

Understanding about God's will in a matter. The Israelites fasted and prayed to discern God's will for them in war (Judges 20:28). The early church fasted and prayed before appointing Elders to receive God's guidance (Acts 14:23).

Waiting upon God's deliverance or protection. King Jehoshaphat called a fast in seeking God's deliverance (2 Chronicles 20:3-4). Ezra called a fast asking for the Lord's protection on his journey (Ezra 8:21-23). Esther called a fast as she prepared to speak to Xerxes (Esther 4:16). Paul fasted while waiting for restoration (Acts 9:9). In each case, leaders utilized fasting to help cultivate a dependence upon God.

Expressing grief over sin and repentance. Repentance is a change of mind and direction and fasting has historically been an indication of one's resolve to follow God. The Israelites fasted in repentance of their idolatry (1 Samuel 7:6). Jonathan went without food in grief over his father's shameful behavior (1 Samuel 20:34). Through the prophet Joel, God commanded the people to fast in repentance (Joel 2:12). The Ninevites fasted in grief over their sin (Jonah 3:5). At the same time, it is important to understand that going without food or water cannot purchase our forgiveness (Ephesians 2:8-10).

Expressing our humility before God. Kings Ahab and David humbled themselves before God through fasting (1 Kings 21:27-29, Psalms 35:13). Fasting, when practiced with the right motives, is a physical expression of humility, just as kneeling or prostrating can reflect humility. We should also understand that fasting can also express pride if our hearts are not truly broken (Luke 18:12), and that we are only promised reward for fasting when we fast with appropriate motives (Matthew 6:17-18)

Preparing for temptation. Jesus fasted in preparation for temptation (Matthew 4:1-11).

Is fasting required of Christians?

Fasting is not required. But Jesus did assume his followers would fast. When Jesus spoke about fasting, he did not say *if* you fast, but "when you fast," indicating that he expected his disciples would fast (Matthew 6:16). Furthermore, Jesus taught that fasting was a response to his absence and a reflection of our longing to be in his presence (Matthew 9:15).

Doesn't fasting send the message that food is bad?

Food is meant to be a source of enjoyment (Ecclesiastes 2:24-25; 5:18, 1 Timothy 4:1-4). When Jesus was tempted by Satan, he did not refuse by saying that bread is bad (Matthew 4:4). In fasting we are acknowledging that we have a need that is greater than food, a need satisfied only by God.

Will we fast in heaven?

We will not fast in heaven. Heaven is described as a time of feasting (Matthew 22:1-14)! Jesus explained that his disciples were not fasting because there was no reason to "mourn," as long as he was with them

(Matthew 9:14-15). In heaven there will be no reason to mourn, only to celebrate (Revelation 7:17).

What do we do while fasting?

Pray! Fasting without prayer is simply dieting. Read Scripture. God speaks through his Word and we are often softened to better responding to his Word when we fast. We should also be careful not to draw attention to ourselves when fasting (Matthew 6:16-18).

Is fasting supposed to be done in secret?

Jesus warns his disciples not to parade their fasting for others to see (Matthew 6:16-18). However, there are community fasts recorded in the Bible (Leviticus 23:27). Joel and Jehoshaphat both called national fasts, and all of Nineveh fasted together (Joel 2:15, 2 Chronicles 20:1-4, Jonah 3:5).

Can we give up things other than food?

Everyone is free to determine the nature of their fast. For this reason, it is popular to abstain from things like watching television or shopping. However, fasting from food uniquely cultivates a hunger for God, because nothing softens our heart as quickly as physical suffering.

What about medication that is taken with food?

If you are on medication that must be taken with food, then we would encourage a partial fast (e.g., drinking only water, eating only fruits and vegetables).

What if we have never fasted before?

As with most disciplines, it is important to allow some time to build discipline. Begin by simply missing one meal, or only eating fruit or vegetables for the day. Over time you will be able to go for longer periods without eating.

Are there any cautions to be aware of?

Biblical fasting is not aimed at losing weight. Those who struggle with eating disorders may need to consider a different discipline.

We should be careful not to cultivate pride when fasting. We are not more spiritual because we fast, and a single fast is not a spiritual cure-all.

Finally, fasting is not a substitute for obedience in other areas. The people of Isaiah's day thought that they could fast while living in disobedience, but that did not please God (Isaiah 58:3b-4).

How long should I fast?

Each person should determine the length of his own fast. I'd recommend starting very slowly and only lengthening your fast when you feel ready. The goal is not to be miserable, but to be reminded of our need for God.

What are the different types of fasting?

Each person is free to define the parameters of his abstinence, and the options for fasting are virtually limitless. Some of the more common fasts include:

No food or drink — This is a radically restrictive fast and should be limited in its scope to two or three days. Going without food and drink can be harmful to your health and should be done rarely. Esther decided to fast for three days abstaining from both "food and water" both "day and night" (Esther 4:15-16). The rabbi Ezra and the apostle Paul also went without food and water for three days (Ezra 10:6-9; Acts 9:9).

No food, water only – this type of fast is more common but should be limited to those who do not need to eat for medical reasons.

Some foods, water only - in this type of fast, the emphasis is placed on restricting one's diet to certain types of food, rather than abstaining completely from eating. Daniel ate fruits and vegetables and drank only water (Daniel 1:16, 10:3). Other restrictions may include going without desserts, or breads, or designer drinks (coffees and alcohol).

What should we expect physically while fasting?

Depending on the length and type of fast, you can expect lightheadedness, dizziness, headaches, or nausea, and even muscle cramps. You may feel more tired than usual, and it will be important to limit your physical activity. Rest as much as your schedule will permit. You may feel unusually impatient, cranky, anxious, and even sad. The first two or three days are usually the hardest in an extended fast. As your fast continues though, you may experience a sense of well-being both physically and spiritually.

What if I fast and nothing good happens?

Jesus promised that those who fast with the right motives will be rewarded (Matthew 6:18). Something good will happen, although the spiritual benefit might not be immediately obvious.

How should I get ready for a fast?

First, begin with prayer, asking God to help you identify the type and length of your fast. Make sure to consult your calendar to see whether social commitments will conflict with the time of fasting. Second, identify when and where you will pray and read scripture while fasting. Many have found it best to pray and read during mealtime. Third, spend some time at the outset confessing sin. Ask the Holy Spirit to convict you of sin and celebrate God's forgiveness (1 John 1:9). Fourth, prepare yourself physically. You may need to see a doctor, especially if you take prescription medication. Eat smaller meals before starting a fast. Avoid high-fat and sugary foods. Finally, begin with an expectant heart. God promises to be found by those who seek him (Matthew 6:18, 7:8, Hebrews 11:6).

How do I finish a fast?

Ending your fast gradually is a good rule of thumb. If you were abstaining from solid foods, begin with several smaller meals of fruits and vegetables or snacks. Light soups are helpful, along with drinking fruit or vegetable juices. Next add in salads and then gradually increase your diet.

Prayers of the New Testament Church

They prayed for their enemies.
But I say to you: Love your enemies and pray for those who persecute you. (Matthew 5:44)

They prayed in secret.
But when you pray, go into your room, close the door and pray to your Father, who is unseen. Then your Father, who sees what is done in secret, will reward you. (Matthew 6:6)

They prayed together.
They all joined together constantly in prayer, along with the women and Mary the mother of Jesus, and with his brothers. (Acts 1:14)

They devoted themselves to the apostles' teaching and to the fellowship, to the breaking of bread and to the prayers. (Acts 2:42)

When they heard this, they raised their voices together in prayer to God. "Sovereign Lord," they said, "you made the heaven and the earth and the sea, and everything in them." (Acts 4:24)

They prayed with sincerity.
And when you pray, do not keep on babbling like pagans, for they think they will be heard because of their many words. (Matthew 6:7)

They devour widows' houses and for a show make lengthy prayers. Such men will be punished most severely." (Mark 12:40)

They prayed to the Father with praise.
"This, then, is how you should pray: "'Our Father, who art in heaven, hallowed be thy name.'" (Matthew 6:9)

They called on God's kingdom to come.
Thy kingdom come, thy will be done on earth as it is in heaven. (Matthew 6:10)

They called on God to meet their daily needs.
Give us this day our daily bread. (Matthew 6:11)

They called on God to forgive their sin.
Forgive us our debts, as we forgive our debtors. (Matthew 6:12)

They prayed for God to provide workers.
Ask the Lord of the harvest, therefore, to send out workers into his harvest field. (Matthew 9:28)

They prayed in faith.
If you believe, you will receive whatever you ask for in prayer." (Matthew 21:22)

Whatever you ask for in prayer, believe that you have received it, and it will be yours. (Mark 11:24)

They prayed to avoid temptation.
And lead us not into temptation, but deliver us from evil. (Matthew 6:13)

Watch and pray so that you will not fall into temptation. The spirit is willing, but the body is weak. (Matthew 26:41)

They prayed for deliverance from demons.
He replied, "This kind of demon can come out only by prayer." (Mark 9:29)

They prayed offering forgiveness.
And when you stand praying, if you hold anything against anyone, forgive him, so that your Father in heaven may forgive you your sins. " (Mark 11:25)

They prayed persistently.
Jesus told his disciples a parable to show them that they should always pray and not give up. (Luke 18:1)

They prayed for justice and vindication.
And will not God bring about justice for his chosen ones, who cry out to him day and night? Will he keep putting them off? (Luke 18:7)

They prayed for faithfulness with perseverance.
Be always on the watch, and pray that you may be able to escape all that is about to happen, and that you may be able to stand before the Son of Man." (Luke 21:36)

Be joyful always; pray continually; give thanks in all circumstances, for this is God's will for you in Christ Jesus. (1 Thessalonians 5:16-18)

We constantly pray for you, that our God may count you worthy of his calling, and that by his power he may fulfill every good purpose of yours and every act prompted by your faith. (2 Thessalonians 1:11)

They prayed for unity among believers in order that unbelievers may find salvation.
My prayer is not for them alone. I pray also for those who will believe in me through their message, that all of them may be one, Father, just as you are in me and I am in you. May they also be in us so that the world may believe that you have sent me. I have given them the glory that you gave me, that they may be one as we are one: I in them and you in me. May they be brought to complete unity to let the world know that you sent me and have loved them even as you have loved me. (John 17:20-23)

They prayed for God's direction in selecting and commissioning leaders.
"Lord, you know everyone's heart. Show us which of these two you have chosen. (Acts 1:24)

They presented these men to the apostles, who prayed and laid their hands on them. (Acts 6:5-6)

So after they had fasted and prayed, they placed their hands on them and sent them off. (Acts 13:3)

Paul and Barnabas appointed Elders for them in each church and, with prayer and fasting, committed them to the Lord, in whom they had put their trust. (Acts 14:23)

They prayed for boldness and signs and wonders.
"Now, Lord, consider their threats and enable your servants to speak your word with great boldness. Stretch out your hand to heal and perform miraculous signs and wonders through the name of your holy servant Jesus." After they prayed, the place where they were meeting was shaken. And they were all filled with the Holy Spirit and spoke the word of God boldly. (Acts 4:29-31)

Elijah was a man just like us. He prayed earnestly that it would not rain, and it did not rain on the land for three and a half years. Again he prayed, and the heavens gave rain, and the earth produced its crops. (James 5:17-18)

They prayed as a ministry priority.
Brothers, choose seven men from among you who are known to be full of the Spirit and wisdom. We will turn this responsibility over to them and will give our attention to prayer and the ministry of the word. (Acts 6:3-4)

They prayed while being persecuted.
While they were stoning him, Stephen prayed, "Lord Jesus, receive my spirit." (Acts 7:59)

So Peter was kept in prison, but the church was earnestly praying to God for him. (Acts 12:5)
I urge you, brothers, by our Lord Jesus Christ and by the love of the Spirit, to join me in my struggle by praying to God for me. Pray that I may be rescued from the unbelievers in Judea and that my service in Jerusalem may be acceptable to the saints there, so that by God's will, I may come to you with joy and together with you be refreshed. (Romans 15:30-32)

Pray that we may be delivered from wicked and evil men, for not everyone has faith. (2 Thessalonians 3:2)

They prayed for healing.
Peter sent them all out of the room; then he got down on his knees and prayed. Turning toward the dead woman, he said, "Tabitha, get up." She opened her eyes, and seeing Peter she sat up. (Acts 9:40)

His father was sick in bed, suffering from fever and dysentery. Paul went in to see him and, after prayer, placed his hands on him and healed him. (Acts 28:8)

Is any one of you sick? He should call the Elders of the church to pray over him and anoint him with oil in the name of the Lord. And the prayer offered in faith will make the sick person well; the Lord will raise him up. If he has sinned, he will be forgiven. Therefore confess your sins to each other and pray for each other so that you may be healed. The prayer of a righteous man is powerful and effective. (James 5:14-16)

They prayed that others might receive the Spirit.
When they arrived, they prayed for them that they might receive the Holy Spirit. (Acts 8:15)

They prayed in and through the Holy Spirit.
In the same way, the Spirit helps us in our weakness. We do not know what we ought to pray, but the Spirit himself intercedes for us with groans that words cannot express. (Romans 8:26)

And pray in the Spirit on all occasions with all kinds of prayers and requests. With this in mind, be alert and always keep on praying for all the saints. (Ephesians 6:18)

But you, dear friends, build yourselves up in your most holy faith and pray in the Holy Spirit. (Jude 1:20)

They prayed for strengthening through the Spirit.
I pray that out of his glorious riches he may strengthen you with power through his Spirit in your inner being, so that Christ may dwell in your hearts through faith. And I pray that you, being rooted and established in love, may have power, together with all the saints, to

grasp how wide and long and high and deep is the love of Christ, and to know this love that surpasses knowledge—that you may be filled to the measure of all the fullness of God. (Ephesians 3:16-19)

They prayed for the salvation of unbelievers.
Brothers, my heart's desire and prayer to God for the Israelites is that they may be saved. (Romans 10:1)

They prayed in lieu of sexual intimacy.
Do not deprive each other, except perhaps by mutual consent and for a time, so that you may devote yourselves to prayer. Even then, come together again so that Satan will not tempt you because of your lack of self-control. (1 Corinthians 7:5)

They prayed in tongues and for interpretation.
For this reason, anyone who speaks in a tongue should pray that he may interpret what he says. For if I pray in a tongue, my spirit prays, but my mind is unfruitful. So what shall I do? I will pray with my spirit, but I will also pray with my mind; I will sing with my spirit, but I will also sing with my mind. (1 Corinthians 14:13-15)

They prayed for spiritual enlightenment.
I pray also that the eyes of your heart may be enlightened in order that you may know the hope to which he has called you, the riches of his glorious inheritance in the saints, and his incomparably great power for us who believe. (Ephesians 1:18-19)

They prayed in joy and with confidence in Christ.
I thank my God every time I remember you. In all my prayers for all of you, I always pray with joy because of your partnership in the gospel from the first day until now, being confident of this, that he who began a good work in you will carry it on to completion until the day of Christ Jesus. (Philippians 1:3-6)

They prayed for love and discernment.
And this is my prayer: that your love may abound more and more in knowledge and depth of insight, so that you may be able to discern what is best and may be pure and blameless until the day of Christ, filled with the fruit of righteousness that comes through Jesus Christ—to the glory and praise of God. (Philippians 1:9-11)

They prayed instead of growing anxious.
Do not be anxious about anything, but in everything, by prayer and petition, with thanksgiving, present your requests to God. And the peace of God, which transcends all understanding, will guard your hearts and your minds in Christ Jesus. (Philippians 4:6-7)

They prayed to live a life worthy of Jesus.
For this reason, since the day we heard about you, we have not stopped praying for you and asking God to fill you with the knowledge of his will through all spiritual wisdom and understanding. And we pray this in order that you may live a life worthy of the Lord and

may please him in every way: bearing fruit in every good work, growing in the knowledge of God. (Colossians 1:9-10)

They prayed with devotion.
Devote yourselves to prayer, being watchful and thankful. (Colossians 4:2)

Night and day we pray most earnestly that we may see you again and supply what is lacking in your faith. (1 Thessalonians 3:10)

They prayed for wisdom.
If any of you lacks wisdom, he should ask God, who gives generously to all without finding fault, and it will be given to him. (James 1:5)

They prayed for opportunities to share the gospel.
And pray for us, too, that God may open a door for our message, so that we may proclaim the mystery of Christ, for which I am in chains. Pray that I may proclaim it clearly, as I should. (Colossians 4:2-4)

Finally, brothers, pray for us that the message of the Lord may spread rapidly and be honored, just as it was with you. (2 Thessalonians 3:1)

They prayed for God's glory.
We pray this so that the name of our Lord Jesus may be glorified in you, and you in him, according to the

grace of our God and the Lord Jesus Christ. (2 Thessalonians 1:12)

They prayed for all in authority.
I urge, then, first of all, that requests, prayers, intercession and thanksgiving be made for everyone—for kings and all those in authority. (1 Timothy 2:1)

They prayed for the consecration of all things.
For everything God created is good, and nothing is to be rejected if it is received with thanksgiving, because it is consecrated by the word of God and prayer. (1 Timothy 4:4-5)

They prayed that others would share their faith.
I pray that you may be active in sharing your faith, so that you will have a full understanding of every good thing we have in Christ. (Philemon 1:6)

They prayed for others to be delivered from sin.
If anyone sees his brother commit a sin that does not lead to death, he should pray and God will give him life. I refer to those whose sin does not lead to death. There is sin that leads to death. I am not saying that he should pray about that. (1 John 5:16)

They prayed for good health and for success.
I pray that you may enjoy good health and that all may go well with you, even as your soul is getting along well. (3 John 1:2)

The Prayer of a Righteous Man

Obedience is important in the work of intercession. James wrote, "The prayer of a righteous man is powerful and effective" (James 5:16). We mistakenly believe that because we cannot earn our way to heaven, but must trust solely in the sacrifice of Jesus on our behalf, that our obedience once we are saved counts for nothing. For this reason, the Apostle James famously said that "faith without works is dead." Our works do not save us, but saving faith always has works, always has obedience.

Why is this the case? Becoming a Christian means being adopted into the family of God, so that prayer is best understood as a child asking something of his father (Matthew 7:9-11). This is important to understand, because while our Heavenly Father is eager to "give good gifts" to his children, he will not reward disobedience. This is not to say that the prayers of the disobedient are never answered. Even disobedient children may receive their requests from time to time. But the most powerful and most effective in prayer are those who are obedient. Jesus said:

> If you remain in me and my words remain in you, ask whatever you wish, and it will be given you. John 15:7 (NIV)

Just as we would not approve of a father's behavior if he did everything a rebellious child wished,

God our Father will not do the bidding of his children who disregard his words. Our obedience does not force God to act as we want, but rather places us in a position of better understanding his will. Obedience allows us to pray more confidently in accordance with his will, as we will have a better understanding of what brings him glory (1 John 3:21-23).

Now lots of people learn of the importance of obedience in the effectiveness of our prayer and immediately feel that perfection is required. But we do not have to be perfect to receive answers to prayer. In fact, it is clear in Scripture that God did not expect that we would be perfect, which is one of the reasons Jesus taught us to pray "Forgive us our debts as we forgive our debtors" (Matthew 6:12). Jesus expected that we would need to regularly acknowledge our sinfulness in prayer. The righteous person, whose prayers are powerful and effective is not a sinless person but a person who acknowledges his sin and is continually turning turn from it. For this reason, James couples confession and effective prayer.

> Confess your sins to each other and pray for each other so that you may be healed. The prayer of a righteous man is powerful and effective. James 5:16 (NIV)

Based upon this verse we must simultaneously be able to affirm the importance of obedience and accept the continuing reality of our sinfulness.

While the burden of perfection is a brutal taskmaster, at the other end of the spectrum too many Christians throw off the call to obedience altogether and simply wallow in a life of sin. As followers of Jesus we are told both to "confess" and to "pray" for one another's healing. We are to admit that we are sinful creatures and seek God's care together.

How then do we grow in power and effectiveness in prayer? It is by admitting our sinfulness to one another and seeking God's healing together. This is why Jesus Christ died in the first place! Jesus died so that we might be healed of the damage done in our lives by sin. Obedience comes by praying for one another's healing, by hearing one another's confession and then praying for one another's faithfulness. This means that we cannot live obedient lives by ourselves. In order to be fully obedient to Christ and grow in effective prayer, we must have someone in our lives to whom we confess sin without fear, and whose confession we in turn can hear and answer with the same gentleness and patience that Jesus shows. So many of us want to grow in power and effectiveness in prayer, but we do not want anyone to know of our sin. We do not want to have to depend upon others. But that is not how God has ordained matters.

Prayer In Jesus' Name

When it comes to Christian prayer, there are few practices as universal as praying in Jesus' name. Praying in Jesus' name can't mean simply tacking the word "Jesus" on to the end of our prayer (Acts 19:23-17). Jesus' name is not a magic word to be recited at the end of a long incantation. Instead, Jesus offers the power of his name to his followers to comfort them as his departure nears (John 14:1-14).

The disciples apparently felt as though they were losing their connection to God because Jesus was leaving them, but he wanted to assure them that they will continue to have access to God by his name. In fact, Jesus wanted them to understand that their access to God the Father would grow stronger, even though he is leaving them. How can that be? How could Jesus guarantee that we will do even greater works when he is no longer here on Earth with us? Because Jesus and the Father are one!

Praying in Jesus' name means recognizing that the one who came to earth and gave his life for us is one with the God who rules the universe, governs all things, and can meet our needs and empower us to do great things. Jesus said "I am in the Father and the Father is in me" (John 14:11), and he explains that because of our access to the Father through him, we will do great things, even greater things than Jesus himself did.

To understand the power of praying in Jesus' name, we must believe that Jesus is himself God. The Jewish exorcists in Acts 19 did not believe that Jesus was God. At best, they believed his name had magic powers. But Jesus claimed to be God saying, "Anyone who has seen me, has seen the Father" (John 14:9). He claimed that the words he spoke were the Father's words (John 14:10) and that the works he did were those given to him by the Father (John 5:19).

Scripture says that there is no other name given under heaven by which people are to be saved (Acts 4:12). And it is our faith in his authority that causes demons to flee, as scripture reports that the disciples returned from their first mission trip rejoicing that even the demons submitted to them in Jesus name (Luke 10:17). It is also our faith in his authority that often draws the ire of those who do not believe that every knee will bow and tongue confess that Jesus Christ is Lord (Philippians 2:10-11).

So Jesus offers his name for far more than "name dropping" purposes. Later in the same evening, while still in the upper room with his disciples Jesus points out that praying in his name assumes a relationship with and through him. He says:

> In that day you will ask in my name. I am not saying that I will ask the Father on your behalf. No, the Father himself loves you because you have loved me and have believed that I came from God. John 16:26-27 (NIV)

Notice that we can go straight to the Father. To pray in Jesus' name is to appeal to God the Father's love for us through a dependence upon what God the Son has done for us through his sacrifice on the cross. Scripture teaches that he is eager to give those he loves every good gift, and we misunderstand the nature of our access to God through Jesus' name when we act as if we must wrestle some particular answer from his hands. It's true that prayer is often described as wrestling, and it can be a labor to wait upon God in prayer. But it is easy to wrongly think that wrestling means overcoming God's purposes and preferences so that we get what we want. That is not at all what prayer is about. God is eager to bless us and prayer is about discovering his purposes and priorities and praying in accordance with his will. This is the third element of praying in Jesus' name.

Praying in Jesus' name means praying in accordance with Jesus' purposes and priorities. Praying in Jesus name is to pray according to Jesus' will. Jesus' will is that we bear fruit, which means that we act in accordance to his character, conduct and concerns. Again, while gathered in the Upper Room and trying to teach the disciples how different things will be now that he was leaving them. Jesus said about prayer:

> You did not choose me, but I chose you and appointed you to go and bear fruit—fruit that will last. Then the Father will give you whatever you ask in my name. John 15:16 (NIV)

Persevering in Prayer

Luke does us a favor at the beginning of this parable by telling us exactly what we are to learn.

> Then Jesus told his disciples a parable to show them that they should always pray and not give up. Luke 18:1-8 (NIV)

In Luke 17, just before offering this parable, Jesus had spent some time talking about the end of the world, his second coming and the establishment of his kingdom on earth. He knew that he would soon be leaving the disciples. The crucifixion, resurrection and ascension are not far off, and he wanted to prepare them. Times are going to be hard, with disappointment and discouragement, rejection and testing, and his prescription for trouble was persevering in prayer.

The widow represents those of us waiting for an answer. She's alone. She's helpless, without any recourse or real power. She's totally reliant upon the judge's mercy and fairness. She is also under attack, and being persecuted. "Grant me justice, against my adversary" she asked. So it's not just that she is alone, dependent and needy, she's also under attack. The pressure is on, life is hard and she is pleading for justice.

It's important to note she is not asking for vengeance, but for justice. You get the sense that she is a righteous woman, falsely accused and wrongly suffering, coming to an unrighteous court. She's easy to identify with because we all have issues in our lives where we feel alone, helpless and needy, issues that only God can help us with. We all, at one time or another have felt under attack, either by people or the circumstances of life, and we are forced to rely upon his mercy and fairness if things are going to get any better, and it's easy in those situations to grow discouraged when the answer doesn't come quickly. When life is pressing in on us, it's easy to grow impatient and discouraged with God's apparent slowness and simply stop praying altogether.

But Jesus says don't give up! How many of us would enter our house, reach for a switch to turn the light on and when it didn't come on, simply give up trying? How many of us would live comfortably in the dark? It's safe to say that none of us would want to live in the dark, and so we would begin immediately trying to figure out the problem. In prayer we are called to possess the same persistence. As we pray, throwing the switch so to speak and wanting an immediate response from God, when the answer doesn't come as quickly as we would like, we aren't to grow content with the darkness. The apostle James confirms that persistence is the foundation to effective prayer writing that "The effective, fervent prayer of a righteous man avails much" (James 5:16).

But what does it mean to be persistent in prayer and at the same time content in our circumstances? Jesus said…

> For some time he refused her pleas. But finally he said to himself, 'Even though I don't fear God or care about men, yet because this widow keeps bothering me, I will see that she gets justice, so that she won't eventually wear me out with her coming!' Luke 18:4-5 (NIV)

The judge of this story is arrogant (not fearing even God) and callus (not caring about the needs of those he has authority over). Jesus is not saying that God is like this judge and that he must be badgered before he will answer. God is in fact the opposite. He will see that they get justice, and quickly.

If you have ever spent any time in a courtroom, you know the important role the character of the judge plays in the justice process. Judges interpret the law and help juries apply the law. Jesus is contrasting the arrogant and callus judge, who grants justice reluctantly, with God who cares for those he has authority over and acts quickly on their behalf. Thus, we can persevere in prayer with confidence in the character of our Judge. In fact, persistence in prayer can co-exist with patience because of our confidence in the good character of God.

Praying in the Spirit

The charge to "pray in the Spirit" comes at the close of Paul's description of the armor of God (Ephesians 6:10-18). Paul explains that we have an enemy—the devil—who is scheming and waging war against us. We are to be prepared for battle, wearing the full Armor of God, which will enable us to stand firm when the day of evil comes. But when and how do we take our stand? Assuming we're wearing the armor, when and how do we utilize it? The answer is in prayer. Is prayer all that believers are to be doing in taking their stand against the spiritual forces of evil in the heavenly realm? Certainly not. But prayer is a primary means by which we experience the victory won for us by Jesus Christ. Prayer is the primary means by which we win the spiritual battles that we face.

Are you plagued by a besetting sin—one from which you can't seem to break free? Prayer is a primary activity by which we gain freedom. Do you have a friend or family member that seems to move further away from Christ? Prayer is a primary activity by which we can fight on their behalf, helping them to experience freedom and blessings. Are you under attack from the enemy and feel overwhelmed by the fiery arrows coming your way? Prayer is a primary means by which we launch a counterattack, standing firm in our faith.

Too often we view prayer as a passive and/or weak activity of last resort, something to be utilized when all other options have been exhausted. Too often we relegate prayer to an activity set aside for little old ladies, who are widowed and/or retired and supposedly have nothing better to do. Prayer is in fact, a primary means by which the men of the church will take their rightful place of leadership and have their greatest influence. We must see prayer as an active means for physically engaging the spiritual forces of evil in the heavenly realms, through which we experience the blessings that the Lord has for us.

But what does it mean to pray in the Spirit? If you're familiar with the New Testament, then you know that prayer "in the Spirit" is a relatively unique phrase appearing only one other time in the New Testament, in the book of Jude 1:20. In many other New Testament passages Paul simply commands us to pray without using the phrase "in the Spirit." So what does this mean? First, to pray in the Spirit is to engage in spiritual warfare during prayer. The context of Paul's encouragement to "pray in the Spirit" is a charge to be prepared for spiritual warfare. We are to be prepared for battle because just as the Israelites were led by God into the wilderness where they met the Amalekites (Exodus 17:8-13), and just as Jesus was led into the wilderness by the Spirit where he was tempted and faced the enemy (Matthew 4:1-11), the Spirit will lead us into battle as well. To pray in the Spirit is to follow the Spirit's leading into battle.

Secondly, to pray in the Spirit is to utilize the armor of God. Again, the context of the admonition to "pray in the Spirit" comes at the end of Paul's charge to put on the full armor of God. This means we are to utilize the armor as we carry it into battle during prayer. For example, to pray in the Spirit we must wear the Belt of Truth in prayer. This will involve confession. Whether it is confessing our sin or our hopes and dreams, praying in the Spirit means opening our self completely and unreservedly to God. If we are not going to tell the truth in prayer, then our prayers will be superficial and perfunctory.

To pray in the Spirit, we must wear the Breastplate of Righteousness. This will involve celebrating the righteousness of God provided to us in Christ (Romans 3:21-26). The good news about telling the truth in prayer is that Jesus has provided salvation for us. We can be completely honest about our sin, because Jesus was a completely righteous sacrifice, who died on our behalf so that we are forgiven.

To pray in the Spirit, we must have our feet "fitted with the readiness that comes from the gospel of peace" (Ephesians 6:15), which means praying for God to send laborers into the harvest field (Luke 10:2), embolden our witness (Acts 4:29) and save lost people (John 1:13). The first step in effectively sharing our faith is not talking to lost people, or even preparing to answer people's objections to the faith. The first step in effectively sharing our faith is prayer.

To pray in the Spirit, we must raise the Shield of Faith, which means we must stand in prayer on God's good character and purposes. This will involve quoting Scripture that tells of God's goodness and his good purposes for his people. We may quote in prayer Jeremiah 29:11, declaring God's intent to prosper his people and to provide a hope and a future. We may quote Romans 8:28, declaring that God works for the good of those who love him and have been called according to his purposes.

To pray in the Spirit, we must wear the Helmet of Salvation, which involves recounting God's work of salvation in our lives and throughout history. Over and over the Israelites, as well as the Church, are told to remember God's works of salvation. Remembering involves retelling and to pray in the Spirit involves remembering God's victory over the enemy in days past. At a most practical level, this will include recounting God's feats of deliverance for the Israelites and his provision for the Church.

To pray in the Spirit, we must wield the Sword of the Spirit. This will involve addressing demonic influences with the truth of God's Word. Our Enemy is called the "father of lies" in Scripture (John 8:44), and renouncing lies believed and announcing the truths in God's Word by which you want to begin living.

Finally, and ultimately, to pray in the Spirit is to appeal to the Spirit's power for victory. To pray in the Spirit is to acknowledge our inability and powerlessness to accomplish any good work, and to wait in faith upon God's deliverance (John 15:5). The Spirit is ultimately and only the means by which we are affective in prayer.

Unanswered Prayer

We know that God always hears the prayers of his people, despite their unrighteousness and because of the righteousness of Jesus (John 14:13-14, 1 Timothy 2:5, Revelation 5:8). However, in some cases God's people may not receive what they requested in prayer.

Prayers may go unanswered if we lack faith.
But when you ask him, be sure that your faith is in God alone. Do not waver, for a person with divided loyalty is as unsettled as a wave of the sea that is blown and tossed by the wind. Such people should not expect to receive anything from the Lord. James 1:6-7 (NLT)

Because of their unbelief, he couldn't do any miracles among them except to place his hands on a few sick people and heal them. And he was amazed at their unbelief. Mark 6:5-6 (NLT)

Prayers may go unanswered if we are disobedient.
If our hearts do not condemn us, we have confidence before God and receive from him anything we ask, because we keep his commands and do what pleases him. 1 John 3:21-22 (NIV)

If you remain in me and my words remain in you, ask whatever you wish, and it will be done for you. John 15:7 (NIV)

Prayers may go unanswered if ask with wrong motives.
You ask and don't receive because you ask with wrong motives, so that you may spend it on your evil desires. James 4:3 (HCSB)

Prayers may go unanswered if we mistreat others.
Husbands, in the same way be considerate as you live with your wives, and treat them with respect as the weaker partner and as heirs with you of the gracious gift of life, so that nothing will hinder your prayers. 1 Peter 3:7 (NIV)

Prayers may go unanswered if God is testing us.
When they came to the oasis of Marah, the water was too bitter to drink. So they called the place Marah (which means "bitter"). Then the people complained and turned against Moses. "What are we going to drink?" they demanded. So Moses cried out to the LORD for help, and the LORD showed him a piece of wood. Moses threw it into the water, and this made the water good to drink. It was there at Marah that the LORD set before them the following decree as a standard to test their faithfulness to him. He said, "If you will listen carefully to the voice of the LORD your God and do what is right in his sight, obeying his commands and keeping all his decrees, then I will not make you suffer any of the diseases I sent on the Egyptians; for I am the LORD who heals you." Exodus 15:22-26 (NLT)

But he knows the way that I take; when he has tested me, I will come forth as gold. Job 23:10 (NIV)

Three times I pleaded with the Lord about this, that it should leave me. But he said to me, "My grace is sufficient for you, for my power is made perfect in weakness." Therefore I will boast all the more gladly of my weaknesses, so that the power of Christ may rest upon me. 2 Corinthians 12:8-9 (ESV)

Prayers may go unanswered because of spiritual opposition.
Then he said, "Don't be afraid, Daniel. Since the first day you began to pray for understanding and to humble yourself before your God, your request has been heard in heaven. I have come in answer to your prayer. But for twenty-one days the spirit prince of the kingdom of Persia blocked my way. Then Michael, one of the archangels, came to help me, and I left him there with the spirit prince of the kingdom of Persia. Now I am here to explain what will happen to your people in the future, for this vision concerns a time yet to come." Daniel 10:12-14 (NLT)

Prayer in Tongues

Speaking in tongues is the biblical term used to describe syllables spoken by, yet unknown to, the speaker (1 Corinthians 12:28). A tongue speaker is defined as one who "utters mysteries" to God (1 Corinthians 14:2-3), and Paul says of those who speak in tongues, "no one understands" them and they speak directly to God (1 Corinthians 14:2). For this reason, speaking in tongues is often described as sounding like gibberish, by both the speaker and the listener, as most unknown languages would sound. But just because something sounds like gibberish, doesn't mean that it is without meaning and value.

There are two biblically described uses for tongues, private use (e.g., in prayer or when singing) and public use (e.g., when addressing the congregation during worship). When used publicly in worship, Paul said that he would rather have five known words spoken to 10,000 words spoken in an unknown tongue (1 Corinthians 14:19). Paul's point seems to be that when in public worship it is wisest to focus on speaking known words, rather than unknown words.

However, the Bible does make some provision for tongues (i.e., unknown words) to be spoken in worship, if they are interpreted. If tongues are spoken publicly, an interpretation is required (1 Corinthians 14:27-28). There needs to be an interpretation simply because no one understands an unknown language unless it is interpreted. Just as God gives the gift of tongues to one, he will also give the gift of interpretation to another (1 Corinthians 12:10). So, while the Biblical directive in public worship is to prefer 5 known words to 10,000 unknown words in a tongue, we do realize that in some cases unknown words, if interpreted, can add value.

When tongues are used privately in prayer or while singing, those praying or singing in tongues are to ask God for an interpretation (1 Corinthians 14:13). While no interpretation is required when tongues is spoken in private, as it is when they are utilized in public worship (1 Corinthians 14:27-28), those praying or singing in private are to ask for an interpretation so that they can understand what they have prayed or sung and be encouraged.

Tongues is a gift given to some by the Holy Spirit.
And in the church God has appointed first of all apostles, second prophets, third teachers, then workers of miracles, also those having gifts of healing, those able to help others, those with gifts of administration, and those speaking in different kinds of tongues. 1 Corinthians 12:28 (NIV)

Tongues is unintelligible, but still profitable.
For if I pray in a tongue, my spirit prays, but my mind is unfruitful. What is the outcome then? I will pray with the spirit and I will pray with the mind also; I will sing with the spirit and I will sing with the mind also. 1 Corinthians 14:14-15 (NASB)

Tongues speakers speak mysteries to God.
For one who speaks in a tongue does not speak to men but to God; for no one understands, but in his spirit he speaks mysteries. 1 Corinthians 14:2 (NASB)

One who speaks in a tongue edifies himself; but one who prophesies edifies the church. 1 Corinthians 14:4 (NASB)

Speaking in tongues is not to be forbidden.
Therefore, my brethren, desire earnestly to prophesy, and do not forbid to speak in tongues. 1 Corinthians 14:39 (NASB)

Known languages are preferable to unknown.
I thank God, I speak in tongues more than you all; however, in the church I desire to speak five words with my mind so that I may instruct others also, rather than ten thousand words in a tongue. 1 Corinthians 14:18-19 (NASB)

Prayer for Healing

While it's true that faith is an essential part of receiving healing (Matthew 15:28, Mark 5:34, Acts 3:16), it is not required that the sick person himself possess the faith. Frankly, God can heal even when the sick person doesn't even recognize him (John 5:13), and/or doesn't possess the ability to exercise faith (John 11:44), or by utilizing the faith of those who are not sick (James 5:14-15). And when the sick person himself does need faith for healing, the good news is that very little is required. Jesus said:

> If you have faith as small as a mustard seed, you can say to this mulberry tree, 'Be uprooted and planted in the sea,' and it will obey you. Luke 17:6 (NIV)

A mustard seed is a tiny seed. Not only is very little faith needed to receive healing, but it's also true that faith itself is a gift from God. Jesus is the "author and the perfecter" of our faith (Hebrews 12:2). For example, after healing a lame beggar, Peter explained that the faith needed for healing was supplied by Jesus (Acts 3:16). Faith is not something that we can or must manufacture, but something that only God provides. So what are we to do if we feel we lack faith? We are to pray and ask for faith. While it is true that the faith comes only from God, this does not mean that we are without responsibility. God is sovereign, providing healing as well as the required faith to receive healing, but we are also invited to ask for what we desire. When we feel we lack faith, we should simply pray and ask God for both the faith and the healing. Jesus said:

> Ask, and it will be given to you; seek, and you will find; knock, and it will be opened to you. For everyone who asks receives, and he who seeks finds, and to him who knocks it will be opened. Matthew 7:7-8 (NASB)

"Help our unbelief," should be the cry of all people before God (Mark 9:21-24). Unfortunately, lots of Christians refuse to pray for the sick because they can't guarantee their healing. But that is simply not an option, as we are told in Scripture to pray for one another's healing and that the prayer offered in faith will make the sick person well (James 5:14-16).

We must remember that Jesus chastised those who demanded that he perform signs and wonders in order for them to believe (John 4:48). We need to be careful that we don't base our faith in God on being healed, but rather on the finished work of Jesus' death and resurrection. The good news of the gospel is that all those who have faith in Jesus' death and resurrection are guaranteed healing in heaven, where there will be no more tears, death, mourning, crying, or pain (Revelation 2:14).

THE MINISTRY
OF
THE WORD

Giving Attention to the Word

Paul wrote, "Do your best to present yourself to God as one approved, a workman who does not need to be ashamed and who correctly handles the word of truth" (2 Timothy 2:15). While Elders do not have to be professional theologians, we are to study in order to lead well. The goal is to use the Scripture to "correct, rebuke and encourage—with great patience and careful instructions" (2 Timothy 4:2).

The following theological statements are meant to define GEBC's beliefs, as well as detail our posture on certain "hot" theological topics (i.e. women in leadership, miraculous gifts, etc.). When fielding questions on theologically contentious issues, remember that our beliefs (head) on any given topic are only a third of the answer needed. A good answer will always address the emotion fueling a question, which includes offering our theological posture (heart) as well as our historical practice (hands). Truth is to be spoken in love (Ephesians 4:15) and our speech should be seasoned with salt (Colossians 4:6).

When addressing a theological "hot topic" make sure to define whether or not this issue is a major (i.e., essential to salvation) or a minor (i.e. not essential to salvation) for GEBC. While a minor doctrine is not synonymous with unimportant, we intuitively know that we can't die on every hill. For that reason, it is helpful to identify four categories of doctrine, which will actually strengthen the church's unity and mission.

- **Essential Doctrine** - those critical to the gospel and the work of salvation (e.g., Deity of Christ). We hold these positions unapologetically and with great conviction.
- **Urgent Doctrine** - non-essential, but vital to the operation of the local church (e.g., mode of baptism, spiritual gifts, women in leadership). These doctrines lead to a practical difference in how we "do" church. We hold these positions with conviction and humility.
- **Important Doctrine** - both non-essential and not urgent to the operation of the local church, but important in forming a coherent biblical worldview (e.g., nature of creation days, millennialism). We hold these positions loosely and treat those with whom with disagree with great gentleness and respect.
- **Unimportant Doctrine** - matters that are neither explicitly commanded nor forbidden, but which people often have passionate opinions about (e.g., alcohol usage). We hold these with the utmost charity toward those with whom we disagree.

Some treat all doctrine as essential, but when placing a doctrine in a category we want to consider; clarity on the topic offered in Scripture, proximity of the topic to salvation, historical position of the church on the topic, as well as the effect upon the church today.

Position on Racial Equality, Justice and Unity

Purpose Statement

The purpose of this paper is to affirm the biblical equality of all people, as well as call for continued work on issues of racial justice and unity. While we celebrate the meaningful strides that have been made on issues of race in America, we also believe there is important work still to be done and that the Church has a vital role to play in this work. We view humanity through the lens of the Gospel, both acknowledging the sobering truth of the wickedness of the human heart brought by the presence of sin, as well as the necessity and availability of God's grace shown towards us in Christ. We recognize there can be a temptation to look away from the sin of racism. We choose to look directly at it, embracing a biblical framework that will guide us toward a deeper understanding of God's desire for equality, justice, and unity among all image- bearers. We are called to this work as followers of Christ. This is Kingdom work.

The Image of God and the Sin of Racism

Scripture teaches that all people are made in the image of God (Genesis 1:26-27), and that the Kingdom of God will include "every nation, tribe, people and language" (Revelation 7:9-10). As a result, all people are inherently valuable and equally valued in God's sight, and those who are trusting in Christ for salvation are "one" (Galatians 3:28). As a response the church is to include all peoples. The multi-racial reality of the gospel was clearly seen in Jesus' efforts to make His ministry inclusive of Samaritans (Luke 10:25-37, John 4:7-10), as well as the Canaanite woman (Matthew 15:21-28). This reality was also demonstrated in the early church where the Spirit was poured out on peoples from many nations (Acts 2:8-12), the prophets and teachers in Antioch were of different races (Acts 13:1). Paul later explained that reconciliation between people groups is a direct result of the gospel's ministry (Ephesians 2:11-13). Admittedly, not everything was perfect in the early church. They had racial issues to address as well. For example, Paul famously confronted Peter in Antioch for drawing back from fellowship with Gentiles, which was little more than a posture of racism on Peter's part, albeit expressed through Jewish ethnic food laws (Galatians 2:11-13).

Racism has often undermined unity within the American Church too. This began with slavery, but sadly did not end with the passage of the Thirteenth Amendment. Racism is any attitude or system of oppression based upon racial makeup (e.g., skin color). Racism is "prejudice plus power," which is aimed at discriminating against a person or group of people (The Color of Compromise, Tisby 16). When racism is present division always results. Even after the Civil War, many of our political, economic, social, and religious institutions, functioned with racist laws, ideologies, policies, and practices, which persisted for decades. Examples include but are not limited to: 1) Jim Crow laws; 2) policies by local school boards designed to thwart desegregation and the U.S. Supreme Court's pronouncement that "separate is inherently unequal;" and 3) the practice of systematically excluding black Americans in some of America's most prominent institutions of higher education, religious organizations, social clubs, and even local facilities such as parks and local sports teams. Although discrimination based on race is illegal in America, the effects of these laws, policies and practices are still too often felt today by many Americans of color. Examples include, among other things, housing and zoning policies, lending practices, the availability of quality education, and aspects of the criminal justice system.

Much of the progress on issues of race has allowed society to see that racism is often more subtle and, in some cases, is even embedded within the normal day to day operations of cultural institutions. This leads to a "racialized society." A racialized society is one that affords different economic, political, social, and even psychological rewards along racial lines. Often referred to as "systemic" racism, statistical evidence for racialization within American society is overwhelming and is seen in black-white inequalities in health, income, college graduation rates, home ownership, and incarceration. As a result, and often without realizing it, people of good faith can sustain a racialized society in some of the ordinary activities of our everyday lives.

As shepherds of GEBC, we write to respond to these tragic realities by denouncing racism and racialization in all forms and naming it as a sin against humanity and God. We write to lament the damage done by racism. We write to call the people of GEBC to repent of any and all racist beliefs, postures and/or practices, and to embrace Christ's teaching to love our neighbor as ourselves (Matthew 22:37-40) and live in unity with one another (Galatians 3:28, Colossians 3:14). Finally, we write to declare our commitment to pursue justice by actively addressing racism and working to strengthen unity within our church and the broader community, thereby empowering the people of GEBC to live as ambassadors of healing, justice, and reconciliation (Micah 6:8, 2 Corinthians 5:18-20).

Biblical Foundations
Biblically, we know that God does not show favoritism toward anyone (Deuteronomy 10:17, Acts 10:34-35, Romans 2:11, Ephesians 6:9) and that we are not to discriminate against anyone for any reason (James 2:1-4). Unfortunately, some have confused God's "choosing" Israel and requiring them to live separated from other nations as an affirmation of racism. However, God's selection of Israel was based not upon any physical attribute or cultural heritage of a people group, but was rather the calling of a singular man, Abram, through whom God decided to bless all peoples of the world (Genesis 12:3, Genesis 18:18).

From our New Testament perspective, we know that God's purposes in keeping Israel separate from other nations was not an affirmation of Israel's racial superiority but was rather a means to ensure that his redemptive work of blessing all peoples would be accomplished through Israel (Romans 9:3-5). Unfortunately, Israel failed to keep the Law of God and their sin created hostility with other nations. If the Law had been kept by Israel, a law which included loving God and all their neighbors (Deuteronomy 6:5, Leviticus 19:18, 33-34), then Israel would have maintained communion with God as well as a good standing with all other people groups.

One implication of the good news of the Gospel is that the dividing wall of hostility that grew between Jews and Gentiles was destroyed through Jesus' ministry (Ephesians 2:14). Part of God's plan in redemptive history was to create one new humanity (Ephesians 2:15-16). This means that all forms of racism are affronts to the work of Christ on the cross, antithetical to the gospel, and contrary to God's work in the world. In fact, all those who have faith in Christ have been given a ministry of reconciliation in which we are to reach out and invite all people into the fellowship of the church (2 Corinthians 5:18-20). This means that it is incumbent on Christians to expose the evil deeds of darkness and call people to embrace the multiethnic reality of Heaven (Ephesians 5:11, Revelation 5:9-10, 22:1-5).

Racism is Sin and the Gospel is Unity
Race is a socio-cultural construct, which is to say that it is people and not God who have elevated certain physical attributes and discriminated against one another based upon those prejudices. While the Bible never speaks against racism directly, there are many vice lists in the New Testament which clearly identify racism as contrary to the character and purposes of God. For example, Paul lists "discord, jealousy, fits of rage, selfish ambition, dissensions, factions and envy" as works of the flesh (Galatians 5:19-21), all of which are involved in racist attitudes and actions. Racism at its core is sinful in its prideful posture, exalting one people group over another, while denigrating or altogether denying the image-bearing capacity of certain groups (Genesis 1:26-27).

Finally, racism is sinful because it opposes the command to love our neighbor as we love ourselves (Matthew 22:37-40). Although racism is a part of the sinfulness that has corrupted our relationships with each other, through faith in Jesus Christ's sinless life, sacrificial death and victorious resurrection, we who were once divided by our sin are now brought into the one family of God, the one body of Christ, and the one community of God's people (Ephesians 2:14-16). Through our mutual faith in Jesus' victory over sin, we not only have peace with God, but we also have peace with one another.

We are committed to treating all individuals as image-bearers of God and to loving all people. We pursue the great multitude from every nation, tribe, people, and language with the good news of Jesus' victory over sin. We believe that making a commitment to racial and ethnic diversity and unity within our congregation, as well as making a commitment to advocating for justice, is central to fulfilling the Great Commission and keeping the Greatest Commandments. We strive to cultivate a community in which all people are loved, respected, and helped in following after Jesus (Matthew 22:37-40, 28:19-20, Revelation 7:9-10).

Confession, Repentance and Commitments
We confess that our priorities as a church specifically and within the larger Church of America generally, have not always demonstrated God's commitment to racial equality, justice, and unity. In this, both individuals within the community and the community as a whole have sinned by committing overt acts of racism in attitudes and actions of discrimination and prejudice, as well as passive acts of racism by failing to advocate for those who were being sinned against. We confess the sin of not only active attitudes and actions of racism, but also passive silence and inaction in the face of racial discrimination, prejudices, and injustice.

We repent of these sins, turning away from both the active and passive sins of racism. We celebrate God's mercy and grace shown toward us in Christ. We celebrate Christ's reconciling death on the cross, and we dedicate ourselves to creating an environment where all people know we are Christ-followers by the way we love one another (Mark 3:24-26, John 13:34-35, Ephesians 2:11-16, 1 John 1:7-10). Toward that end, we make the following commitments:

> **Racial Diversity:** We commit to pursue and welcome all people as image-bearers of God who are uniquely, fearfully, and wonderfully made by and for his glory (Psalm 139:14, Colossians 1:15-17).
>
> **Racial Inclusion:** We commit to include people of all races as full participants within the church as respected, valued, and supported ambassadors of Christ (2 Corinthians 5:18-20). We commit to expose and work to transform attitudes and actions of racism, inequality, and division, while at the same time cultivating hospitable attitudes and actions (Galatians 2:11-13, Galatians 3:28). We commit to nurture the unique talents, experiences, cultural expressions of faith, and perspectives of all peoples in an effort to enjoy the varied reflections of the family of God (Romans 12:3-8, 1 Corinthians 12:12-13).
>
> **Racial Justice:** We commit to act for what is right, equitable, and fair in our church body, as

well as the broader communities in which our church is located (Psalm 89:14, Micah 6:8, Matthew 23:23, Luke 10:25-37). We commit to fight the good fight of faith, advocating for the marginalized and oppressed (Psalm 146:7-9, Proverbs 17:15, Mark 10:42-45, Acts 6:1-7).

Lament for the Sin of Racism: We commit to mourn with those who mourn, continuing in repentance over the sins of racism committed within our country. While we are not all equally guilty of the sins of racism, we raise our voices to repent as members of a nation that is guilty, recognizing our responsibility for bringing change. Just as Ezra had not been personally culpable for the sins he confessed, he nonetheless accepted responsibility for the sins that his community had committed (Ezra 9:5-7). And just as Daniel confessed the sins of his nation, although he was not personally guilty of committing the sins he named, we too confess and repent of the sins we have collectively committed (Daniel 9:8). In confession, Nehemiah went so far as to not only acknowledge the sins of the community, but to personally identify with sins committed by the broader community (Nehemiah 1:4-7).

Pray: We commit to pray "against the spiritual forces of evil," which are at work in the sinful activities of racism (Ephesians 6:12). We commit to pray for both the healing and full restoration of the victims of racism, as well as for the forgiveness of racists, asking that God grant them the gift of repentance. It's our prayer that "godly sorrow" will lead to repentance in our lives and healing in our nation (2 Corinthians 7:10). We ask that God make us one in faith, affection, and goals by the Holy Spirit (Psalm 133:1-3, John 17:20-23, 1 Corinthians 1:10, Ephesians 4:11-13).

Conclusion

Finally, we stand with and for those who are and have been the target of racism, believing that it is incumbent on the followers of Christ to stand up and defend the rights of the oppressed. We are also calling for change. Change in the hearts and minds of citizens and leaders to strengthen the work of justice and put an end to all forms of racism. Realizing that inaction in the face of racism is participation in evil, we want to act. Christians are to love their neighbor in word and deed, even as they love themselves (Mark 12:31).

Position on Miraculous Gifts

In general, the Elders want to exercise care to simultaneously permit the appropriate expressions of the Holy Spirit's activity within the church while ensuring that everything is done "decently and in order" (1 Corinthians 14:40) and that we avoid the clearly problematic excesses that sometimes accompany charismatic practice. Generally, we believe the church is best served by Dr. Robert Saucy's position described as "open but cautious." This seems to represent a good balance that:

- Remains open to the possibility of the miraculous gifts but with
- Strong caveats about classical Pentecostal theology and with
- Careful warnings about the application of "revelatory speech" (tongues and prophecy).

The Gift of Tongues

Doctrinally, we do not subscribe to a "second blessing" that suggests the baptism of the Holy Spirit occurs after or separate from justification/salvation. We also do not subscribe to an "evidence" doctrine that suggests speaking in tongues accompanies the filling of the Spirit. While tongues were used by God as a sign of authentication in the early church, we don't see that as an application or necessity today.

In practice, considering the variety of manifestations of tongues described in the New Testament, we believe that the most defensible contemporary application of tongues is in private prayer and worship for personal edification. GEBC does neither encourage nor discourage this practice, following the Pauline guideline that we should "Seek not, Forbid not." While not discouraged, biblical teaching regarding the private use of tongues clearly identifies its limitations. It is not by itself to be considered a sign of increased spiritual maturity or faith, does not represent a necessary post-salvation experience or one in which others are to be encouraged to similarly practice it. Those who do not practice tongues should never be made to feel as though they are lacking giftedness by the Holy Spirit. Therefore, we do not believe that others should be: encouraged to seek the gift of tongues or that it should be promoted by the leadership of the church, whether staff or volunteers. The Holy Spirit remains sovereign in his giving of the gifts.

While positions differ on the current applicability of tongues and their interpretation in public worship, the conditions Paul attaches to their exercise in 1 Corinthians 12-14 suggests a high level of caution should be exercised. Since the individual who feels led to speak in tongues cannot know for sure that someone will be similarly led to interpret the tongues, Paul's guidelines would appear to suggest that they should not speak publicly. As a result, we discourage the public expression of tongues just as we discourage spontaneous "prophetic" speech in our public worship.

The Gift of Healing

In general, we believe that God continues to provide miraculous healing as part of his sovereign will. But God does not and, in fact, at no point in redemptive history has provided temporal healing as an "ordinary or typical" guarantee in his relationship with his people. While ultimate healing is ensured in our resurrection, temporal healings result from God's sovereign activity as a result of God's compassion, his provision of signs to unbelievers and to accomplish eternal purposes that result in his own glory. GEBC makes it clear that while we believe that God heals, we do not subscribe to a "name it - claim it" theology that suggests that healing is only contingent on the faith of the recipient, or purity or some other feature linked solely to human rather than divine activity. We are asked to pray believing but to always rest in the knowledge that God's goodness, wisdom, and justice result in what ultimately best fulfills his purposes.

In practice, we believe that the Elders can and should be called on to pray for and anoint with oil those who are sick and all believers are invited to pray for their own healing and intercede on behalf of others. While "our ways are not God's ways...our thoughts aren't his thoughts," we have complete confidence in God's goodness, his power, his love and his justice.

On this basis, the Elders do not support public services devoted specifically to the exercise of healing gifts or the claim that individuals permanently possess a "gift of healing" that they can willfully use to become the agent of healing for those that they are called on to pray for. Therefore, a service to seek God's healing would be permissible as long as it was made perfectly clear that there is no guarantee of healing and whether God chooses to heal is a function of his will not our action or gifts of healing.

The Gift of Prophecy

As noted above, we generally discourage spontaneous "prophetic speech" in our public worship for the same reasons as discouraging tongues in public worship. The Elders also recognize their responsibility to evaluate prophecy in accordance with the Scriptures (see, for example) 1 Corinthians 14.

"Other Views"

The authors of *Are Miraculous Gifts For Today: Four Views*, edited by Wayne Grudem, recognize that there are a variety of views circulating within the evangelical world with which NONE of the authors would agree. The Elders agreed with the authors of the Book in rejecting the following positions:

- If a person has not spoken in tongues, he or she is not truly a Christian and does not have the Holy Spirit.
- Tongue speakers are more spiritual.

- If someone who is prayed for is not healed, it is probably the fault of the sick person for not having enough faith.
- God wants all Christians to be wealthy today.
- It is always God's will to heal.
- If we simply speak a "word of faith," God will grant what we claim.
- There are apostles today in the same way that Peter was an apostle.
- If we are guided by the Holy Spirit, we do not need to follow Scripture.
- We should follow anointed leaders, even if they deny the inerrancy of Scripture.
- Speaking in tongues is usually demonic.
- In guiding us, the Holy Spirit never uses our intuitions, promptings, and feelings.
- God should not be expected to heal today in answer to prayer.
- God never works miracles today because those ceased with the apostles.
- Charismatics and Pentecostals are not evangelical Christians.
- The charismatic movement is part of the New Age religion.
- The Third Wave movement (or the Vineyard Movement) is nonevangelical (or is a cult).
- Charismatics are generally anti-intellectual.
- The faith of Cessationists is dry intellectualism.

- It is legitimate to criticize another position by telling anecdotes of mistakes made by untrained laypersons.

Current Posture

In discussing these issues, the Elders recognized that there were a variety of different views within the congregation, and while we most closely identify with the "open but cautious" position, we hold it as a "non-essential." Accordingly, we do not hold this position in a way that seeks to divide with others who draw a different conclusion from Scripture.

In addition, the Elders recognized the importance of consistency in teaching. Accordingly, the Elders believe that care should be exercised in teaching to promote consistency and clarity and avoid unnecessary confusion.

Finally, the Elders discussed whether any of us believed God was calling us to "evolve" or change our position from its current one to some other position; the Elders do not sense such a call to change at this time.

Summary: "Are Miraculous Gifts for Today" Four Views, edited by Wayne Grudem

Cessationism

The cessationist position argues that miraculous gifts are not "normative" today. Gifts such as prophecy, tongues, and healing were confined to the first century and used to help establish the churches. With the church established, and Scripture fully revealed, the need for and availability of these gifts passed. This does not preclude God performing miracles. It merely states that God no longer gifts individuals with the ability to perform such miracles. It's not a view "against" the work of the Holy Spirit, but rather a view that sees God-imposed parameters on the Spirit's current operation (e.g., 1 Cor. 14:33, 40). Accordingly, the "baptism of (or in) the Holy Spirit" takes place at conversion, not after conversion. To maintain the continuation of revelatory gifts means new, inerrant, revelation of God. This stands in contradiction to the concept of the closed canon.

Pentecostal & Charismatic

"Pentecostal" refers to any who trace their origin to the Pentecostal revival in 1901 and hold the following doctrines.
1. All the gifts of the Holy Spirit are for today.
2. Baptism in the Spirit is an empowering experience after conversion to be sought by all.
3. When baptism in the Holy Spirit occurs,

people will speak in tongues as a "sign" that they have received this experience.

Charismatic refers to those who trace their roots to the charismatic renewal effort of the 1960s and 1970s and who seek to practice all the spiritual gifts. Among charismatics there are differing viewpoints on whether baptism in the Holy Spirit comes after conversion and speaking in tongues is a necessary sign of baptism in the Spirit.

Both groups generally agree that Acts establishes patterns which are normative. Accordingly, they teach that: the "sign gifts" continue and are necessary in revealing God's will to His people; in particular, tongues is normative (or highly desirable); healings of all types ought to be expected and/or sought; and miraculous gifts ought to be manifest in the operation of the church as a normal practice.

Third Wave

In the 1980s a third renewal movement arose, so called by mission professor C. Peter Wagner. He referred to the Pentecostal renewal as the first wave of the Spirit's work in the modern church, and the charismatic movement as the second wave. The Third Wave encourages the equipping of all believers to use spiritual gifts and says that the proclamation of the gospel should be accompanied by "signs, wonder, and miracles," according to the New Testament pattern.

They teach, however, that: baptism in the Spirit happens at conversion and subsequent experiences are better called "fillings" or "empowerings." The Vineyard Church is an example of the Third Wave Movement. A criticism of some in the Third Wave Movement is that they may tend towards emphasis on the operation of the Spirit and power to the exclusion of doctrinal consistency.

Open but Cautious

I fourth position is held by those who are convinced the gifts are neither a first-century phenomenon nor comfortable with the doctrine or practice of those who emphasize such gifts today. They are open to the possibility of miraculous gifts today, but cautious in their exercise. They do not think speaking in tongues is ruled out by Scripture but want modern utilization to conform to biblical guidelines. They think churches should emphasize evangelism, Bible study, and faithful obedience, rather than miraculous gifts. Yet they appreciate some of the benefits in worship passion that the Pentecostal, charismatic, and Third Wave churches have brought to the evangelical world.

Briefly put, their view is that the Bible neither explicitly states that any gifts will pass away, nor that they will continue. Therefore, the issue is not whether God still works miracles, but whether all the miraculous gifts seen in the early church of the New Testament are normal for the regular operation of the entire church age.

Summary: "Four Views on Hell"
Edited by Stanley Gundry and Preston Sprinkle,

Introduction
All the contributors to this volume believe in Hell. The authors differ on the nature of Hell.

Position #1 – Eternal Conscious Torment (ECT), by Denny Burk

ECT makes sense because of the seriousness of sin. To sin against an infinity glorious being is an infinitely heinous action and requires an equally infinite and terrible punishment. With a proper view of God's glorious character in perspective, ECT is not a source of embarrassment for Christians, but will ultimately result in more of God's praise (Revelation 19:3). Burke assess 10 passages of Scripture, noting in each that separation is final, unending, and just. Here are eight.

> Matthew 18:6-9
> - Final Separation - Hell is presented as the worse of two possible destinations.
> - Unending Experience – "eternal" fire and "life" in Matthew always refers to unending (Matthew 7:14, 19:16, 17, 29, 25:46), which is the same as in Daniel 12:2.
> - Just Retribution - punishment of eternal fire is presented as justified and retributive.

Matthew 25:31-46

- Final Separation – Both sheep and goats are separated finally and completely.
- Unending Experience – Goats and sheep both have eternal experiences.
- Just Retribution - "Punishment" (*kolasis*) in Matthew 25:46, appears two other times in the New Testament. While Universalists say that the semantic range of this word would allow for it to be translated as "correction," there are no instances of this type of translation in the Bible or related ancient literature. Further, the same word is used to describe the punishment prepared for the devil and his angels, which is certainly not corrective.

Mark 9:42-50

- Final Separation - one destination described as "life" and the other as "hell."
- Unending Experience - Unending torment, in which the worm does not die and the fire does not go out, a quote of Isaiah 66:24.
- Just Retribution – Reward is defined as recompense, but also punishment (2 Macc. 8:33, Isaiah 40:8, Rev. 22:12). Likewise the recompense for stumbling and/or causing others to stumble is Hell.

2 Thessalonians 1:6-10

- Final Separation - There are only two destinations described.
- Unending Experience - those who do not know God receive "eternal destruction." While Annihilationists would argue that "destruction" means the condemned "cease to exist," that is never the meaning in any of New Testament passages (1 Corinthians 5:5, 1 Thessalonians 5:3, 1 Timothy 6:9).
- Just Retribution - God will "pay back." The view here is retributive justice.

Jude 7

- Final Separation - the wicked will be punished as Sodom and Gomorrah was, and the righteous escape as Lot did.
- Unending Experience – punishment and life are both eternal
- Just Retribution - The punishment of Sodom and Gomorrah was tied directly to the behaviors of their citizens, and the punishment of eternal fire will be the same.

Jude 12-13

- Final Separation - Those "wandering stars" are sent into "blackest darkness."

- Unending Experience - The darkness has been reserved "forever."
- Just Retribution - Failing to reflect the light of Christ (wandering stars), brings darkness.

Revelation 14:9-11
- Final Separation - Those who worship the beast and those who do not have different experiences.
- Unending Experience - "will rise for ever and ever," and will have "no rest day or night."
- Just Retribution - Those who worship the beast receive their punishment accordingly

Revelation 20:10, 14-15.
- Final Separation - Anyone not found in the "book of life" is separated eternally.
- Unending Experience - It's clear that the devil, the beast and his prophet are experiencing the same "day and night" (i.e. eternal) torment that those who worship the beast receive (Revelation 14:11).
- Just Retribution - There is no mention of redemption, only retribution

ECT exalts both God's mercy and his justice. It rightfully teaches us to fear God (Romans 2:5-8).

POSITION #2 – Terminal Punishment (TP), by John Stackhouse

Terminal punishment is the theory that those who do not accept Jesus' atoning sacrifice must make their own atonement for sin by suffering in Hell. Once they have suffered sufficiently for their sins, they are annihilated (i.e. done away with permanently, never to exist again). Stackhouse begins by defining terms, as he understands them. Hell is:

1. the destination of those who reject God,
2. a place of fire, and fire refines and consumes,
3. a dump, where evil is removed and destroyed.

Having a destination for those who reject God is congruous with the goodness of God in that it respects the freedom of human choice. Having fire in Hell is congruous with the justice of God in that it punishes and eradicates all sin, as well as all sinners. Hell as a dump demonstrates that God intends to remove and destroy evil from his presence. Stackhouse claims that the doctrine of Hell is generally resisted for two reasons.

1. because we make little of sin, evil and the damage it does, and
2. because we can't imagine ECT. He suggests TP as a middle way, a theory that makes much of sin and is more easily embraced.
3. TP is supported by the best exegetical work.

When the Bible speaks of God as "eternal," it means forever. But when it speaks of mountains (Genesis 49:26) or ordinances/rituals (Exodus 12:24-25) or the Temple (1 Kings 8:6, 12-13) as eternal, it means something else, namely something that these things represent. The word translated as "eternal" in the New Testament can be translated as "everlasting," or "of the age to come," which means that Hell could have a qualitative, rather than quantitative, nature.

Further, the word "eternal" can reference the consequence of an event. In other words, the implications of an event can be "without end." For example, in Hebrews 6:2 "eternal judgment" is a reference to the consequences of God's judgment that extends throughout eternity. And Hebrews 9:11-12 references "eternal redemption," which is an ongoing outcome of a singular event, Christ's death, and resurrection. Further, 2 Thessalonians 1:9 references "eternal destruction," which notes the ongoing consequences of destruction brought in judgment. Finally, in Mark 3:29 the nature of "eternal sin" is not sin that continues to be acted out, but rather the consequences of the sin that continue to be experienced. In the same way, Stackhouse proposes that "eternal suffering" is not the continual experience of pain, but rather the continual consequence of a judgement that is without end.

Stackhouse also believes that the words destruction and death in the New Testament always mean just that, complete destruction, and cessation of life. Thus, the lost are consigned to termination. Over and over in Scripture the wicked are eventually done away with according to Ps. 1:4-6, Psalm 37:9,22,38. Sodom and Gomorrah's destruction is offered as an example of the annihilation that unrepentant humans can expect 2 Peter 2:6. Surely "our God is a consuming fire" (Hebrews 12:29), which results in the non-existence of those he judges. In other words, God consumes the wicked and they are no longer in existence. And in Revelation the best understanding of the "second death" is ultimate disappearance (Rev. 19:20). Even the torment that is described as lasting "forever and ever" (Rev. 20:10) does not necessarily include mankind. Finally, the notion of ultimate destruction and complete annihilation fits with the "gift" notion of eternal life (John 3:16, 1 Cor. 15:50-54). In other words, apart from God's gracious intervention, no one is immortal, no lives eternal, all are annihilated.

> NOTE: Sprinkle rebuts this at the end of the book, pointing out that *if* "eternal" is qualitative (e.g. *full* life) when describing the believer's experience in Heaven (John 3:16, John 17:3), then it certainly doesn't exclude a quantitative reality (i.e. everlasting) for those in Heaven. In other words, if eternal isn't addressing an "everlasting" experience for the righteous, then it isn't prohibiting an everlasting experience for the wicked in Hell.

The suffering in Hell is commensurate to the sin one has committed. Just as Jesus did not suffer eternally on the cross, humans need not suffer eternally in Hell. Finite beings commit a finite amount of sin and need only suffer a finite amount as a result in order to atone for their sin. Death (Romans 6:23), meaning annihilation, is the outcome for those who decide to atone for their own sin.

> NOTE: Once we atone in Hell for our sins, then why can't we be restored to a relationship with God in heaven? If guilt is "purged" through suffering in Hell, might atonement result in redemption? Where is the justice of God, if he is destroying those whom have atoned for their sins?

> NOTE: Just because fire is depicted as refining and consuming, does not mean that it only refines and consumes in Hell. Fire also tortures (Luke 16:19-31).

POSITION #3 – A Universalist View, by Robin Parry

Universalism is the view that in the end God will reconcile all people to himself. Universalists believe that sin separates us from God, draws God's just judgment and condemnation, but that God will save all.

Parry begins by saying that *prima facie* readings of Scripture will yield conflicting interpretations. To resolve these conflictual interpretations, Parry suggests a "gospel hermeneutic." Parry's contention is that Universalism makes the most sense, given the overall plotline of the gospel. As examples Parry notes that "reconciliation" definitionally requires "making peace," and thus excludes ECT and TP (Colossians 1:19-20). Parry asserts that you can't claim God is reconciling all things, if some of those things are separated from God eternally and being tormented.

Parry next works to define God as one who is both just and loving, and he claims that these attributes are never in competition with each other but are always complementary. He describes God's punishment of sin as both retributive (getting what one deserves) and restorative (putting things right). Retributive and restorative punishment provide the necessary complements between justice and love. Parry sights the many oracles of coming destruction against the nations in the Old Testament, which are immediately followed with the promise of restoration. Parry suggests that for this reason we can imagine that punishment in Hell is of this same type, both retributive and restorative.

Next Parry addresses the possibility of post-mortem conversion, beginning with an admission that there are no Scriptures that describes such. He also quickly notes that there are not Scriptures that repudiate such possibility. Finally, he concludes that believing in post-mortem conversion opportunities unifies Hell's reality and God's love for all people. Parry next addresses "Tricky Texts."

In explaining Mark 9:42-50 Parry notes that:

1. there is no consensus on Gehenna's nature
2. the worms and fire imagery does not require an eternal activity. It may mean simply that they are active until they complete their judgment.
3. everyone being salted might note their being purified, which salt does.
4. while Jesus is not discussing post-mortem conversion here, that his description of Hell does not rule it out as a possibility.

In explaining Matthew 25:31-46 Parry notes that:

1. "eternal" is also translated in some NT texts as "an age to come" such that this passage refers to the "punishment of an age to come" and "life of an age to come." He does not believe that "eternal" notes length, but is rather talking about the "quality" of the time. He compares

this with "eternal" description of Sodom and Gomorrah's fire in Jude 7, which is not quantitative, but rather a qualitative.
2. Punishment is not eternal in length, and cannot be, because it lacks any Christ-centered theological basis. Thus, there is no gospel hermeneutic for everlasting punishment.

In explaining 2 Thessalonians 1:5-10 Parry notes that:

1. "punishment of eternal destruction" may very well mean "punishment of an age to come," again a qualitative comment, rather than quantitative
2. Simply because Paul does not present post-mortem conversion does not mean it isn't available.

In explaining Revelation 14:9-11, 20:10-15 Parry notes:

1. these passages are the strongest support for ECT
2. situating these passages in the literary context means admitting that both are followed by universalist guarantees of salvation for the damned (15:3-4 and 21:24-25)

Parry closes with an explanation of free will, which basically notes people stay in Hell only as long as they can take the suffering. God's Spirit, according to Parry, provides increasing appreciation of the truth, ultimately and finally convincing all people. People are fully free, and God fully wins.

> NOTE: Universalism seems to be a description of God torturing the unrepentant into submission.

> NOTE: if post damnation salvation is a reality, then why isn't it clearly celebrated in Scripture as the victory that you say it would be?

> NOTE: What are we to make of the fact that those who worship the beast receive as punishment "no rest day or night"? (Revelation 14:11)

> NOTE: the word "eternal" used in Jude 21 is the same one used to describe the nature of the fire in Jude 7.

> NOTE: What are we to do with all the references in the NT that describe God's judgment of the wicked as final? (Matthew 7:19, 27, 13:40, 48, 15:13, 21:41, 44, 24:51, Luke 13:7, 28, John 15:6, 2 Peter 2:6, Jude 7)

POSITION #4 – Hell and Purgatory, By Jerry Walls

Walls points out that there is a fair bit of debate as to whether this doctrine rightly relates to Hell, or is better situated in a discussion of Heaven, in that purgatory is actually a place of refinement for those destined by God for Heaven. Purgatory is as a place of prolonged labor, in which one who died in a state of grace, works out their sanctification, having failed to do so on earth during life.

In this respect Purgatory is not a place of second chances, for those who die unrepentant, such that they can change their mind in Hell and begin a journey to Heaven. Purgatory is necessary because nothing unclean will enter heaven (Rev. 21:27), and only holiness qualifies us to see the Lord (Heb. 12:14). Of course, Protestant theologians have historically answered this question by explaining God's powerful and immediate transformation of the soul upon death, thus making one ready in an instant for heaven.

Within Catholic doctrine, purgatory took on a "satisfaction" role, in which one was made to satisfy the wrath of God against sin. However, Protestants in no way have to accept a satisfaction theology in order to embrace a sanctification theology for purgatory.

There is no explicit support for the doctrine in Scripture. However, Walls argues, it is an outgrowth of things implied in Scripture. Walls primary Scriptural reference is 1 Corinthians 3:11-15, and he admits that it may not be talking about purgation.

D.A. Carson on Hell

Summary of Chapter 13: "On Banishing the Lake of Fire," from "The Gagging of God: A Christians Confronts Pluralism"

The parallelism of eternal life and punishment is a decisive description of two ongoing realities, one of blessing and one of punishment (Matthew 25:46). The phrase "their worm does not die" implies that the existence of the worm and those punished are perpetually united (Mark 9:48). The "smoke of their torment rises for ever and ever" (Revelation 14:11) is describes an experience that lasts forever.

Further, Revelation 20:10 describes the devil as thrown into the Lake of Fire. If one sentient being is consciously tormented forever, how are humans a special case? Why would the Lake of Fire not consume Satan, while consuming all others? Matthew 25:41 also describes the devil as experiencing eternal conscious punishment. It's hard to think that the same context wouldn't mean to describe the same experience for humans when using the same words, only five verses later in Matthew 25:46.

Finally, if some sin is "eternal sin" (Mark 3:29) that "will not be forgiven, either in this age or in the age to come" (Matthew 12:32), it appears the impact of some sin continues, thus the punishment for such sins should continue. This supports the idea that sinners continue to sin in Hell (Revelation 20:11).

Francis Chan on Hell

Summary of "Erasing Hell," by Francis Chan & Preston Sprinkle

Chapter 1: Does Everyone Go To Heaven

Universalists argue that Philippians 2:11 states that "every tongue will confess that Jesus Christ is Lord," but Paul is here quoting Isaiah 45:23, a passage in which only some embrace salvation. Further, Philippians 1:28 and Philippians 3:19-21 says that those who oppose the gospel will face "destruction."

Universalists argue that "all will be made alive" is an affirmation that all will receive eternal life. But the very next verse makes it clear that Paul has only believers in mind. In fact, everyone who opposes God will be destroyed (1 Corinthians 15:22-26). "All" often denotes a large number of people, not "everyone."

Universalists argue that in I Timothy 2:4, Paul states that God "wants all people to be saved," but in this context, "all" means all types of people, just as Paul says we are to pray for "all people," but what he really means is types of people, "for kings and all those in authority" (1 Timothy 2:1-2).

Finally, no Scripture says there is a postmortem opportunity for salvation. In fact, Luke 13:22-30, describes a time when the "door is shut" and all opportunities for being saved are closed.

Chapter 2: Has Hell Changed Or Have We

First-century Jews would have understood Daniel 12:2 describing that some are raised to "shame and everlasting contempt." These who were raised had been held in Hades/Sheol until judgment.

The apocryphal book 4 Ezra, which was written in the first-century AD, describes Gehenna (Hell) as a place of fire and torment, from which there is no return. Many other extra-biblical writers also testify that this was the general understanding of the first-century Jews. While no first-century Jews thought one might return from Hell, some did believe that souls were annihilated in Hell.

No one in the first century thought that Hell was actually like a garbage dump, as Gehenna might have functioned. It should be noted that there is zero evidence that Gehenna was a garbage dump during Jesus' day. The first reference to Gehenna as a dump comes in 1200AD, which is 1000 years after Jesus died. But just because someone refers to a highway as a parking lot, doesn't mean that the speaker believes it is a parking lot, but rather that the traffic is bad there.

Gehenna was understood by first-century Jews as a place where the bodies of the wicked would be cast according to Jeremiah 7:29-34, 19:6-9, 32:35, and a place of fiery judgment for the wicked.

Chapter 3: What Jesus Actually Said About Hell

Jesus didn't reject the popular notion of Hell that was circulating in the first century. Remember, it was common for Jesus to overturn culturally accepted teachings. But he didn't do that when it came to Hell. For Jesus Hell is a place of that God consigns those he judges (Matthew 5:22, Matthew 23:33).

Jesus described Hell as a place of darkness and fire
- Matthew 13:30 – weeds (non-believers) will be burned
- Matthew 13:40-43 – law breakers will be placed in the fiery furnace, a place of weeping and gnashing of teeth (Matthew 13:49-50)
- Matthew 18:8-9 – "fire of Hell" is a real possibility for those who fall to temptation
- Matthew 8:11-12 – "thrown into outer darkness" will be the experience of some
- Matthew 22:13 and Matthew 25:30 both speak of darkness in Hell

Jesus described Hell as a place of eternal punishment
- Matthew 25:41 – "everlasting fire"
- Matthew 25:46 – "everlasting punishment"
    - *kolasis*, the Greek word for punishment appears 3 other times in the NT and clearly means

"punishment" in all other places. So, it cannot mean "correction," or a more temporary experience. Ten commentators from different theological backgrounds and fifteen Bible translations in five different languages and no one translates it as "correction."
- "everlasting" consistently refers to the ongoing punishment of the devil in 25:41, as well as the ongoing punishment of the wicked 25:46. While it is true *aionoios* doesn't always means everlasting, it must in this case because of the life believers receive and the punishment that the devil receives is clearly everlasting.

Chapter 4: What Jesus' Followers Said About Hell

Paul never used the word Hell but talked about the fate of the wicked more than any other NT author. He talked about the fate of the wicked more than the reward of the righteous (2 Thessalonians 1:6-9). 2 Peter and Jude both read like a chapter from Dante's Inferno. Themes include punishment, judgment, condemnation of the wicked and retributive suffering. Revelation offers the starkest description. Themes include God's wrath, anger, and torment by fire.

Sam Storms on Hell

Summary from book titled, "Tough Topics 2: Biblical Answers to 25 Challenging Questions,"

Chapter 12: Does Hell Last Forever?

The most descriptive passage of the eternality of Hell is found in Revelation 14:11, in which it says those in Hell will have "no rest day or night." Regarding the Terminal Punishment (TP), Storms notes that destruction can occur without extinction.

Regarding the TP claim that the fire and the worms of Hell live eternally, while humans in Hell are destroyed, this carries the metaphor of fire and worms too far. Both fire and worms are metaphorical descriptors of the nature of suffering. After all, how could Hell be a place of "utter darkness" if it has fire in it. And clearly, there is no purpose in a metaphor for suffering continuing eternally, if the purpose for which it is offered is destroyed at some point.

Regarding the Universalist claim that *aion* can mean a limited period of time. The evidence is split on this, with some contexts rendering a "limited time" interpretation, while others rendering an "eternal" interpretation. What is important to note though is that some passages do in fact require an "eternal" interpretation of meaning (e.g. 2 Corinthians 4:18, Luke 1:33, Hebrews 1:8-12, Romans 16:26). Contra Rob Bell, the Bible does speak in "forever" categories.

Matthew 25:46 is one of those contexts in which "eternal" is required for best interpretation.

Regarding the Universalist claim that redemption is possible in Hell and the TP claim that sin can be personally atoned for in Hell, Revelation 22:11 indicates that sin continues in Hell. Beside, once sin is atoned for why can't sinners be restored to a relationship with God in heaven? If guilt is purged through suffering in Hell, might atonement in Hell result in redemption? Regarding the Universalist claims that Christ's victory requires redemption for all, couldn't that argument be extended to Satan's redemption too.

Chapter 13: Will the Horror of Hell Ruin the Happiness of Heaven?

The song of heaven recounts our redemption and that we have been ransomed "from ever tribe," (Revelation 5:9). While apparently aware that we are not in hell, we are aware of hell as that from which we have been saved. And in Revelation 18:20 the saints are called to rejoice over the judgment of Babylon. Jeremiah 51:48 affirms that some are called to sing over the suffering of Babylon, and the same is true eschatologically. Finally, in Revelation 19:3-4 we learn that "Hallelujah" (i.e. praise to God) is the appropriate response to the eternal judgment against Babylon, and God's angels and Jesus are aware of the realities of Hell, while living in Heaven (Revelation 14:10).

Tim Keller on Hell

Summary from "The Reason for God: Belief in an Age of Skepticism"

Chapter 5: "How Can A Loving God Send People to Hell?"

Not all modern cultures take offense at divine judgment. In the west, we love divine forgiveness, love and mercy. While in the east, they love divine judgment and are repulsed by the call to turn the other cheek. The truth is God's love and judgment, will offend something within each culture.

Ultimately, it is God's love and judgment, that gives us hope that all things will one day be put right. And without this hope, humanity would brutalize one another. To make his point, Keller notes that it is always the godless societies (communist, Nazi) that commit the most crimes. The doctrine of Hell thus curtails injustice.

Finally, Hell is permission, given by God, to continue on the trajectory of self-absorption. For example, the Rich Man in Luke 16 never asks to get out of Hell, but that Lazarus would serve him and his family. In this respect, Hell is the "greatest monument to human freedom," as God gives them over to their desires (Romans 1:24). It is simply inaccurate to picture God as casting people into Hell, even while they cry out for salvation.

Finally, Keller maintains that the belief in a God of love without judgment requires more faith than a belief in God who is both loving and just. He maintains that there is simply no evidence for such in the natural order of things, and no textual support of such in any of the major world religions. It simply exists as a preferential opinion of modern westerners.

Position on Women in Leadership

We believe men and women are created in the image of God, equal in worth and value before God, and have distinct roles in home and church as designed by God. We believe gender roles were established at creation, are hierarchical and complementary, continue in effect today and are intended as a blessing. We believe all spiritual gifts listed in Scripture are available without respect to gender, that both men and women are encouraged to exercise their gifts as the Spirit leads, but that Scripture reserves the office of Elder and the weekly preaching ministry within the local church for men. This position is best described as a complementarian position. We hold this position based upon our understanding of the following Scripture:

- Genesis 2:18-25: where we see God's design at creation included both relational hierarchy (male headship) and complementarity (gender specific roles).
- Genesis 3:9-20: where we read that God's design for relational hierarchy and complementarity were undermined by sin.
- 1 Corinthians 11:3, Ephesians 5:22-33: where we read that Christ's redemptive work includes the restoration of hierarchy and complementarity in relationship.

- 1 Timothy 3:1-7, Titus 1:6-9: where we read that Paul limited the Elder office to men.
- 1 Timothy 2:12: where we see Paul reserves the most authoritative teaching role (i.e. weekly preaching ministry) within the church for men.

Defining Complementarian and Egalitarian

The two positions on women in ministry are "egalitarian" and "complementarian." Egalitarians believe God created men and women as equals, that both were charged with the responsibility to rule over creation, and that sin corrupted God's design of equality. Sin's entry resulted in hierarchy, where men oppress women and women resist men. Christ's work on the cross is intended to remove the effects of sin and restore God's design of equality. For egalitarians, Galatians 3:28 expresses the ideal: "There is neither Jew nor Greek, slave nor free, male nor female, for you are all one in Christ Jesus." (NIV)

Complementarians hold that God created men and women equal in value but distinct in roles, that men are given the responsibility of leadership in home and church and women are to support and assist men. Sin's entry into the world corrupted God's design resulting in oppression of women by men and a rebellion of women against men's authority. Christ's ministry is meant to remove the effects of sin and restore the care of women by men and the assistance of men by women. Ephesians 5:22-27 details the hierarchical ideal for complementarians.

Wives, submit to your husbands as to the Lord. For the husband is the head of the wife as Christ is the head of the church, his body, of which he is the Savior. Now as the church submits to Christ, so also wives should submit to their husbands in everything. Husbands, love your wives, just as Christ loved the church and gave himself up for her to make her holy, cleansing her by the washing with water through the word, and to present her to himself as a radiant church, without stain or wrinkle or any other blemish, but holy and blameless. Ephesians 5:22-27 (NIV)

The egalitarian position is described in an article titled "Men, Women and Biblical Equality," offered by Christians for Biblical Equality. The complementarian position is described in "The Danvers Statement," written by The Council on Biblical Manhood and Womanhood.

Identifying Hierarchy in Old and New Testament

We believe the equality of genders does not preclude one exercising authority over another, that men are called to lovingly lead in home and church, while women are called to willingly submit to and assist their loving leadership. These gender roles were designed to complement one another and bless humanity. Arguments for both complementarian and egalitarian positions hinge on identifying God's design at creation, and in Genesis 1-3 we see hierarchy in the following ways:

- In created order – Adam was created before Eve (Genesis 2:18-25).
- In responsibility for the law – The prohibition against eating from the "tree of the knowledge of good and evil" was given to Adam, not Eve (Genesis 2:17).
- In authority within the Garden – Adam named all of the animals (Genesis 2:20) and he named Eve (Genesis 2:23, 3:20).
- In women's specified role of helpmate - Eve was created second and with a distinct role of support (Genesis 2:18).
- In responsibility for sin's entry into the world - When sin entered the world God looked for man first, not woman (Genesis 3:9).
- In God's judgment of Adam for abdicating his leadership – Adam was judged in part for his failure to lead in the Garden (Genesis 3:17).
- In sin's destructive impact upon marriage – Adam and Eve's complementary roles were negatively affected, as sin pitted them against one another (Genesis 3:16).

As one studies the New Testament, the restoration of hierarchy as God's intended design is clearly identified in the following ways:

- Through role differentiation in the Trinity – God is the head of Christ, and the Son willing submitted to the Father (1 Corinthians 11:3, Philippians 2:6-7).
- Through the nature of Christ's ministry – Christ is the head of man, and man is identified as the head of woman (1 Corinthians 11:3).
- By Jesus' role in salvation – as second Adam, Jesus reverses the effects of the first Adam's sin (Romans 5:12-21, 1 Corinthians 15:22, 45-49).
- Through the Church's relationship with Christ – Male headship in marriage mirrors Christ's headship over the church (Ephesians 5:25-31).
- Through Church ministry – Prayer, prophecy, teaching and leadership are all affected by hierarchy (1 Corinthians 11:2-16, 14:34-36, 1 Timothy 2:11-12, 3:1-7, Titus 1:5-9)

While egalitarians believe the New Testament references to hierarchy are culturally bound, the New Testament authors present a hierarchal interpretation of Genesis 1-3, and God would not allow the New Testament to misinterpret the Old Testament. To deny the biblical teaching of hierarchy, in our view, undermines the authority of Scripture.

Reserving the Office of Elder for Men

We believe the doctrine of hierarchy (male headship in home and church) is taught throughout

Scripture as a transcultural principle, and requires men to assume the primary responsibility for leadership, teaching and care giving in home and church. We believe Scripture reserves the office of Elder for men, and we hold this position for the following reasons:

- The testimony of Scripture - The most explicit texts relating directly to male headship within the church are: 1 Corinthians 11:2-16, 14:34-36, 1 Timothy 2:11-15, 3:1-7, and Titus 1:6-9. In addition, it is notable that Israelite priesthood was exclusively male (Exodus 28, Leviticus 9) and all twelve apostles were male.
- The practice of Jesus, Paul, and the early church - While both Jesus and Paul elevated the role of women in ministry beyond their culture, and while there were certainly prominent women ministering within the early Church, neither Jesus nor Paul removed the practice of male headship and there are no examples of women Elders in the New Testament.
- The link between male headship in the home and church - The Biblical connection between home and church suggests that the headship of husband at home implies the headship of men at church (1 Corinthians 11:3).

For a more detailed presentation of male headship in home and church we recommend Alexander Strauch's book titled Biblical Eldership (Lewis and Roth), and Vern Sheridan Poythress's article titled "The Church as Family," from Recovering Biblical Manhood & Womanhood (Crossway). For a more detailed consideration of interpreting and applying cultural versus transcultural commands see Craig Blomberg's interpretation of 1 Corinthians 11 as offered in The NIV Application Commentary (Zondervan). A modern equivalent to braided hair and gold jewelry may be a bikini thong, something that flaunts femininity and demonstrates arrogant disregard for one's marriage vows and the integrity of the community of faith.

Identifying Culturally Conditioned Commands

One of the challenges in interpreting the Bible is identifying which commands are culturally conditioned, meaning temporary demonstrations of a Biblical mandate, and which are transcultural, meaning permanent demonstrations of a Biblical mandate. Concerning women in ministry, complementarians and egalitarians agree that Paul prohibited women from speaking in church while men were teaching (1 Corinthians 14:34, 1 Timothy 2:11), praying and prophesying with their heads uncovered (1 Corinthians 11:5), and wearing braided hair, gold jewelry, pearls or expensive clothes (1 Timothy 2:9). In the ancient world, these behaviors were thought to undermine male headship (demonstrations of rebellion against male authority and/or feminine immodesty). When interpreting these passages most complementarians and egalitarians agree that submission and modesty are the focus of Paul's aim for women and that each generation of Christians must identify culturally appropriate demonstrations of these principles.

Identifying Transcultural Commands in the Bible

While both complementarians and egalitarians generally agree that Paul's prohibition against a woman praying or prophesying with her head uncovered (1 Corinthians 11:3-5) was culturally conditioned, complementarians consider Paul's prohibition against women teaching and exercising authority (1 Timothy 2:12) as transcultural, even though both prohibitions are directly linked to God's design of hierarchy within creation (1 Timothy 2:13-14).

Complementarians make this distinction for a couple of reasons. First, the primary purpose for wearing head coverings was to demonstrate an acceptance of God's hierarchy in male headship. At the same time, wearing head coverings are not an essential "ministry" of the church, and the underlying principle of submission to male authority can be upheld in other modern and more culturally appropriate ways. On the other hand, the primary purpose for prohibiting women from teaching and exercising authority over men, was to reserve these functions for male leaders. Teaching and exercising authority are vital and ongoing methods for accomplishing God's work through the church, and there are no substitute means for upholding the principle of male headship in these areas. Therefore, to overturn God's prohibition against women teaching and exercising authority over men undermines the functions of male headship itself, while allowing women to demonstrate submission in ways other than wearing head coverings does not.

Finally, to affirm the permanent validity of a command it must be tied to at least one of three unchanging objects: 1) the nature and/or character of God, 2) the created order as designed or intended by God, or 3) the message of the Gospel. The prohibitions against women teaching and exercising authority over men should be interpreted as transcultural in that the functional complementarity of men's and women's roles is tied directly to the:

- Nature of God, as reflected in the Trinity (1 Corinthians 11:3, Philippians 2:6-7).
- Design of God as established at creation (Genesis 2:18-25, 1 Timothy 2:13).
- Salvation of God as illustrated in the family and church (Ephesians 5:25-31).

Interpreting and Applying 1 Timothy 2:12

Paul writes in 1 Timothy 2:12, that a woman must be "silent." Although we know that Paul does not have in mind the complete "silence," in that he gives permission for them to both pray and prophecy (1 Corinthians 11:3-5), exactly what he is prohibiting is hotly debated. While all the spiritual gifts are available without respect to gender, and both men and women are encouraged to exercise their gifts as the Spirit leads, we believe that Paul's dual prohibition in 1 Timothy 2:12 is aimed at reserving a specific type of authoritative teaching role just for men, a role that is most clearly identified in the weekly preaching ministry of the local church. We believe this for the following reasons.

The grammar and syntax of 1 Timothy 2:12.

1 Timothy 2:12 includes two separate verbs (to teach or exercise authority) whose meaning is best understood when interpreted together. A paraphrase of the verse might read, "I do not permit a women to hold the authoritative teaching position in the church." In other words, not all teaching positions within the church are equally authoritative, and while women are free to hold some teachings positions, Paul limits the most authoritative teaching position to men, a role that we believe is most clearly identified in the weekly preaching ministry of the local church.

Robert Saucy, in Women and Men in Ministry (Moody), points out that "it is generally agreed that [two verbs] being joined together by the Greek term *oude* ("or"), are closely related ideas, where in many instances the latter activity appears to further elaborate or extend the first..." (306). And while the use *oude* is strongly debated among theologians, Saucy's conclusion is that the teaching proscribed is one that "uniquely" carries authority.

The overall focus of the book of 1 Timothy.

The focus of 1 Timothy overall and of the Pastoral Epistles in general is not to exclude women from all teaching positions, but to strengthen the Elder's role of authoritative teaching. The apostle Paul writes to Timothy, the leader of the church in Ephesus, calling him to "command certain men not to teach false doctrine" (1 Timothy 2:3), and to make sure that those approved as Elders are in fact able to "teach" (1 Timothy 3:2). Timothy's challenge was cultivating leadership capable of guarding the doctrine against heresy, and for that reason the book reads much like a "leadership manual." Setting apart for the Elders a specific authoritative teaching role, which in our contemporary setting is most closely associated with the weekly preaching ministry of the church, was aimed at strengthening the doctrinal integrity of the church.

John Stott also holds this position, writing in his book titled Decisive Issues Facing Christians Today (Revell), "I believe that there are situations in which it is entirely proper for women to teach, and to teach men, provided that in so doing they are not usurping an improper authority over men" (277). Craig Blomberg also holds this position, believing that Paul is aiming at restricting only the position of senior pastor, as teaching Elder, to men. Blomberg's position is presented in an article titled "Neither Hierarchicalist Nor Egalitarian: Gender Roles in Paul," which is an appendix article in the book titled Two Views on Women in Ministry (Zondervan)

Considering the Whole of the New Testament

Beyond our interpretation of 1 Timothy 2:12 as reserving the authoritative teaching role of weekly pulpit ministry for men, we believe that there are other Scriptural indications that women are to play a vital role in the teaching ministries of the church. For example:

The semantic range for the word "teach" in the New Testament is broad.

A study of the usage of the word "teach" in the New Testament reveals that not all teaching is equally authoritative and that there are different types of teaching roles. The teaching described in the Pastoral Epistles, particularly 1 Timothy 2:12, possesses a much greater authority and responsibility than other types of teaching. For example, when Paul describes the corporate assembly in worship he writes, "Each one...has a teaching" (1 Corinthians 14:26), and although we do not know the nature of this teaching or even how it took place there does not appear to be any gender restriction implied, giving women the freedom to address the congregation, during corporate worship, with men present.

For a survey of the meaning of "teaching" within the New Testament see Saucy's book titled *Women and Men in Ministry* (Moody). Saucy summarizes his position writing, "most interpreters understand Paul as prohibiting women from that 'teaching' that is done in the capacity of a leader of the church" (307). Further, Wayne Grudem, in his book titled The Gift of Prophecy in 1 Corinthians (University Press of America) identifies different levels of authoritative speech in Paul's writings, with authoritative speech having "the right to enforce obedience or belief" (73).

The evidence that women shared in the teaching ministry of the early church.

Even though the final responsibility for the teaching ministry in the early church rested with male Elders, it is clear that women actively participated in teaching the men. For example, Priscilla taught Apollos (Acts 18:24-26) and Luke even lists Priscilla's name before her husband, Aquila's, suggesting she was the more prominent of the two, and because Scripture gives no indication that this was an exception, we may assume that it occurred on other occasions.

The affirmation that women may prophesy in corporate worship.

The context of the passages addressing the "silence" of women are all placed within discussions of appropriate behavior within worship (1 Corinthians 11:2-16, 14:34, 1 Timothy 2:8-15). Clearly these passages do not teach that women may not "utter any sound" in a church since that would conflict with Paul's recognition that a woman may prophesy (1 Corinthians 11). In fact, when Luke announces the Spirit's arrival he affirms that both "sons and daughters" will prophecy (Acts 2:17). Further, in Acts the four daughters of Philip the evangelist were named as "prophetesses" (Acts 21:9), and the apostle Paul even gives guidelines for women when prophesying in public worship (1 Corinthians 11:5). Therefore, we believe that women may address co-ed adult audiences through prophecy, but only in such a way that does not undermine the authoritative teaching and leadership role of the Elders.

The probability that prophecy included prepared instruction.

The gift of prophecy exercised within corporate worship by both men and women, most likely included spontaneous "inspired" communication, as well as prepared instruction and exhortation from the Scripture. The means women could have prepared a message to be delivered in the corporate assembly, which might have included reading or quoting Scripture, as well as explaining Scripture and offering examples of application for the Christian community. Thus, women could exercise their gift of prophecy as long as they demonstrated an acceptance toward male headship (1 Corinthians 11).

In his book titled Prophecy In Early Christianity and the Ancient Mediterranean World (Eerdmans), David Aune presents six basic forms of prophetic speech, whose purposes included exhortation, admonishment, judgment, consolation and instruction and whose function served a purpose similar to our modern preaching role.

Craig Blomberg's conclusion that prophecy could be both "spontaneous 'inspired' utterances," as well as "those into which previous thought and preparation had been given" (344-345), leads him to believe that Paul is tacitly giving approval for women to preach God's Word, albeit under male authority. Wayne Grudem, in his book titled The Gift of Prophecy in 1 Corinthians (University Press of America), describes the function of prophecy as similar to that of teaching/preaching in that the spiritual growth and strengthening of the listeners is the goal and the content may include doctrine (185).

Holding "Non-essential" Beliefs

At GEBC the issue of women in ministry is considered a "non-essential," as we do not believe that one's salvation is affected by holding either position. Therefore, we do not require an affirmation of complementarianism in order to become a member, or even to serve within the church. At the same time, this is an important topic and one about which many feel passionate. Therefore, our posture is one of:

Humility and a commitment to avoid portraying those who disagree with us as less godly. We realize that:
- Both positions are capable of constructing sound arguments from the Scripture.
- We come with personal history, biases and the abiding presence of sin.

- Our differences on non-essentials should not undermine our unity.

<u>Integrity</u> and a commitment to interpret Scripture without shaping it to fit our personal desires. We realize that we must:
- Allow the Bible to communicate its message, and not force it to communicate ours.
- Submit to the Bible's mandates, including an openness to having our minds changed by the Bible.
- Be willing to accept the Bible's silence and/or ambiguity when it does not address all our concerns or answer all our questions.
- Be committed to the intention of the author/s, rather than twisting their words in order to fit our position. These "methodological" commitments are adapted from the NIV Application Commentary on Genesis, written by John Walton (189).

<u>Sensitivity</u> and a commitment to fully understand what is at stake from both perspectives. We realize that:
- There has been a history within the church of women being abused in the name of complementarian theology. This is not God's intent and cannot be tolerated.

- Neither position is simply seeking control or power, but each sincerely believes their position is God's ideal and they long for what is best.
- All Christian women are gifted and called into ministry and the church must encourage their involvement if we are to fully glorify God.

Conclusion

We believe that God created both men and women in his image and with equal value in his sight. As a complementarian church, we believe all of us are called and enabled through the Holy Spirit to use our gifts and yet, in the home and church, we believe that God has reserved unique roles for men and women. It is our prayer that these gender specific roles will be the blessing that God intended them to be and that everyone will be encouraged and empowered to fully exercise their gifts and influence in the ministries of GEBC. Recognizing that the role of women in ministry issue can be a challenging topic for churches to navigate successfully, the Elders conclude our yearlong study of the issue with a posture of humble conviction on this important but non-essential issue. Our posture is ideally reflected in Augustine's historic statement, "In essentials unity, in non-essentials liberty, in all things charity."

Position on Church Discipline

Discipline is a vital part of disciple-making. Included in discipline is all types of encouragement, correction and rebuke, which is aimed at strengthening the faith of the individual and the community. Much like an iceberg, most discipline goes unseen, or is never registered as discipline, in that it happens quickly, quietly and subtly. Some discipline though is seen and is even done publicly.

The Purpose of Church Discipline:

Discipline within the church is primarily designed to correct and restore God's children when they fall into sin (Matthew 18:15-20). Rather than being punitive, we lovingly confront each other so that we will walk rightly with our Lord (Hebrews 10:24).

The Posture of Church Discipline:

We approach the issue of discipline with humility, recognizing that all are sinners, saved by grace (Galatians 6:1-2). The more we get to know the Lord, the more we recognize both how far we fall short of his standards, and the danger of seeking to correct minor issues in others while ignoring the greater issues within ourselves (Matthew 7:1-5). We approach each other with patience, recognizing that we are all "in process" (Romans 15:1).

At the same time, we also approach the issue of discipline with authority, recognizing the link between our actions on earth and the spiritual reality in Heaven (Matthew 18:18-20). We also handle discipline matters without fear, as we are charged with the protecting the church, and unaddressed sin compromises the whole. (1 Corinthians 5:6-7)

The Plan of Church Discipline:

First, in private: The offended party must first meet privately with the offender, seeking their repentance (Matthew 18:15). Discussions with other persons are out of bounds at this point, and amount to gossip, which is sin and destructive to the process of seeking repentance and restoration.

If necessary, then with witnesses: If the offending party remains unrepentant, the offended person should meet again privately with the offender along with two or three witnesses. This is designed to establish the validity of the offense and provide a stronger call to repentance (Matthew 18:16).

If necessary, then to leadership: If the offending party remains unrepentant, the offended person should bring the matter to the church (Matthew 18:17). In the governmental structure of GEBC, this step is accomplished first by bringing the matter to the Elders or pastor. The Elder or pastor involved will meet with the offended party to determine the appropriate action. Issues in this regard brought to the pastoral staff are reviewed (at a minimum) with the Senior Pastor, and also with the Elders as deemed appropriate by the Senior Pastor. Matters brought to an Elder are reviewed by at least one other Elder. In the event that repentance is evidenced, we rejoice in the completion of the process. If the offending party remains unrepentant, the matter is discussed with the entire Board of Elders for determination of further proceedings

Finally, to the congregation as a whole: If after all attempts above have failed, the offender is to be treated as a non-Christian and removed from the membership of the church (Matthew 18:17, 1 Corinthians 5:12-13). Again, the point of this step is to bring the person to repentance and to protect the integrity of the church. The scope of public disclosure regarding the circumstance is determined by the Board of Elders in light of the facts. The determination is based on seeking accountability for the offender and openness and integrity within the body; the scope of disclosure is generally determined by the scope of the offense. As would be the case with all non-Christians, members of GEBC would be encouraged to pursue the person urging them to repentance. If repentance follows, the person is to be lovingly restored into the community (2 Corinthians 2:5-6)

Church Discipline of Leadership:

Additional care is exercised in discipline of church leaders. Note 1 Timothy 5, when addressing this issue in the context of establishing the importance and honorability of serving as an Elder:

First, we are not to address charges against

leaders without the testimony of at least two witnesses (1 Timothy 5:19). This is important as leaders are subject to misunderstanding and even to slander in the fulfillment of their roles.

Second, if a leader sins and violates the conditions of their office (e.g. the requirements of 1 Timothy 3), we are to rebuke the leader publicly for the purpose of both pursing repentance by the offender and as an example to the congregation (1 Timothy 5:20). As is the case in general church discipline matters, the scope of public disclosure is determined by the Elders in light of the facts and a determination is based on seeking accountability for the offender and openness and integrity within the body. The scope of disclosure is generally determined by the scope of the offense and those impacted by the offense.

We recognize the higher standard placed on leaders and our responsibility to exercise church discipline without regard to the temporal consequences (1 Timothy 5:21) and we are fully committed to Biblical instruction regarding the handling of sin within the body and particularly within leadership as obedience to God, honor for the Church and reputation of our Lord Jesus and in the loving pursuit of repentance and restoration for those within the body who fall.

All leaders (including staff, Elders or other lay leaders) in an unrepentant state are not allowed to lead until healthy. If repentance follows the discipline process, we exercise caution in restoring the person in question to a leadership position (1 Timothy 5:22).

Position on Hermeneutics

"Hermeneutics" is the discipline of interpreting and applying Scripture. While we realize that these instructions will not answer all interpretive questions, we want the congregation to be equipped to understand Scripture's meaning so that they can apply it to their lives.

Authority of Scripture

We believe the Bible is God's "special" revelation in that God revealed himself to particular authors, who wrote his message of salvation (Hebrews 1:1-2). We believe the Bible is inspired by God, and the only infallible rule for faith and practice (2 Timothy 3:16). By "inspired" we mean the supernatural influence of the Holy Spirit upon the authors of Scripture rendered their writings an accurate record. By "rule" we mean the Bible has the authority to require change in our lives. Studying the Bible results in changed lives as we apply its truth (Hebrews 4:12).

Interpreting Scripture

First, we should come prayerfully, inviting God to teach through the work of the Holy Spirit (John 16:13), and believing that God longs to reveal himself to us (James 1:5-8). Scripture is a unified and understandable whole, accessible to all who believe. Thus, interpreting Scripture includes a commitment to accept its testimony at face value, doing our best to read and understand the text as the author intended it to be read. Second, we should work to accurately interpret God's word (2 Timothy 2:15) and avoid imposing our personal pre-suppositions upon the text. A diligent study should include:

- Reading the passage in context, reviewing the surrounding verses, paragraphs, and chapters, and the book's larger place within the canon of Scripture, as well as the book's literary form (genre), whether poetry, letters, historical narrative, gospel, apocalyptic, etc.
- Identifying the cultural context of the author and audience. Scripture was written within a particular time in history, and fully applying Scripture requires understanding the author's original message to his original audience in their historical context.
- Researching the grammar used within the passage, looking for any comparisons or contrasts and identifying basic grammatical structures. Noting word usage (i.e. definitions, key words or repeated words or phrases), indications of literal or figurative intent based on the context, and perhaps original language translation, will also help to clarify meaning. Recognizing that Scripture is made up of words means that a good understanding of the meaning of words and their order is vital to an

accurate interpretation and application in our contemporary setting. While knowing the original biblical languages is certainly helpful, today's English translations are highly accurate and a breadth of meaning can be gained simply by comparing various translations.

- Researching complementary passages of Scripture. While some Scripture may be difficult to understand, it never ultimately contradicts itself. The best interpreter of Scripture is Scripture. When a passage is difficult to understand, use the Scripture that is clearest to interpret what is less clear, as well as explicit passages to interpret the implicit.

Third we should come believing, possessing a confidence that Scripture has a message for us today. Despite being written for an ancient audience Scripture still speaks to us today. In this step the goal is to answer the question, "What does the text mean?" For example, if a particular verb tense was noted and recorded as an observation, now we ask what the use of that particular verb tense tells us. A present progressive tense might highlight an on-going work God is doing, or an imperative tells us this is a command, not just a suggestion! Below is an example.

> And my God will meet all your needs according to his glorious riches in Christ Jesus. Philippians 4:19 (NIV)

Observations through study:
Paul was a "servant of Christ" (1:1) From the book of Acts we know that he was taking the gospel to people beyond Jerusalem as a missionary to gentiles.

- Paul was writing to believers in Philippi (1:1).
- Paul acknowledged the gifts that they had sent to meet his need (4:14, 18).
- Paul affirmed that the gifts were "pleasing to God" (4:18).
- "God will meet" - God is the one who supplies for all needs (WHO)
- "God will meet" - indicates certainty, and timing to be future (WHEN)
- "all your needs" – not some but all and not wants, but needs (WHAT)
- "according to his glorious riches in Christ Jesus" - denotes the source (HOW)

Possible conclusions and applications:

- "all your needs" - God's provision is comprehensive
- "according to his glorious riches" - God's provision is abundant
- "in Christ Jesus." - Christ is the one through whom the riches are available
- Giving a sacrificial offering pleases God.

Applying Scripture

Here the question, "What does this mean <u>for me</u>?" is considered. An "action" step is not always required by a passage. Sometimes Scripture is simply illustrating the character of God in order to strengthen our faith, rather than calling us to action. Turning to our example, some clear application points are:

- We can give of our finances to support ministry without worry, because God has promised to meet all our needs. Do we trust in our portfolios or in God to supply our needs?
- God is pleased when we financially support ministry. Are we an example to our children of trust in God for his supply?
- We can be generous financially in supporting ministry because we know God will meet our needs. Am I obediently sharing in supplying the needs of those who are sharing the gospel here and around the world?

After learning from God's Word, we should immediately go back to prayer (where we started) as we seek God's help through the Holy Spirit to start making the necessary changes -- whether in our perceptions of God or in our actions.

R.C. Sproul on Hermeneutics

Summary of Sproul's
"11 Practical Rules for Interpreting the Bible,"
from the book titled "Knowing Scripture"

Read the Bible like any other book – it is not like any other book, but it is at the same time a book. For example, the Bible has verbs and nouns and pronouns and for that reason understanding the rules of grammar and syntax helps in making sense of its message. The Bible also has different types of literature (ex. history, prophecy, poetry, law, letters), which are different in nature and purpose and thus require different methods of interpretation. Each of the books within the Bible was also written within a particular historical context by a particular author with a unique perspective and understanding both help in understanding God's message through them.

Read the Bible passionately and intimately – although the books of the Bible were not written to us, they were written for us. The Bible is God's story of saving work in the world and was meant to be received and applied personally by all who believe. For this reason, the Bible is interpreted best as we are able to enter the story fully, allowing it to impact our mind, will and emotions.

Interpret story by the didactic – although the stories in Scripture communicate something about God's saving work in the world, many are simply descriptions of the fallenness of humanity, rather than prescriptions for godly living. This can make it hard to identify doctrine and biblical ethics when interpreting stories. Generally, an accurate interpretation of biblical stories will be corroborated by those sections of Scripture that are didactic. Much of Paul's writings are didactic. In short, ethics and doctrine within biblical story will be affirmed within the broader biblical teachings.

Interpret the implicit by the explicit and the obscure by the clear – although the basic message of the Bible is clear and can be understood by anyone able to read, not all parts of the Bible are equally clear. For this reason, it's important that what is explicitly stated, be utilized to interpret whatever is unclear.

Determine carefully the meaning of words – although words have meaning on their own, only the context in which a word is used can determine the specific meaning of word. For this reason, when doing word studies make sure to understand the range of meaning that a word can have and look at the different contexts in which the word is used.

Note the presence of parallelisms – parallelism involves a linking of thoughts, as it identifies similarities or differences between ideas. Three basic types of parallelism are:

- Synonymous parallelism – presents the same thought in a different way. (Proverbs 19:5
- Antithetical parallelism – presents a contrast

between two thoughts. (Proverbs 13:1)
- Synthetic parallelism – presents expectation and fulfillment (Psalm 92:9)

Note the difference between proverb and law – although proverbs are truisms, they are not to be considered universal laws. Ancient proverbs reflect principles that are wise guides for living, however they are not promises that bind God to act in a certain way. The classic example is "Train up a child in the way he should go, and when he is old, he will not depart from it" (Proverbs 22:6). This is not a law guaranteeing our children's future behavior, but an admonition to train our children in godliness because it will generally bring a good outcome.

Observe the difference between the spirit and the letter of the law – although obedience to God's Word is very important there is a tendency to go beyond what is commanded in Scripture, effectively missing the spirit of God's command. For example, the importance of resting on the Sabbath (Deuteronomy 5:12), has been interpreted to mean you can't do any number of things that might actually be restful. Jesus was careful to nuance the difference between the spirit and the letter of the law, indicating that the law is a call for heart transformation and not simply outward obedience (Matthew 5:27-28).

Be careful with parables – Jesus taught with parables, but it was clear that he used parables to conceal truth from some while revealing it to others

(Mark 4:10-12). The safest way to handle parables is to avoid allegorizing and look for one primary message or central point.

Be careful with predictive prophecy – if we examine how the New Testament treats Old Testament prophecy, we discover that in some cases an appeal is made to fulfillment of the letter, such as the birth of the Messiah in Bethlehem, and in others fulfillment has a broader scope, such as the fulfillment of Malachi's prophecy of Elijah's return (Malachi 4:5-6, Matthew 11:13-15).

Interpret the Bible with a posture of humility – humility is not synonymous with doubt or timidity. We don't have to hold our convictions tentatively, but we need to avoid arrogance and be open to learning from others. We also need to recognize that not all beliefs are equally important and on lesser points of doctrine and/or interpretation we must hold them loosely.

Summary of Explaining Hermeneutics:
A Commentary on the Chicago Statement of Biblical Hermeneutics. International Council on Biblical Inerrancy, 1983.

Article I
We believe the authority of Scripture is the authority of God and is attested to by Jesus. Whatever the Bible affirms, God affirms. Jesus confirmed the authority of Old Testament (cf. Matt. 5:17-18; Luke 24:44; John 10:34-35), and he promised the same for the New Testament (John 14:16; 16:13). To reject the authority of Scripture is to impugn the authority of Christ.

Article II
As Christ is both God and Man, so Scripture is God's Word in human language. We deny Christ entails sin and that Scripture entails error. Both Christ and Scripture were conceived by the Holy Spirit, using fallible agents. Both produced a divine and human (theanthropic) result; one a sinless person and the other an errorless book. Christ is one person uniting two natures and Scripture is one written expression uniting two authors (God and man).

Article III
We believe Jesus is the central focus of Scripture. Jesus taught that he is the Bible's central theme (Matt. 5:17; Luke 24:27, 44; John 5:39; Heb. 10:7).

Article IV

We affirm that the Holy Spirit who inspired Scripture acts through it today to work faith in its message. The Spirit never teaches anything contrary to Scripture.

Article V

The Holy Spirit enables believers to appropriate and apply Scripture. While non-Christians may understand the meaning of Scripture, they will not accept its message apart from the Holy Spirit's help.

Article VI

The Bible expresses God's truth in propositional statements, and the biblical truth is both objective and absolute. To suggest that the Bible contains mistakes, but that these are not errors so long as they do not mislead, is contrary to both Scripture and ordinary understanding.

Article VII

We affirm that the meaning expressed in each biblical text is single, definite, and fixed. We deny that the recognition of this single meaning eliminates the variety of its application.

Article VIII

We affirm that the Bible contains mandates that apply to all cultural and situational contexts and other mandates which apply only to particular situations. We deny that the distinctions between the universal and particular mandates of Scripture can be determined by cultural and situational factors.

Article IX
Hermeneutics helps with all that is involved in understanding the Bible. We deny that the message of Scripture derives from the interpreter's understanding.

Article X
Scripture communicates through a variety of literary forms: parables, satire, irony, hyperbole, metaphor, simile, poetry, and even allegory (e.g., Ezek. 16-17). The limits of language is not inadequate to convey God's message.

Article XI
Translations can communicate across all cultural boundaries. The Bible's meaning is not so tied to culture that meaning in other cultures is impossible.

Article XII
Only functional equivalents faithful to the content of biblical teaching should be employed. We deny the legitimacy of methods which either are insensitive to the demands of cross-cultural communication or distort biblical meaning in the process.

Article XIII
Awareness of literary categories is essential for proper exegesis. When the prophet speaks of "trees clapping

their hands" (Isa. 55:12) this is clearly poetry and not prose. Yet, some take Jonah to be an allegory when he is presented as historical (Mat. 12:40-42).

Article XIV
We affirm that the biblical record of events corresponds to historical fact. However, a parable must not be understood to represent historical facts.

Article XV
The Bible is to be interpreted literally, which will consider all literary forms in the text. The correct interpretation discovers the meaning in its grammatical forms and historical, cultural context.

Article XVI
Critical techniques can determine the canonical text and its meaning. Yet, no method of criticism can question the truth or integrity of the writer's expressed meaning. Critical methods can establish which of the texts are copies of the original, but not call into question whether something in the original text is true.

Article XVII
We affirm the unity, harmony and consistency of Scripture and declare that it is its own best interpreter. Scripture may not be interpreted in such a way as to suggest that one passage contradicts another.

Article XVIII
The Bible's own interpretation of itself is always correct. We deny the writers of Scripture always understood the full implications of their words. Scripture has only one meaning, but it is important to acknowledge that God may have had more in mind than the prophet did.

Article XIX
Scripture is not required to fit pre-understandings, inconsistent with itself, such as naturalism, evolutionism, scientism, secular humanism, and relativism.

Article XX
We affirm God is the author of all truth, and all truths cohere, and that the Bible speaks truth on every issue it addresses. We affirm that extra-biblical data has value for clarifying what Scripture teaches, and for prompting correction of faulty interpretations. We deny that extra-biblical views can disprove Scripture. All truth is God's truth and God never affirms contrary propositions.

Article XXI
We affirm the harmony of special with general revelation. We deny that any scientific facts are inconsistent with the meaning of Scripture.

Article XXII
We affirm that Genesis 1-11 is factual. We deny Genesis 1-11 is mythical and that science may be invoked to overthrow what Scripture teaches.

Article XXIII
We affirm the clarity of Scripture and specifically of its message about salvation from sin. We admit that some passages are less clear, as well as less relevant, as the Bible's central saving message.

Article XXIV
We affirm no one is dependent on biblical scholars for understanding of Scripture. We deny that a person should ignore the study of biblical scholars.

Article XXV
We affirm that only preaching which sufficiently conveys the divine revelation is that which faithfully expounds Scripture as the Word of God. We deny the preacher has any message apart from Scripture.

Position on Marriage, Divorce, & Remarriage

Purpose Statement

This paper grew out of the Elders' desire to 1) strengthen the marriages of GEBC and the integrity of our community of faith, 2) combat the decay of the institution of marriage and 3) support and encourage the pastoral staff of GEBC in their efforts to care for fractured marriages and prepare engaged couples for a life-long marriage commitment.

While this paper intentionally avoids offering specific directives in particular scenarios, our hope is that providing clarity on God's design for marriage will deepen conversations, provide direction in the process of prayer and decision-making and raise the quality of pastoral care in these difficult situations.

The Sanctity of Marriage

Marriage is a relationship ordained by God and established at creation, and Jesus referred to the creation narrative as the foundation for our understanding of marriage (Genesis 2:18-25, Matthew 19:4-6). Designed by God, marriage is to be a monogamous, lifelong, heterosexual union, that promotes holiness, as well as represents symbolically and mysteriously the relationship between God and his people (Isaiah 54:5, Jeremiah 3:20, Ezekiel 16:8, Hosea 2:14-23, Ephesians 5:21-33). When a man and woman are united in marriage, they are to provide a living example of Christ's love for the world. Marriage is to be a living metaphor of Christ's union with the Church, His spiritual bride, a picture of something far larger than mere human devotion (Ephesians 5:21-33).

When marriages succeed in creating a loving environment for spouses to live within, then we can see clearly the attributes of God's patience, kindness and selflessness toward each of us played out in a concrete manner. When marriages fail to demonstrate Christ's selfless and sacrificial love the witness of Christ's Church is weakened. For this reason, God directs believers to marry only other believers (2 Corinthians 6:14) and not divorce (Malachi 2:14-16, Matthew 19:6).

The Permissibility of Divorce

The Bible presents marriage as a union which should be indissoluble (Matthew 19:6). For this reason, divorce is always outside the design of God, in that it is contrary to God's commandment to "leave and be united" (Genesis 2:24) and breaks the bond of two becoming one (Matthew 19:4-5). For that reason, Paul wrote plainly that divorce should not happen among God's people (1 Corinthians 7:10-11). The Bible presents divorce as the product of sin, whether in one or both spouse's lives. Jesus interpreted Moses' allowance for divorce as the result of hard heartedness (Matthew 19:8). This means that divorce is never morally neutral, and every divorce demonstrates a failure to live out the gospel message of forgiveness and reconciliation.

Although we realize that there is much debate over the biblical permissibility of divorce, specifically in situations involving adultery, abandonment, and/or abuse (Matthew 5:32, 19:9; 1 Corinthians 7:15), we believe that God always desires reconciliation between spouses. For this reason, as shepherds we never recommend divorce and always encourage patience and hope in God's ability to heal and restore a marriage relationship. In some circumstances however (e.g. physical or emotional abuse), it may be best for spouses to separate for a season (1 Corinthians 7:5), and the church body should support the efforts of restoration throughout a season of separation. Separation is best utilized with an eye toward devotion in prayer and ultimately marital reconciliation.

At the same time, we do realize that divorces still occur within Christ's community. A mature Christian may be forsaken by a disobedient or unbelieving spouse. Two professing believers may drift so far from the Lord that they no longer acknowledge the authority of the Lord or the binding nature of their marriage covenant. The good news of the Gospel is that there is no unpardonable sin once confession and repentance have taken place (1 John 1:9). Therefore, while we will fight for the preservation of marriages, we will also eagerly extend grace to those who divorce, realizing that God longs to do a work of repair and restoration in their lives. The church, as God's family, is called to minister forgiveness, discipline, healing, and restoration whenever possible.

The Advisability of Remarriage

Considering the Bible's position on the sanctity of marriage and the sinful implications of divorce, we encourage caution in remarriage for the following reasons:

- Those divorcing are directed to either remain unmarried or to be reconciled to their spouse (1 Corinthians 7:10-11).
- Although divorce severs a marriage legally, it does not break the marriage bond from a biblical perspective. Those remarrying commit adultery (Mark 10:11-12, Luke 16:18), unless the marriage bond was broken by marital unfaithfulness (Matthew 5:32, 19:9), or the one remarrying is a widow or widower. The marital bond is the spiritual union established through sexual intimacy, as "two become one" (Genesis 2:24, Matthew 19:5, Mark 10:8).
- "Marital unfaithfulness" (NIV) is described not as a reason to divorce or remarry, but only as breaking the marital bond (Matthew 5:32, 19:9).
- Scripture places a high priority on forgiveness and reconciliation (Matthew 6:14-15, 2 Corinthians 5:18).

Again, although we realize there is much debate over the biblical permissibility of divorce in situations involving adultery, abandonment, and/or abuse (Matthew 5:32, 19:9; 1 Corinthians 7:15), we believe it is the responsibility of each Christian to search the Scriptures and wrestle with God in prayer over whether their divorce was biblically permissible before considering remarriage. GEBC staff and Elders are eager to help parishioners wrestle with these issues, providing support through Bible study and prayer.

Further, nothing in Scripture indicates that conversion alters the advisability of remarriage, as God's design for marriage, and the priority of forgiveness and reconciliation supersedes participation in the church (Matthew 19:4-6). Finally, if one does remarry, believers should only marry other believers (1 Corinthians 7:39, 2 Corinthians 6:14-15), and once remarried they should not divorce (1 Corinthians 7:27).

The Process of Restoration in Fellowship

God's people are to be a part of the process of restoration of broken relationships. Specifically, those who are mature in the faith are to help restore those who fall into sin (Galatians 6:1). In the process of restoration, we are restored from our sinfulness to fellowship with God and others. This will require reconciliation (2 Corinthians 5:16-21), which involves seeking for forgiveness (Matthew 5:23-24), as well as granting forgiveness to others (Matthew 6:14-15; 1 John 1:7, 2:9). While restoration in fellowship doesn't require that ex-spouses remarry, it does allow members of the body of Christ to take communion in good conscience (1 Corinthians 11:27-30).

Realizing that the failure of a marriage always involves both spouses, even though blame is rarely shared equally, confession and repentance are a necessary part of the process of restoration for all involved (James 5:16; 1 John 1:9). Confession is the process of acknowledging one's sin, and repentance is the process of forsaking the sin. This process takes time and should involve someone who is spiritually mature to provide guidance (Galatians 6:1). The work of restoration is aimed at preserving the unity and the testimony of the Church (John 17:23).

The Process of Restoration to Ministry

Once a process of restoration in fellowship has been completed, restoration to positions of ministry leadership and/or teaching can be sought. While the process of restoration can vary, it will generally include meeting with pastoral staff and/or Elders for prayer and instruction from Scripture, as well as submitting to ongoing accountability.

Certain leadership roles within the church are reserved only for those who, if married, possess strong marriages. While many churches take the position that individuals who are divorced and/or remarried can never again serve as Elders, ministry leaders, teachers, or pastors, our interpretation of the relevant passages in Timothy and Titus does not inherently exclude such individuals once they have completed a careful process of restoration. Paul wrote to Timothy that Elders and deacons (i.e. ministry leaders) must be "above reproach." Among the characteristics of being above reproach, Paul required that a leader be "the husband of one wife" (1 Timothy 3:2, 12), a phrase that is typically interpreted as focusing on marital fidelity ("a one-woman man"). The text also requires that leaders be "able to manage" their own household well (1 Timothy 3:4-5, 12). Further, Scripture explains that those who teach the Word of God will be judged more strictly (James 3:1). Therefore, it is important for those leading and/or teaching to be diligence in the process.

Conclusion

While Christians disagree on these matters, it is our prayer that this paper strengthens our fellowship by offering biblical guidelines for GEBC. Whether in premarital counseling, marital crisis, divorce proceedings or marital restoration, we are eager to support and encourage one another in the bond of unity and pray that GEBC is a community of love and grace.

Position on Fornication and/or Cohabitation

Couples wanting to be married at GEBC by our staff must complete a pre-marital counseling. If it is discovered during the process that an engaged couple is either having sexual intercourse or living together the pastoral staff of GEBC will speak with the couple about:

- God's design of sex creating a union between two people (1 Corinthians 6:16).
- God's prohibition against sex outside of marriage. Fornication is defined as "sexual intercourse between persons not married to each other," which the Bible condemns (Matthew 15:19, Mark 7:21, John 8:41, Acts 15:20, Acts 15:29, Acts 21:25).
- Death brought by sin. Fornication brings death into our lives, negatively impacting us, as well as others, as it creates an unsafe environment for intimacy (1 Corinthians 6:15-20).
- God's grace available to all those who repent. The good news of the Gospel is that the death and resurrection of Jesus Christ provides forgiveness and restoration to all who trust in Jesus (1 John 1:9).
- The importance of abstaining from sexual intercourse until married and for those who are cohabiting to live separately until married.

Finally, it is the practice of GEBC to not marry any Christians refusing to abstain from sexual intercourse prior to marriage. The Elders believe that Christians refusing to abstain from sexual intercourse outside of marriage, once they are made aware that the activity is sinful, have a heart and/or maturity issue that indicates they are most likely not ready for marriage (1 John 3:9). Christians are expected to represent Christ publicly (2 Cor. 5:20), living above reproach (1 Thess. 5:22) and a refusal to do so should be addressed before facilitating marriage.

Position on Marriage, Gender, and Sexuality

We believe that the term "marriage" has only one meaning: the uniting of one man and one woman in a single, exclusive union. (Genesis 2:18-25) We believe marriage was ordained for the mutual help of husband and wife, for the increase of mankind and of the church through a holy seed; and for preventing of uncleanness. (Genesis 1:28, 2:18, 9:1; Malachi 2:15; 1 Corinthians 7:2, 9; Ephesians 5:28; 1 Peter 3:7) We believe that it is lawful for all sorts of people to marry, who are able with judgment to give their consent. (Hebrews 13:4; 1 Timothy 4:3; 1 Corinthians 7:36–38; Genesis 24:57–58) Yet, it is the duty of Christians to marry only in the Lord. (1 Corinthians 7:39) We believe that marriage ought not to be within the degrees of consanguinity or affinity forbidden by the Word. (Leviticus 18:6–17; 24–30; Leviticus 20:19; 1 Corinthians 5:1; Amos 2:7) Nor can such incestuous marriages ever be made lawful by any law or consent of parties, so as those persons may live together as man and wife. (Mark 6:18; Leviticus 18:24-28.)

We believe that God intends sexual intimacy to occur only between a man and a woman who are married to each other. (1 Corinthians 6:18; 7:2-5; Hebrews 13:4) We believe that any form of sexual immorality (e.g. adultery, fornication, homosexual behavior, bisexual conduct, bestiality, incest, and use of pornography) is sinful and offensive to God. (Matthew 15:18-20; 1 Corinthians 6:9-10.)

We believe that God wonderfully and immutably creates each person as male or female. We believe that God's original and ongoing intent and action was the creation of humanity manifest as two distinct sexes, which was affirmed by Jesus Christ himself in his teaching correcting abuses of divorce stating, "at the beginning the Creator 'made them male and female'" (Matthew 19:4; Mark 10:6.) We believe in the equal dignity and worth of male and female and the importance of not fostering confusion between male and female. (Romans 1:26-27; Galatians 3:28) These two distinct, complementary genders together reflect the image and nature of God. (Genesis 1:26-27) Rejection of one's biological sex is a rejection of the image of God within that person. We believe that in order to preserve the function and integrity of Glen Ellyn Bible Church as the local Body of Christ, and to provide a biblical role model to the Church's members and the community, it is imperative that all persons employed by the Church in any capacity, or who serve as volunteers, agree to and abide by this Statement on Marriage, Gender, and Sexuality. (Matthew 5:16; Philippians 2:14-16; 1 Thessalonians 5:22.)

We believe that every person must be afforded compassion, love, kindness, respect, and dignity. (Mark 12:28-31; Luke 6:31) Hateful and harassing behavior or attitudes directed toward any individual are to be repudiated and are not in accord with Scripture nor the doctrines of Glen Ellyn Bible Church.

Position on Stewardship

The Bible gives lots of attention to money. Sixteen of the thirty-eight parables told by Jesus concerned money and/or possessions. One out every ten verses in the Gospels deals with money. Why is this? Scripture indicates that there is a fundamental connection between our spiritual well-being and how we handle our finances. We cannot divorce our faith and our finances, any more than we can separate our sexuality and our spirituality (1 Corinthians 6:19), or our willingness to forgive others and our wanting to be forgiven by God (Matthew 6:15).

Our faith and our finances are necessarily and inseparably linked. For this reason, churches should give lots of attention to the issue of financial stewardship. Moreover, the American church should give it even greater attention, because Jesus described wealth as one of the largest barriers to entering heaven (Matthew 19:23-24). According to Jesus the poor have a spiritual advantage over the rich. Wealth is spiritually dangerous. We can't claim to both love God and money (Matthew 6:24). As people who claim to love God, hating money means that we recognize the love of money as a root of all kinds of evil (1 Timothy 6:10), and it means that we have rejected the pursuit of money for the sake of our souls.

Paul wrote that we are to "excel in this grace of giving" (2 Corinthians 8:7). Whatever our annual income, we are not only to give, but we are to excel in the grace of giving. For most American's this will mean giving far more than the Old Testament tithe (i.e. 10%). Bear in mind that the average American Evangelical gives only about 2.5% of their income. So to the question "How much do I have to give?" I'm increasingly tempted to answer, "Well, how risk averse are you?" In other words, does the reality of Hell and the possibility of spending eternity there scare you a lot, or just a little? Or we might ask, "What's your pain tolerance? Is eternal torment something you estimate you can withstand, or would you rather insulate yourself against that experience? And you may say, "That's crazy. We are saved by grace, apart from anything we do!" Exactly! That's why asking, "How much do we have to give?" is completely off the mark.

Let there be no misunderstanding, following Jesus means giving all that you have to him and his kingdom. Nothing that we have is ours and his Kingdom's interests are to be funded by our material wealth. Obviously, this does not mean we're to give until we cannot pay our bills. But it does mean that we are to curb our spending so that we can give more to his Kingdom's efforts!

Jesus is not primarily concerned about our taking longer or more luxurious vacations, or the additions that we want to put on our house. Jesus is concerned about the least and the lost, and if we have truly experienced God's grace then we will share his concern and store increasing amounts of our treasure in heaven (Matthew 6:20).

Stewardship is the wise management of the resources given to us by God (ex. time, talents, treasure). The goal of our stewardship is God's glory and our joy (Matthew 25:14-30). Poor stewardship is an indication of spiritual issues (ex. unwillingness to trust and/or submit to God). Helping people understand the importance of stewardship is a responsibility of leadership. Below are some Scripture references on stewarding our money.

- Abraham tithed (Genesis 14: 18-20)
- God's people gave abundantly (Exodus 36:4-7)
- Giving leaders are encouraging (1 Chronicles 29:9,14)
- Giving is rewarded (Proverbs 3:9-10)
- Greed is never satisfied (Ecclesiastes 5:10)
- Giving is a way to test God (Malachi 3:6-11)
- Failing to give is cheating God (Malachi 3:8-9)
- Giving invests in eternity (Matthew 6:19-21)
- We cannot serve God and money (Matthew 6:24)
- It is hard for a rich man to enter heaven (Matthew 19:23-26)
- We cannot serve two masters (Luke 16:13-15)
- Generosity is rewarded by God (Luke 6:38)
- Generosity was a part of the spread of the gospel. (Acts 2:44-47)

- Generosity empowered the spread of the gospel. (Acts 4:34-35)
- Lying about one's giving was condemned by God. (Acts 5:4-5)
- Christians are to be disciplined in their giving. (1 Corinthians 12:1-2)
- Generosity is a sign of grace at work in our lives. (2 Corinthians 8:1-4)
- Christians are to excel in the grace of giving. (2 Corinthians 8:7)
- We can test the sincerity of our love by comparing it to the generosity of others. (2 Corinthians 8:8-9)
- Paul boasted in the Corinthians' eagerness to give. (2 Corinthians 9:1-2)
- Paul told the Corinthians to be ready to give. (2 Corinthians 9:5)
- We get out spiritually, what you put in financially. (2 Corinthians 9:6)
- We should not give out of compulsion. (2 Corinthians 9:7)
- We can give confidently that God will provide. (2 Corinthians 9:8-9)
- We are made rich by God in order to be generous. (2 Corinthians 9:10-11)
- Giving meets needs and results in God's praise! (2 Corinthians 9:12)

- Generosity results in God's praise. (2 Corinthians 9:13-15)
- Paul directs us to support the work of ministers. (Galatians 6:6)
- Greed is a sign of no inheritance in the kingdom. (Ephesians 5:5)
- We are to actively put to death greed. (Colossians 3:5)
- Freedom from the love of money is a sign of maturity. (1 Timothy 3:2-3)
- Paul directs us to support the local church. (1 Timothy 5:18)
- People who want to get rich fall into temptation. (1 Timothy 6:6-9)
- Love of money is a root of all kinds of evil. (1 Timothy 6:10)
- Love of money is a sign of the last days. (2 Timothy 3:1-5)
- Contentedness grows out of a confidence in God. (Hebrews 13:5)
- Jesus is worthy to receive all our wealth. (Revelation 5:11-12)

Encouraging Excellence in Giving

The Bible gives lots of attention to money, because our faith and our finances are necessarily and inseparably linked. In fact, Jesus described our wealth as one of the potentially largest barriers to entering heaven (Matthew 19:23-24). For this reason, Paul wrote that we are to "excel in this grace of giving" (2 Corinthians 8:7). Encouraging people to excel in the grace of giving takes tactical intentionality on the part of church leadership. Below is summary of our efforts toward this end.

- We provide a weekly encouragement to give as a part of Sunday worship.
- We create digital access to make giving easy
    - Giving link on top of website
    - Giving slide in welcome slide rotation on Sunday
    - Giving information/code/link in bulletin
    - Giving QR codes in lobby
- We send email/letters encouraging giving.
    - Quarterly letters to members, with their giving statement
    - Annual and/or semi-annual giving encouragement from Elder Chairman (June/Dec)
    - Letter to first-time givers - regardless of amount donated
    - Thank you/acknowledgement for all stock/asset donations

- - Letter about ways to give as we end the year (Nov)
  - Letter to non-GEBC families who attend Recess/Reckless (Dec) about the importance of supporting the church's ministry
- Annual CareCenter Coat Drive Special Project fundraising encouragement (Oct)
- Giving updates at Congregational meetings (May/Nov)
- Video encouraging year-end giving (Nov)
- Preaching on generosity and sacrificial giving as it comes up in the Scripture
- Capital campaign fundraising (e.g. ENGAGE 2020, REACH)
- Regular "thank you" and giving encouragement communication from Senior Pastor and/or Lead Pastor. The Senior Pastor does not know how much anyone gives but actively cultivates a giving dialogue with congregants. The Lead Pastor does know how much people give, assess giving patterns and encourages the Senior Pastor to shepherd congregants accordingly.
  - Giving is a gift that should be cultivated (Romans 12:8)
  - Giving is relational, a natural part of the discipleship dialogue.
  - Not talking about giving as a Church may be an indication of idolatry
  - 1 Timothy 6:17-19 those who are rich are to be uniquely encouraged to give
  - Acts 20:35 more blessed to give than receive

Position on Music and Worship

Jesus said, "Love the Lord your God with all your heart and with all your soul and with all your mind. This is the first and greatest commandment." Worship is at the center of everything that the church believes, practices and seeks to accomplish. It is the responsibility of the Body of Christ, and will be the eternal occupation of every believer. Our goal is to help people develop a lifestyle of worship. Our mission is to build a worship experience that encourages every believer and seeker to have an encounter with the person of Jesus Christ as they participate in corporate worship. We will create that environment by:

- Remembering that it is God Almighty that we seek to please. He is the audience. The congregation and leadership are the participants. Our task is to follow biblical instruction to bring sacrifices of praise and worship that honor Him, rather than seeking to satisfy the preferences of the participants.
- Working toward excellence in everything we do. Our God deserves nothing less.
- Striving to create an atmosphere that serves both the believer and the unbeliever. This includes words that are understood by all, a balance of musical style, and a warm and friendly attitude.
- Using many worship forms such as varied

styles of music (both vocal and instrumental), drama and art to bring worshipers into God's presence, with a strong emphasis on praise.

- Structuring services that teach the congregation to joyfully participate, not passively observe.
- Being bold, innovative, sensitive, reverent, relaxed and joyful, open to creative ideas (new or traditional), flexible and patient, allowing people to worship God without the fear of being judged by others.
- Edifying the Body of Christ, equipping them for service, with a prayerful spirit permeating our times with God in worship and the ministry that grows from it.
- Our services will be intentionally thematic and authentic, yet open to the changes the Holy Spirit may bring about. We will constantly evaluate and seek to always be improving. Truly our deepest desire is to give "blessing and honor and glory and power" to Him who sits on the throne forever and ever.

Explanation of GEBC's Statement of Faith

1. **We believe that the Scriptures of the Old and New Testaments are given by inspiration of God and are the only infallible rule of faith and practice (2 Timothy 3:16, 17).** By "inspiration of God" we mean that God directed human authors, working through their unique personalities, particular writing styles and within their specific cultural settings, to communicate his message. By "infallible" we mean that the Bible is inerrant, true and reliable in all that it addresses. We believe that a lack of modern reporting precision within Scripture, irregularities in grammar or spelling and observational descriptions of nature, as well as the reporting of falsehoods, the use of hyperbole and round numbers, the topical arrangement of material, variant selections of material in parallel accounts, or the use of free citations does not undermine the truthfulness or reliability of Scripture, but is rather a reflection of ancient writing standards through which God has chosen to reveal himself. When there are apparent errors or contradictions we encourage diligence in study, realizing that all truth is God's truth and he cannot contradict himself, as well as humility in making assertions, realizing that we are finite in

our understanding and ability and that more data may change our understanding on an issue. By "rule of faith and practice" we mean that when the Bible is correctly interpreted it is to be believed in all it asserts and obeyed in all that it commands. Finally, while we recognize that good hermeneutical principles are needed to interpret and apply the Scriptures accurately, we also recognize that no interpretive framework will ever remove the need for faith, in that Scripture clearly reports miraculous occurrences, which cannot be explained away by any amount of reasoning (ex. Incarnation, Resurrection, Ascension, Pentecost, etc).

2. **We believe in one God, the Creator and Ruler of the universe, existing in a divine and incomprehensible Trinity: the Father, the Son Jesus Christ, and the Holy Spirit, each possessing divine perfection.** We believe there is one God (Deuteronomy 6:4), the Creator (Genesis 1:1) and Ruler of the universe (Colossians 1:17), existing in a divine and incomprehensible Trinity (Matthew 28:19, John 1:1,3, John 4:24). By Trinity we mean that God is made up of three, eternally existing persons, who carry out distinct roles within the work of creation and redemption. The three persons in the Trinity are God the Father, God the Son and God the Holy Spirit. By divine we

mean that each person within the Trinity is equally God. By incomprehensible we mean that we cannot fully comprehend all that there is to know about any one person within the Trinity, or the nature of the relationships within the godhead (ex. how the three persons maintain perfect unity, while possessing distinct identities). However, incomprehensibility does not mean that we are without any understanding. We can know much about the three persons within the Trinity and the nature of their relationship, and on that basis we deny Modalism (i.e. one God appearing in different modes), Arianism (i.e. a denial of the full deity of the Son and Holy Spirit), Subordinationism (i.e. a denial of equality among the person of the Trinity), and Tritheism (i.e. the belief there are three Gods). We believe in God the Father, an eternal spirit (John 4:24), who is perfect in love (1 John 4:8), seeking worship (John 4:23) and hears and answers prayer (Matthew 6:7-9, Luke 11:13). We believe in God the Son, Jesus Christ, eternally existing (John 1:1-3), born in the flesh (Matthew 1:23), lived and died sinless (Hebrews 4:15), raised from the grave (1 Corinthians 15:6), and living to make intercession for those being saved (Hebrews 7:25). We believe in God the Holy Spirit, eternally existing, who came from the Father and the Son (John 14:15-17), convicts the world of sin, righteousness and judgment (John 16:8-11), who indwells, gifts, empowers, sanctifies (John 7:38-39, 1 Corinthians 12:4-6, Acts 1:8, Galatians 5:16, Romans 8:5) seals Christians (2 Corinthians 1:22, Ephesians 1:3), and prays for Christians (Romans 8:26), all the while enabling us to bear fruit (Galatians 5:22-23).

3. **We believe that our first parents were created holy and upright, that they fell from this condition, and that, in consequence, the whole human race is by nature dead in trespasses and sins (Romans 5:12; Ephesians 2:1,2).**

    We believe that God created the universe as "good," that is without the presence of sin (Genesis 1:31), including our first parents, who were named Adam and Eve (Romans 5:12), who were created in God's image (Genesis 1:27) and were blessed by God (Genesis 1:28). We believe that Eve was deceived by Satan (1 Timothy 2:13-14), and that together our first parents disobeyed God's command (Genesis 2:17) and fell from sinless perfection into corruption (Genesis 3:1-13, 2 Corinthians 11:3). We believe that the sinfulness of our first parents resulted in the corruption of the whole human race, passing the guilt of, enslavement to, and condemnation for sin to their posterity (Ephesians 2:1-3). As a result, all of humanity is sinful by nature, as well as by action, and thus dead spiritually and needing to be born again (Ephesians 2:1-3, John 3:5-7).

4. **We believe in the incarnation, death and bodily resurrection of the Son of God and that salvation is attained only through repentance and faith in Him (Acts 4:12).** We believe that God the Father sent God the Son, Jesus, who was conceived by God the Holy Spirit and born to a virgin named Mary from Nazareth (Matthew 1:23, Luke 1:34-35, Galatians 4:4). By incarnation, we mean that God himself came in the flesh as God the Son, at one and the same time fully God and fully human (John 1:14, Philippians 2:6-8, 1 Timothy 2:5, Hebrews 2:14-17). We believe that Jesus lived without sin (Hebrews 4:15) and then willingly died on a cross (Matthew 28:5) and was buried (John 10:18, John 19:40-41) according to God the Father's purposes in redemption (Luke 24:25-26, Acts 2:23) in order to provide forgiveness of sin for all who trust in him (Romans 3:25). We believe that Jesus bodily rose from the grave on the third day (Matthew 28:6, Romans 4:25, 1 Corinthians 15:4) and is now returned to the Father and exalted (Philippians 2:9-11). After being raised

from the grave and before returning to the Father, Jesus gave many convincing proofs of his bodily resurrection (Acts 1:3, 9-11), at one time appearing to over 500 people (1 Corinthians 15:6). By salvation we mean that work initiated and completed by God (Philippians 1:6) in which we are delivered from God's wrath and an eternal condemnation in Hell due to us because of our sin (Ephesians 2:3-6, Romans 5:9, 1 Thessalonians 1:9-10) and joined to the family of God and guaranteed an eternity in Heaven (2 Corinthians 1:22, 5:5). By faith we mean that forgiveness of sins and the gift of eternal life is received by all who trust only in the sacrificial death of Jesus on their behalf (John 3:16, Acts 4:12, Romans 3:23-26). Finally, we believe that one's trust in Jesus' death and resurrection is evidenced in repentance, a turning from willful sin toward a submission to Christ as Lord (Matthew 3:8, 3:11, Luke 3:8, 5:2, Acts 5:31, 11:18, 2 Corinthians 7:9-10).

5. **We believe that every believer can and should be assured of his or her salvation, having God's Word as authority for such assurance (1 John 5:11-13).** A believer's assurance of salvation can be addressed both objectively and subjectively. From an objective perspective, our assurance of salvation is based

upon the character of God and his purposes to save all those whom he has sovereignly predestined to be conformed to the likeness of his Son (John 6:37, John 10:28-29). In this respect, our assurance is separate from our feelings, as well as our behavior, whether good or bad, and rests solely on the power of God to deliver from death all whom he has determined to save (Romans 8:28-30). Those whom God predestined, he also "seals" for salvation by depositing within them the Holy Spirit (Ephesians 1:13-14, 2 Corinthians 5:5). God, having begun this work himself, also finishes the work of salvation himself (Philippians 1:6, Hebrews 12:2, 1 John 5:11-13). While our objective assurance is based upon God's purposes and power to save, apart from anything we have done, are doing, or will do, his purposes and power do not work apart from our faith. God's salvation always evidences itself through a personal expression of faith in those being saved and thus always produces some form of obedience, however small it may be (James 2:17-26, 1 John 2:19).

From a subjective perspective, assurance of salvation is a measure of one's feelings of confidence in right standing before God. All who are presently trusting in Jesus' death for the forgiveness of sin have a Scriptural basis for having feelings of confidence in their justification (Colossians 1:23, Hebrews 3:14, Hebrews 6:12). Scripture also indicates that all who are born again receive the testimony of the Holy Spirit speaking to their heart (Romans 8:15-16, 1 John 4:13, 1 John 5:9-10), which may result in feelings of assurance regarding one's salvation. Finally, Scripture teaches that those who evidence the genuine work of the Holy Spirit in their lives; including good works (Matthew 7:16-20, Galatians 5:22), dependence upon Jesus and connection to his people (John 15:4-7, 1 John 2:23-24, 1 John 4:6), as well as obedience to God's commands (James 2:17-18, 1 John 2:4-10, 1 John 3:14-17), may possess feelings of assurance regarding their salvation.

While having feelings of assurance is appropriate and comforting for those born again, Scripture also teaches that it is entirely possible to inappropriately possess feelings of assurance concerning salvation, and cautions us that some who feel confident will in fact not enter the kingdom of heaven (Matthew 7:21). Scripture also teaches that some who are born again may lack feelings of assurance for any number of reasons, many of which are outside their control. For example, we may lack feelings of assurance because of psychological damage caused during past negative experiences, which creates an inability to feel confident in God's love (Romans 8:39). We may also lack feelings of assurance due to suffering, whether physical suffering due to illness or spiritual suffering due to attack by the enemy. For this reason, James writes that we are to count suffering as a joy, allowing the experience of suffering to produce in us maturity (James 1:1-8). Finally, disobedience may undermine our feelings of assurance. While perfection is neither expected nor required in the Christian life (Philippians 3:12, 1 John 1:8-10, 1 John 2:1), those who fall into sin may lack feelings of assurance of their salvation because of the work of sin in their lives, which causes us to have disbelieving hearts (Galatians 5:16-18, Hebrews 3:12-13, 1 Peter 2:11).

6. **We believe that the Church of Jesus Christ is made up of all true believers, irrespective of color, race or denomination (1 Corinthians 12:13).**

By Church we mean the one universal Church, made up of all those, in every time and place, who have believed in Christ, and been united to one another through faith by the Spirit into one Body (1 Corinthians 12:13, Colossians 1:18, Ephesians 1:22, Ephesians 3:6, Ephesians 4:15-16, Ephesians 5:23: Galatians 3:28). While the universal Church is "invisible" and isn't exclusively associated with any individual church, fellowship, denomination or sect, believers are urged to actively associate with a "visible" local church fellowship in public worship (Hebrews 10:25), Holy Communion (1 Corinthians 11:23-26), teaching (Acts 2:42) and service (Ephesians 4:11-13, Titus 2:14).

7. **We believe in the Holy Spirit as a divine person indwelling all believers as our instructor, comforter and guide (John 14:26; Galatians 5:18).** We believe that the Holy Spirit is a divine person, the third person within the triune God (Deuteronomy 6:4) and an eternal and equal member with God the Father and God the Son (2 Corinthians 13:14), possessing every divine attribute and sharing in all power and glory. We believe that the Holy Spirit indwells all believers, taking up residence and living within all who are born again by his power (John 1:13, Romans 8:9-11, 1 Corinthians 6:19-20). We believe that the Holy Spirit teaches (John 16:8-11), comforts (John 14:16, 26, John 15:26-27) and guides (Galatians 5:18) all who are born again. We believe that it is through the presence and power (Acts 1:8) of the Holy Spirit that the born again receive gifts for ministry (1 Corinthians 12:7-10), bear fruit in ministry (Galatians 5:22-26) and

continue in faith (Ephesians 1:13-14, 2 Corinthians 5:5, Philippians 1:6).

8. **We believe in a separated walk of life according to (2 Corinthians 6:17,18 & 2 Corinthians 7:1.)** By separated walk we mean that those who are born again do not merely give intellectual assent to the truths of Scripture, but also live according to the Scripture, evidencing a change of mind, heart and behavior that separates them from the sinful ways in which the world is living (John 3:19-21, 2 Corinthians 6:17-7:1, Hebrews 11:24-26, 1 John 5:1-4). We believe that the Holy Spirit is the decisive agent in this life-transforming work, but that we are called to cooperate with the Holy Spirit, by submitting to his leadership in our lives and pursuing holiness through obedience to the Scriptures (Matthew 3:8, John 14:15-21, John 16:3-14, Romans 6:11-13, Romans 8:29-30, Philippians 3:12, 2 Thessalonians 2:13, Hebrews 6:1, Hebrews 13:21, 2 Peter 2:11). This call to live a separated life of holiness is outlined in the book of Galatians 5:13-26, as the Apostle Paul encourages Christians not to use their freedom in Christ as a license to continue in sin. Instead, we are to "walk by the Spirit" and not to gratify the desires of the flesh.

9. **We believe in the eternal bliss of the redeemed in Heaven and in the eternal punishment of the lost in Hell (John 3:36; Luke 16:22, 23).** By the "redeemed" we mean all those who have trusted in Jesus' death and resurrection for the forgiveness of sin and eternal life (John 3:36). We believe that when the redeemed are made absent from the body through death that they enjoy an eternity with Jesus in Heaven (Luke 23:43, 2 Corinthians 5:8). In describing Heaven as "eternal bliss" we mean that it is a paradise (Luke 23:43, Hebrews 12:22-23), a place of unparalleled beauty, far better than our current state and where all our needs are met (Philippians 1:23, 2 Corinthians 5:1-9, Revelation 6:9-11) through a state of perfect communion with God and in worship together (Revelation 4:8, 21:3-4, Jude 1:24).

By the "lost" we mean all those who have not trusted in Jesus' death and resurrection for the forgiveness of sin and eternal life (John 3:36). We believe that when the lost are made absent from the body through death they are consigned to punishment in Hell, which is an eternal separation from God (Matthew 25:46, Luke 16:22-24, Hebrews 9:27, Revelation 14:9-11, Revelation 19:1-3).

10. **We believe in a personal Devil who goes about as "a roaring lion" and as "an angel of light," seeking whom he may devour (1 Peter 5:8, 2 Corinthians 11:14).**

    By "personal Devil" we mean that he is a created being with a will and a character. His character is evil (Matthew 13:28-29, John 8:44, 2 Thessalonians 2:18, Revelation 12:9-10), and his will is to discourage, deceive and destroy God's people (John 10:10, 2 Corinthians 11:14). Although defeated by the death and resurrection of Jesus Christ (Colossians 2:15), the Devil continues as the active enemy of God's people until the final judgment by God (Matthew 25:41, 1 Peter 5:8, Revelation 20:10). For this reason, Christians are to wear the armor of God in order to combat the Devil's evil schemes (Ephesians 6:11, James 4:7).

11. **We believe in the angels as God's ministering spirits (Hebrews 1:14).** By "ministering spirits" we mean that angels serve God's purposes and people (Hebrews 1:14). "Angel" means "messenger," which gives some indication of their role in ministering to God's people. Steven and Paul both note that the Old Testament law was delivered to humanity by angels (Acts 7:53, Galatians 3:19). The names of a few angels are offered in Scripture. Michael is described as an

"archangel," or chief angel (Jude 9), while Gabriel often delivers special messages (Daniel 9:21, Luke 1:26). Angels may appear in human bodies (Genesis 18:3, Numbers 22:31, Mark 16:5, Luke 24:4, Hebrews 13:2), however they are described as "spirit" beings (Hebrews 1:14) and for this reason are most often not seen by us (2 Kings 6:17). Scripture seems to indicate that angels are assigned to care for children (Matthew 18:10), as well as deliver God's people (Acts 12:7), and carry out God's judgment (Acts 12:23). While angels are spirit beings, they are not all-knowing (Matthew 24:36, 1 Peter 1:12) or all-powerful (Daniel 10:13). Angels are not to be worshipped (Colossians 2:18), but are rather worshipers of God (Isaiah 6:3, Luke 2:13-14, Revelation 5:11-12).

12. **We believe in the personal and premillennial return of our Lord Jesus Christ (I Thessalonians 4:16, 17).** By "personal" we mean that Jesus will come again to the earth visibly and physically (Matthew 24:44, Acts 1:9-11, Hebrews 9:28, James 5:7-8), in power and with great glory (1 Thessalonians 4:16-17, Titus 2:13). By "premillennial" we mean that Jesus Christ's second coming will precede and usher in a millennial reign on earth (Revelation 20:1-6).

HISTORY AND PHILOSOPHY OF MINISTRY

History at GEBC & BBC

September 29, 1943 was the founding date of GEBC, the product of a merger between two small churches—the First Evangelical Lutheran Church and the Gospel Tabernacle. Both churches had a desire to proclaim the good news of Christ in their community and around the world. First Evangelical Lutheran Church began in 1912 and was part of the North Illinois District of the German Evangelical Synod. The Gospel Tabernacle grew out of several evangelistic tent campaigns held in Wheaton and Glen Ellyn during the summer of 1931. The second pastor of Gospel Tabernacle, Bob Cook, brought an emphasis in ministry to children and students, along with his friend, Torrey Johnson (founder of Youth For Christ). These two churches merged in their common commitment to reach their community with the Gospel.

Everett Black served as Senior Pastor from 1966-1982 and during his tenure the current worship space was built in 1968 for $300,000. Gary Gulbranson served as Senior Pastor in the 1980's, during which time GEBC experienced significant growth, which brought additional services and the construction of Rathbun Hall in 1989. In 1994 Jim Cofield began serving as Senior Pastor, and during his tenure the facilities were updated (e.g., air conditioning was installed, the basement was remodeled, and the worship center was upgraded), as well as retiring outstanding debt.

Kelly Brady became Senior Pastor in 2004, having already served as the Student Ministries Pastor and Family Life Pastor for a decade. In 2006 Kelly published *Following Jesus*, which explains GEBC's Disciple-Making philosophy of ministry. In February 2010, pastors Brian From and Dave Schubert were sent out, along with 72 adults and children, to plant Four Corners Community Church in Downers Grove, Illinois. In 2019 the church completed a $3,300,000 building remodel and addition of a Welcome Center, adding 5000 sq. feet.

In November 2021, the Elders of GEBC cast the vision to become a multi-church ministry. This vision is aimed at mobilizing the people of GEBC to reach more people in the county follow Jesus. Just six months after the vision was cast, GEBC was approached by Poplar Creek Church (PCC) in Bartlett, asking if they could become the first campus. After fourteen months of prayer and many conversations, the leadership of both churches believed it was God's will for PCC to become GEBC's first campus, and together we launched the REACH capital campaign in July 2022. The goal was to raise $700,000 in order to help in paying off the mortgage of PCC. That goal was reached, PCC's mortgage was paid off and on February 1, 2023 the two churches became one.

As we look ahead, we are thankful for our heritage and God's faithfulness. We are also excited about to help more people follow Jesus. We believe that the best days for God's church are before us!

Multi-Church Ministry Vision

After years of prayerfully considering the best strategy aimed at helping to reach DuPage county with the gospel and making more disciples, the Elders cast a multi-church ministry vision in November 2021.

Multi-Church is best understood as multiple churches working together to make more disciples. This vision is more effective in disciple-making because it:

- overcomes the geographic barriers at 501 Hillside Avenue in Glen Ellyn.
- requires an increase in equipping and sending, which means that more people will utilize more of their gifts. In fact, 79% of multi-church ministries report that leadership development has increased through multi-church ministry.
- prioritizes an increase in proclaiming the gospel and reaching new people. In fact, multi-church ministries report a 33% average attendance growth.

Multi-church ministry is an effective and proven means for making more disciples because it:

- builds on existing church strengths while making available a new church experience in a specific geography.

- allows for expansion at reduced costs through sharing essential services (e.g., human resources, marketing, accounting).
- utilizes staff synergy and increases staff support and accountability.
- capitalizes on the advantages of both larger and smaller churches by providing a breadth of programming, as well as the depth of relationship.

Multi-Church ministry means meeting in many different locations, but sharing:
- One Mission – Helping people follow Jesus.
- One Philosophy of Ministry – Proclaim, Restore, Equip and Send
- One Theology – Statement Of Faith
- One Budget – all contributions go into a common fund.
- One Board – one board of Elders governs all churches.
- One Staff – each church has dedicated staff, but all staff are employees of one church.
- One Preaching Focus – each campus has a preacher, but the preaching focus each week is shared across churches.
- One Administrative Office – all accounting, banking, human resources, and IT are centralized.

History of the Bible Church Movement

Glen Ellyn Bible Church and Bartlett Bible Church are protestant churches. All Protestant churches trace their heritage to a split from the Catholic Church in the sixteenth century. To be protestant is to be in the line of churches "protesting" certain Roman Catholic practices and beliefs and calling for reformation. The "Five Solas" were the backbone of the Protestant Reformation.

- **Soli Deo Gloria** – God's glory over all others, particularly the papacy, which the reformers saw as usurping God's power and wisdom.
- **Sola Gratia** – God's grace alone provides salvation, which the reformers felt stood in contradiction to the Catholic teaching on the necessity of works in salvation.
- **Sola Scriptura** – God's Word alone is authoritative, which opposed Catholic teaching that only those in Apostolic succession (i.e., priests) can interpret and apply God's Word.
- **Solus Christus** – Jesus is the only mediator between God and man, which the reformers believed was undermined by the Pope.
- **Sola Fide** – Justification comes through faith in Christ alone, which the reformers believed was undermined by the Catholic Church's teaching on merit-based righteousness.

Protestants further split from one another into many denominations (e.g., Lutheran, Presbyterian, Methodist, etc.). However, the Bible Church Movement is a part of the "non-denominational" movement. While colonial American had many denominations, some embraced congregationalism, which emphasized a form of church governance that was shared among the attending local congregants. The First & Second Great Awakenings (18th–19th Century) further propelled the rise of independent churches, by emphasizing mass evangelism rather than denominational loyalty. Then in the 1920s–1940s, theological liberalism spread in Protestant denominations, leading many doctrinal conservatives to leave mainline denominations. The Bible Church movement emerged as a response to rise of theological liberalism, which rejected biblical inerrancy and the importance of evangelism, while promoting higher biblical criticism and a social/ethical gospel. The slogan "no creed but Christ, no book but the Bible" was the cry for many, as they rejected denominational structures and creeds, choosing instead independent church governance and an emphasis on Scripture.

Glen Ellyn Bible Church began in 1943, a member of the Independent Fundamental Churches of America (IFCA), which was founded as a network of independent, theologically conservative, evangelical churches that emphasize expository preaching (verse-by-verse teaching of the Bible), overseas mission and children's ministry.

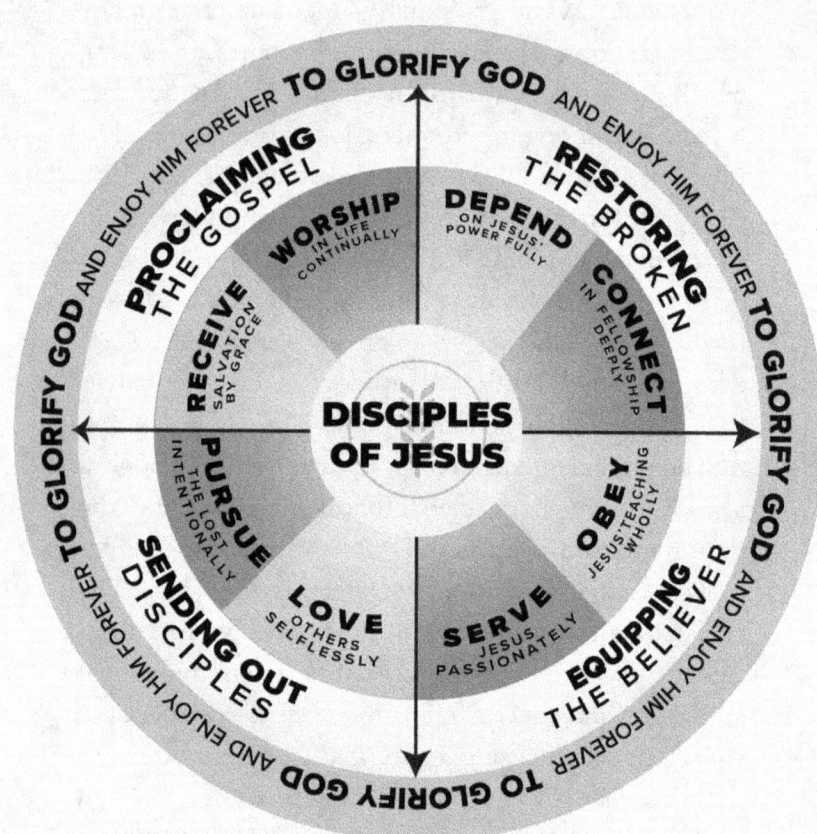

The Disciplemaking Message

We were created to glorify God and enjoy him forever!

Written in 1647 the Westminster Shorter Catechism declares that the chief end of man is to "glorify God" and "enjoy him forever"! Of course, the Westminster Assembly was not the first to identify this truth. The apostle Paul declares this truth writing,

> For by him all things were created: things in heaven and on earth, visible and invisible, whether thrones or powers or rulers or authorities; all things were created by him and for him. Colossians 1:16 (NIV)

God created the universe and everything in it for his glory. All of history is designed to be a living canvas that displays his magnificence and illustrates his beauty and brilliance. Understanding that we were created by him and for him frees us from the perilous pursuit of happiness and personal fulfillment, and it inspires us to pursue God's glory (1 Corinthians 10:31).

Of course this begs the obvious question, "How do we bring glory to God in all that we do?" We bring glory to God by reflecting the character, conduct and concerns of God's Son, Jesus Christ. Paul wrote of Jesus, "He is the image of the invisible God, the firstborn over all creation" (Colossians 1:15). Simply put, we bring glory to God by bearing the image of his Son, by emulating Jesus' attitudes and actions in every area of our lives.

This is what it means to be a disciple, to learn from Jesus and model our lives after his, and the good news of the gospel is that anyone committed to following Jesus will find life to the full. Jesus said, "I have come that they may have life, and have it to the full" (John 10:10). But Jesus also said, "For whoever wants to save his life will lose it, but whoever loses his life for me will find it" (Matthew 16:25). In other words, all of the assurances and benefits offered in the gospel presuppose a life fixed upon bringing God glory by following Jesus Christ, and none of the assurances or benefits makes any sense apart from that commitment. God sent Jesus Christ so that we could forever see, savor and show God's glory, by experiencing his salvation and living in the fullness of his life. If we resist or refuse to bring God glory by following after his Son then we miss out on the "fuller" life that he promised.

The Disciplemaking Methods

We make disciples by imitating Christ's disciple making activities.

The Elders of GEBC have identified four activities modeled by Jesus and embraced by the early church that are essential to the disciple making effort.

Proclaiming the Gospel (Romans 10:14)
We proclaim that salvation is by God's grace through faith in Jesus Christ and call all people to live lives of worship.

Restoring the Broken (Galatians 6:1-2)
People are restored primarily through their dependence upon the Holy Spirit and a connection in fellowship with other believers.

Equipping the Believer (Ephesians 4:11-13)
Believers are equipped through God's Word for obedience and called to lives of service using their spiritual gifts.

Sending out Disciples (Matthew 28:18-20)
Disciples are a people sent out. We are to pursue the lost intentionally and love others selflessly.

Proclaiming the Gospel

John the Baptist came preaching, "Repent, for the Kingdom of heaven is near" (Matthew 3:1-2). Jesus followed him with the same message, "preaching the good news of the kingdom" (Matthew 4:23). Preaching the good news was the direct charge given to the twelve disciples, as they were first sent out by Jesus (Matthew 10:7-8), as well as an essential tool in the early church's effort to spread the gospel. Peter said to the people gathered in Cornelius' house, "He commanded us to preach" (Acts 10:42).

Peter goes on in this passage to explain that the gospel is an invitation to escape certain judgment. Like Peter, we are commissioned by Jesus to proclaim the gospel. "Go and make disciples of all nations," Jesus said (Matthew 28:19). We are God's ambassadors and proclaiming the good news of God's grace and calling all people to live lives of worship is to be a primary activity of the church.

When Cornelius heard the gospel from Peter he was transformed immediately. We read, "While Peter was still speaking these words, the Holy Spirit came on all who heard the message. For they heard them speaking in tongues and praising God." (Acts 10:44, 46) The point is not that everyone who receives Christ will speak in tongues. The point is that as the Church is faithful in proclaiming God's grace, it will always produce lives that bring God praise.

Restoring the Broken

When sin entered the world, we lost our capacity to be the image bearers God intended (Genesis 1:26). Humanity is broken and in need of restoration. The good news is restoration can be experienced through faith in Jesus (Luke 4:17-19).

God's goal in restoration is that we would be holy, just as he is holy (1 Peter 1:16). In the process of transformation those things we once had no interest in, and no desire to experience, often become attractive. We grow to desire sobriety, rather than drunkenness, honesty, rather than dishonesty, modesty and fidelity, rather than immodesty and promiscuity, or to express ourselves more fully in worship or to understand God's Word better. Paul wrote, "if anyone is in Christ, he is a new creation" (2 Corinthians 5:17), which describes the begin of the process of being restored as image bearers.

Restoration comes to us as we depend upon the Holy Spirit's work in our lives and connect with other believers in intimate relationships. Paul wrote, "Brothers, if someone is caught in a sin, you who are spiritual should restore him gently" (Galatians 6:1). Being the church of God's design means helping one another become God's image bearers. We cannot expect to experience the restoration of Christ, without intimate relationships with other believers. Part of God's remedy for our struggles is a deep connection with other believers (James 5:14-15).

Equipping the Believers

Jesus said, "Now that I, your Lord and Teacher, have washed your feet, you also should wash one another's feet" (John 13:14), and equipping the saints to obey Jesus' teaching and emulate his life of service is an essential activity of the Church.

God has provided for the equipping of all believers through the gifts that he has given to the church. Apostles, prophets, evangelists, pastors and teachers are gifted to help "prepare" others for service (Ephesians 4:12). The word Paul uses for "prepare" is the Greek word *katartismon*, which comes from a verb meaning to repair. This verb is used in Mark 1:19 to describe the mending of fishing nets, and in Galatians 6:1 to describe the process of restoring someone caught in sin. The picture is of people using their gifts to strengthen one another for lives of obedience and service. In some cases that will simply involve instruction, and that particular function is the responsibility of those given the gift of teaching. In other cases preparation will involve correction and even healing, which might involve the gift of mercy or faith. But the goal is that the people of God live lives of obedience and find their place of service.

Paul wrote, "Then we will no longer be infants, tossed back and forth...blown here and there by every wind of teaching" (Ephesians 4:14). Immaturity brings instability, and it is our responsibility to help one another build gain sure footing on God's Word.

Sending Out Disciples

Jesus describes our Heavenly Father as seeking the lost (Luke 14:22-24). In the Old Testament, God sent Moses to deliver the Israelites from bondage, and he sent prophets to call the Israelites back to himself. In the New Testament, God sent his Son to die on a cross, and Jesus sent out his first twelve disciples, as well as seventy-two latter, on trips with the message God's Kingdom is near (Matthew 10:7-8, Luke 10:1, 3). At the end of his ministry, Jesus commissioned all of his followers to go and make disciples of all nations (Matthew 28:19-20), and the early church set apart missionaries for the purpose of carrying the gospel to foreign lands (Acts 13:2-3). Disciples are a people sent out, and sending out disciples is an essential activity of the Church.

The good news is we are not sent out alone. Jesus promises to be with us always (Matthew 28:20), and to provide us with the power from Spirit of God, power specifically for the purpose of being witnesses (Acts 1:8). The church is to send disciples out with the authority of Jesus (Matthew 28:18) and power of Jesus Spirit (Acts 1:8), to demonstrate the selfless love of Jesus and pursue the lost. In other words, the Holy Spirit is not given simply for our benefit, so that our influence and kingdom can grow larger and more prosperous. The Spirit's transforming work is to empower us for sharing the gospel.

The Disciplemaking Mission

We glorify God by making disciples of Jesus Christ.

When Simon Peter and his brother Andrew heard Jesus' invitation to, "Come, follow me" (Matthew 4:19), there was no mistaking the call. These first-century Jewish men knew exactly what Jesus was suggesting they do. Jesus was inviting them to disrupt every aspect of their lives and to enter into one of the most intimate of relationships, that of discipleship.

In that first-century world disciples were those that detached themselves from their own way of life and reattached themselves to a rabbi (teacher). So complete and total was a disciple's commitment to the rabbi that it became the preeminent reality of their life and the defining element of their personality, and the nature of what it means to be a disciple has not changed in over 2000 years.

Accepting the invitation to follow Jesus still requires this type of first-century commitment. Jesus is still looking for men and women who will disrupt their entire life, attach themselves to him in an intimate relationship, and learn from him, reflecting his person and carrying out his purposes. In fact, one of the last things that Jesus said to his disciples was go and make more disciples (Matthew 28:18-20), and it is this Great Commission that fuels the activity of the church today.

GEBC's mission is to make disciples of Jesus

Christ, both locally and globally, by helping people connect with Jesus in an intimate relationship and teaching them to reflect his character, conduct and concerns in every area of their life. Toward this end, the Elders of GEBC have identified eight essential attributes that Scripture indicates all disciples should possess as followers of Jesus Christ and all our efforts as a community of faith are focused on helping cultivate these attributes in the lives of our congregants. Disciples are those who…

- Receive salvation by grace (John 3:16).
- Worship continually (John 4:23-24).
- Depend on Jesus' power fully (John 15:5).
- Connect in fellowship deeply (Acts 2:42-47).
- Obey Jesus' teaching wholly (Matthew 7:24).
- Serve with Jesus passionately (Luke 14:27).
- Love others selflessly (Matthew 22:36-40).
- Pursue the lost intentionally (Matthew 28:18-20).

Jesus is the visible "image of the invisible God" (Colossians 1:15), and nothing brings greater glory to God than our bearing his image and helping others do the same. As a disciple making church, all our efforts are focused on helping cultivate these eight attributes in the lives of our congregants so that we may more fully bear Christ's image. On the following pages is a synopsis of each of the 8 Attributes of disciple.

Receive Salvation by Grace.

Grace is unmerited favor and the journey of following Jesus begins, continues and ends by receiving God's grace. The apostle Paul writes,

> For it is by grace you have been saved, through faith—and this not from yourselves, it is the gift of God— not by works, so that no one can boast. Ephesians 2:8-9

We are saved by our faith in God's gracious forgiveness of our sin provided through Jesus Christ's death on the cross. Unfortunately, many Christians accept the grace of God offered for salvation only to later adopt a works righteousness mentality in following after Jesus. Whether trying to consciously earn God's approval, or simply wanting to feel better about themselves, many Christians lapse into performing works of righteousness, believing that they will somehow be able to earn God's favor. A longing for self-righteousness though is one of the greatest hindrances to a life of discipleship, and it is important to understand that there is no bait and switch in Christianity. It's not grace to start the journey and works righteousness to finish. A life of following Jesus Christ requires a dependence upon the grace of God from start to finish. Paul writes of God's sovereign and gracious work in our lives in the book of Philippians.

> In all my prayers for all of you, I always pray with joy because of your partnership in the gospel from the first day until now, being confident of this, that he who began a good work in you will carry it on to completion until the day of Christ Jesus. Philippians 1:4-6

God began the "good work" Paul says, and it is God that will "carry it on to completion." The bad news about Jesus Christ's death on the cross is that it strips us of our self-righteousness. We cannot depend upon ourselves for salvation. At the same time, the good news of Jesus Christ's death on the cross is that it frees us from the guilt and shame of our sinfulness. In other words, we can do nothing to make God love us more than he already does, and we can do nothing to make him loves us any less. Disciples are those who have received God's unmerited favor through Jesus Christ's death on their behalf and are depending upon his favor as they daily follow after him.

Worship in Life Continually

Worship is much more than singing on Sunday morning. Worship is a lifestyle of honoring God above all others, and a life of worship is the natural response of one who has received God's grace. In fact, as the grace of God becomes more deeply understood, then our response of worship will become more and more pronounced. The apostle Paul draws a direct link between God's mercy in our lives and our response in worship writing:

> Therefore, I urge you, brothers, in view of God's mercy, to offer your bodies as living sacrifices, holy and pleasing to God—this is your spiritual act of worship. Romans 12:1

Worship is not to be a part of our lives as disciples. Worship is our life as disciples, which means we can no longer segment our lives between spiritual and non-spiritual activities. Everything we do is to be a spiritual act of worship.

Unfortunately, the temptation in life is to spend our time and energy navigating the path of least resistance and greatest pleasure. The world tells us to seek greater comfort and success, but in so doing our purpose becomes self-centered, while the disciple's life is to be Christ centered, honoring him rather than looking for ways to be honored. For example, worship is telling the truth, even though it may appear easier to simply tell a lie. Worship is working diligently at the office, although everyone else may be loafing. Worship is sharing your faith, even when others might ridicule or reject you. Worship is forgiving, and even pursuing others with love, all though they have hurt you. Worship is giving sacrificial amounts of money to your church, even though the world encourages us to indulge ourselves.

Every aspect of our life is to bring him glory and honor and praise, and as we experience God's grace it will transform every activity of our lives into an activity of worship, which will provide eternal purpose and temporal meaning. King David expresses his complete abandon in worship when he writes…

> Come, let us bow down in worship, let us kneel before the Lord our Maker; for he is our God and we are the people of his pasture, the flock under his care. Today, if you hear his voice, do not harden your hearts. Psalm 95:6-9

One of the biggest barriers to worship in our lives is "hardened hearts." Another way to say that is pride, a refusal to bow, trust and abandon our self to God honoring activities. To cultivate a passionate lifestyle of worship will take great humility, because God must become the focus instead of us. God is calling us to honor him above all others in every area of our lives.

Depend on Jesus' Power Fully

The power that raised Jesus Christ from the dead is available today, power to overcome sinful habits and experience real and lasting change, power for healing, both physically and emotionally, power to endure suffering and remain faithful despite hardship. To access that power we must cultivate our connection to Jesus. Jesus said:

> I am the vine; you are the branches. If a man remains in me and I in him, he will bear much fruit; apart from me you can do nothing. John 15:5 (NIV)

Jesus is describing the most intimate of relationships, the deepest of connections and one of total dependence upon him. The apostle Paul also uses this vine and branches imagery when talking about what Jesus' death has meant for you and me. Paul writes in the book of Romans that we are like branches "grafted" into the vine of God (Romans 11:17). Grafting is when a branch is placed into an opening that has been cut in the bark of another vine. Although separated from God at one time by our sinfulness, through Jesus' death on the cross an opening has been made and we, "as dead branches," can now be plugged into the life-giving relationship and power of the vine of Jesus Christ.

As a grafted branch remains intact in the vine it draws the nutrients it needs to bear fruit. Fruit represents any good work—any God honoring thought, action or attitude—and fruitfulness is the inevitable outcome of a connection with the presence and power of Jesus' Spirit (Galatians 5:22-23).

It is the remaining though that is difficult. Life is hard and disciples of Jesus Christ face trials like everyone else in the world. That is the very reason Jesus offers this metaphor on the eve of his death. He knows that in a few hours, after he is arrested, tried, crucified and buried, that the disciples will be discouraged in their faith and tempted to disconnect themselves from him. But Jesus said to them:

> But the Counselor, the Holy Spirit, whom the Father will send in my name, will teach you all things and will remind you of everything I have said to you. Peace I leave with you; my peace I give you. I do not give to you as the world gives. Do not let your hearts be troubled and do not be afraid. John 14:26-27 (NIV)

God's Spirit is the life giving presence and power that we as branches receive through a connection to the vine, and it is only through the Holy Spirit's movement and work in and through us that we bear any fruit at all. Apart from cultivating our connection to him we can do nothing.

Connect in Fellowship Deeply

Biblical fellowship will require more of us than simply meeting together on Sunday morning. Sharing a pew with someone for an hour and exchanging pleasantries will not create the fellowship God longs for each of us to experience. Luke wrote in the book of Acts of the deep connection the earliest community of believers shared.

> They devoted themselves to the apostles' teaching and to the fellowship, to the breaking of bread and to prayer. Everyone was filled with awe, and many wonders and miraculous signs were done by the apostles. All the believers were together and had everything in common. Acts 2:42-44. (NIV)

Luke goes on in this chapter to describe exactly what he meant when he wrote "they devoted themselves to...the fellowship." He meant that they worshiped together at the Temple each day. They met in homes for the Lord's Supper, ate together and shared their financial resources. We will never become the people that God longs for us to be, or a community that effectively bears witness to his presence and power, without connecting in fellowship deeply, because it is through deep relationships with one another that we draw the strength and encouragement needed to grow in the faith.

When connected to others we bear more fruit, we're more likely to overcome pitfalls, avoid temptations and we are not easily overpowered when attacked by discouragement and doubt (Ecclesiastes 4:9-12). The writer of Hebrews warns us writing:

> Let us not give up meeting together, as some are in the habit of doing, but let us encourage one another—and all the more as you see the Day approaching. Hebrews 10:24-25 (NIV)

This "Day" approaching is a direct reference to the future day of judgment in which all believers are called to give an account of how they spent their time, talents and treasure. Simply put, connecting in fellowship deeply helps us stay on track spiritually, and helps us avoid wasting our lives. You might say that Christianity is a team sport, a group effort, and for these reasons we strongly encourage everyone at GEBC to participate in a small group, which meet in private homes during the week.

Obey Jesus' Teaching Wholly

Jesus said, "If you love me, you will obey what I command" (John 14:15), and the Apostle Paul linked God's grace directly to a life of obedience.

> For the grace of God that brings salvation has appeared to all men. It teaches us to say "No" to ungodliness and worldly passions, and to live self-controlled, upright and godly lives in this present age. Titus 2:11-12 (NIV)

In other words, the more of God's grace we experience, the more obedience we will demonstrate. We are saved by grace, apart from anything we do, but we are saved for "good works," which come as we obediently follow him.

> For it is by grace you have been saved, through faith—and this not from yourselves, it is the gift of God— not by works, so that no one can boast. For we are God's workmanship, created in Christ Jesus to do good works, which God prepared in advance for us to do. Ephesians 2:8-10 (NIV)

Our English word for poem comes from the Greek word translated as "workmanship." We are God's poem, a custom designed, one-of-a-kind, original masterpiece, created for the very specific purpose of doing good works—that is for living obediently. In fact, God has prepared in advance the works of service we are to be doing, which begs an obvious question. Are we doing what we were created for? The answer is "No!" if we are not living in obedience to Jesus' teaching.

Even Jesus had to live obediently. He modeled obedience to the Father when he prayed in Gethsemane, "not my will but yours be done" (Matthew 26:39). Jesus went to the cross out of obedience to the Heavenly Father's will for him, and each of us must demonstrate a Gethsemane posture in life. Anyone who would follow after Jesus must deny themselves, pick up their cross and follow him daily (Luke 9:23). Jesus said:

> Therefore everyone who hears these words of mine and puts them into practice is like a wise man who built his house on the rock. The rain came down, the streams rose, and the winds blew and beat against that house; yet it did not fall, because it had its foundation on the rock. But everyone who hears these words of mine and does not put them into practice is like a foolish man who built his house on sand. The rain came down, the streams rose, and the winds blew and beat against that house, and it fell with a great crash. Matthew 7:24-27 (NIV)

Serve with Jesus Passionately

The night before his crucifixion, while gathered in the Upper Room for his Last Supper with the disciples, Jesus provided a tangible demonstration of his love for all of us by washing the disciples feet. John is very methodical in his description of Jesus' actions that evening, noting that...he got up, took off his robe, wrapped a towel around his waist, poured water into a basin, and began to wash the disciples' feet. John wants us to see the very intentional posture of service that Christ had, a posture that he told the disciples they would only understand later, as the reality of the cross unfolded (John 13:12-17)

As Disciples of Jesus Christ we are commanded to follow his example in foot washing. We are to get up from the table just as he did, wrap a towel around our waist, find the nearest basin and kneel to care for others! We are to lay aside our claim to position and power and authority and assume a posture of humble service. Paul writes in Philippians chapter two that we should have in us the same attitude that was in Christ, who although equal with God did not consider equality with God something to be grasped. Instead of asserting his authority he served others selflessly. As disciples this is to be the very core of our conduct, just as it was Christ's, who did not come to be served but to serve others.

We keep this commandment to wash others' feet by meeting one another's physical needs. In other words, we shouldn't over spiritualize this passage and lose sight of the fact that Jesus actually scrubs the dirt off the disciple's feet. There are many basic physical needs that we can help provide for others, everything from food and shelter to clothing. We also keep this command to wash one another's feet by meeting one another's spiritual needs. In other words, we shouldn't under spiritualize this passage either and lose sight of the fact that Jesus uses this physical activity to represent a spiritual reality, which will include activities like: praying for another, teaching the Bible to one another, listening to and encouraging one another and hearing one another's confessions.

    Bear in mind that John is very careful to point out that Judas Iscariot, the betrayer, is present for the foot-washing portion of the evening. He's mentioned prominently throughout the passage. It is as if John wants us all to know that "Yes, Jesus washes even Judas' feet," and all the while knowing full well that Judas will soon betray him for 30 pieces of silver. The promise of God for those who will kneel and serve is blessings. Jesus says to his disciples, "Now that you know these things, you will be blessed if you do them" (Luke 13:17).

Love Others Selflessly

Jesus said, "By this all men will know that you are my disciples, if you love one another" (John 13:35). In other words, outside of love for one another we are unrecognizable as Christians.

As Christians, we often talk about the love of Jesus. Many books are written, songs sung and sermons preached explaining the impact of his suffering on our behalf. Much of our sharing about the faith is even non-verbal, including the jewelry we wear such as crosses and placing bumper stickers on our cars. But showing Christ's love toward others will ultimately involve much more than simply talking about it or wearing jewelry. Showing Christ's love to others will ultimately involve action, which will be risky and costly, as we set our needs aside to meet their needs. Jesus said to his disciples, "I'm sending you out like sheep among wolves" (Matthew 10:16), which was not meant to villainize non-believers. What Jesus meant was that showing God's unconditional love to others is going to be difficult. Some will take advantage of you and others will outright reject you. Paul wrote that he considered his experience as a Christian much like that of "a sheep being led to slaughter, because he faced death daily in order to share with others the love of God" (Romans 8:36).

What if the vision statement at GEBC was "Living as Sheep Among Wolves"? Our church logo could be a picture of a large wolf with a little sheep's tail hanging out of its mouth. With this picture in mind it is easy to see why we are often tempted not to show love toward others. We can feel too busy, or believe we are too important, or simply feel that it's too big an inconvenience or sacrifice. But we are called to embrace God's purposes, his agenda, and his plans, even when they conflict with our own. Jesus said: "Whoever finds his life will lose it, and whoever loses his life for my sake will find it" (Matthew 10:39).

While loving others does not earn our salvation, it is one way to experience the significance of the salvation offered to us through Jesus' suffering on our behalf. Love was risky and costly for the Good Samaritan who paid for a strangers healing (Luke 10:25-37). Stopping along the road, kneeling to help the victims of this world gives us the opportunity to better experience the suffering that Christ experienced on our behalf. Selflessly loving others helps us identify with the sacrificial love Jesus showed toward each of us. It is a strange paradox but by identifying with the suffering victim we live. It's a backward, unpredictable truth, which Paul highlights when he writes: "the message of the cross is foolishness to those who are perishing, but to us who are being saved it is the power of God" (1 Corinthians 1:18). Loving others and identifying with the suffering of others makes us better able to enter the reality of His grace at a deeper level. Paul even prayed that he would know the power of Christ's resurrection, sharing in the fellowship of his sufferings (Philippians 3:10).

Pursue the Lost Intentionally

Jesus died for us "while we were still sinners," (Romans 5:8). In other words, when we had no interest in him, Jesus Christ left heaven and pursued us, giving his life so that our sin might be forgiven (Romans 8:3). The pursuit of the lost is a powerful spiritual change agent, and we have been commissioned to "go" (Matthew 28:19).

Yet many Christians often struggle with believing that Jesus has the authority to command the obedience and worship of everyone in the world. While disciples are those who have acknowledged the authority of Jesus, many baulk at going out into the world and declaring him as King to others. Do we really believe that our neighbors and the people of our nation and the other nations of the world must forsake their own authority and submit to the authority of Jesus Christ in their lives?

> Then Jesus came to them and said, "All authority in heaven and on earth has been given to me. Therefore go and make disciples of all nations, baptizing them in the name of the Father and of the Son and of the Holy Spirit, and teaching them to obey everything I have commanded you. And surely I am with you always, to the very end of the age." Matthew 28:18-20 (NIV)

Jesus claimed that he had been given all authority, and Paul wrote that one day "every knee will bow and tongue confess that Jesus Christ is Lord" (Philippians 2:10). The claims of Scripture do not allow us any other option, but to believe that *all* must receive Jesus Christ as Savior and submit to him as Lord or their life. As Christians we look foolish if after reading Jesus' claim that "no one comes to the Father but through him" only to suggest that Jesus might not be right for everyone (John 14:6).

Only as we fully believe the claims of Christ, that he is the King of Kings and the Lord of Lords, will we find ourselves getting up and crossing restaurants, or office buildings, or oceans to talk to people about saving faith. It is the knowledge of his authority that fuels our eagerness and confidence in pursuing the lost.

The good news for those who do "go" in obedience to his commission is that we carry with us his promise. Jesus said, "surely I am with you always, to the very end of the age" (Matthew 28:20). Wherever we go, whatever we face, whomever we talk with, we can be confident that Jesus is with us! The one with all authority has given us all of his presence, and it is his Holy Spirit, his presence within us, that will convince others of their need for him (John 16:7-9). If we will believe in his authority and obediently act on his commission to go into all the world and pursue the lost, then we can be confident that his presence will go with us.

The Disciplemaking Means

We grow by opening ourselves to the Holy Spirit.

While we realize that spiritual new birth and growth as disciples of Jesus Christ are brought by the Holy Spirit's work in our life, we also understand that we are capable of both cooperating with, as well as resisting, the Spirit's work. Toward that end we have identified the following means for making ourselves available to the work of the Holy Spirit.

- Follow the Lord in baptism.
- Celebrate communion regularly.
- Attend corporate worship weekly.
- Study Scripture faithfully.
- Intercede for the saints continuously.
- Serve regularly, employing our gifts in a ministry.
- Give sacrificially and cheerfully of our income.
- Incorporate our faith in daily conversations, looking for opportunities to share the gospel.
- Participate in a small group or other spiritual accountability relationship.
- Participate in a short-term (3-10 days) cross-cultural mission trip.

THE CONSTITUTION OF GEBC

The Constitution of Glen Ellyn Bible Church

The name of this church shall be "Glen Ellyn Bible Church," incorporated in the state of Illinois.

ARTICLE I   PURPOSE

Glen Ellyn Bible Church (the Church) is organized and operated exclusively for religious purposes in accord with Sec. 501(c)(3) of the Internal Revenue Code of 1986 (or a corresponding provision of any future United States Internal Revenue law, referred to in this document as the "Code"). More specifically, the Church is organized to help people follow Jesus by proclaiming the gospel, restoring the broken, equipping the saints, and sending out disciples.

ARTICLE II   STATEMENT OF FAITH

1. We believe that the Scriptures of the Old and New Testaments are given by inspiration of God and are the only infallible rule of faith and practice (2 Timothy 3:16, 17).
2. We believe in one God, the Creator and Ruler of the universe, existing in a divine and incomprehensible Trinity: the Father, the Son Jesus Christ, and the Holy Spirit, each possessing divine perfection.
3. We believe that our first parents were created holy and upright, that they fell from this condition, and that, in consequence, the whole human race is by nature dead in trespasses and sins (Romans 5:12; Ephesians 2:1,2).
4. We believe in the incarnation, death and bodily resurrection of the Son of God and that salvation is attained only through repentance and faith in

Him (Acts 4:12).
5. We believe that every believer can and should be assured of his or her salvation, having God's Word as authority for such assurance (1 John 5:11-13).
6. We believe that the Church of Jesus Christ is made up of all true believers, irrespective of color, race, or denomination (1 Corinthians 12:13).
7. We believe in the Holy Spirit as a divine person indwelling all believers as our instructor, comforter, and guide (John 14:26; Galatians 5:18).
8. We believe in a separated walk of life according to 2 Corinthians 6:17,18 and 2 Corinthians 7:1.
9. We believe in the eternal bliss of the redeemed in Heaven and in the eternal punishment of the lost in Hell (John 3:36; Luke 16:22, 23).
10. We believe in a personal Devil who goes about as "a roaring lion" and as "an angel of light," seeking whom he may devour (1 Peter 5:8, 2 Corinthians 11:14).
11. We believe in the angels as God's ministering spirits (Hebrews 1:14).
12. We believe in the personal and premillennial return of our Lord Jesus Christ (I Thessalonians 4:16, 17).

ARTICLE III — ORDINANCES

SECTION 1. BAPTISM

The ordinance of baptism of believers shall be by immersion based on the individual's confession of faith as witnessed by the Senior Pastor or others as approved by the Senior Pastor.

SECTION 2. LORD'S SUPPER

A. This church welcomes participation in the

Communion Service by all who have accepted Jesus Christ as their personal Savior through faith in His blood shed for their sins and who demonstrates a newness of life by practical obedience to Him.

B. The Lord's Supper shall normally be observed monthly.

ARTICLE IV   FINANCES

This church believes that the Bible teaches that the proper method of financing the Lord's work is by tithing and by the free will offerings of consecrated believers. Accordingly, this church shall primarily rely on tithing and free will offerings for its financial support, and may also receive funding from other gifts, events and sources as deemed appropriate by the Elders and to the extent consistent with its operation as a church and applicable law.

ARTICLE V   MEMBERSHIP

SECTION 1.   QUALIFICATIONS AND PROCEDURE

A. A Christian believer may be received into regular membership in this church upon sharing his or her testimony of faith in Jesus Christ with representative members of the Board of Elders.

B. Each candidate for membership shall receive a copy of the Constitution to be read before giving his or her testimony to the Elders. It is necessary for the candidate to give written assent to the Constitution.

C. Upon the recommendation of the Board of Elders, the church shall receive the candidate into membership in the presence of the congregation.

D. The Senior Pastor and his wife shall automatically become members when the Senior Pastor assumes his duties.

SECTION 2. TYPES
  A. Regular - Regular membership provides all the rights, privileges and responsibilities of this church, except that the right to vote is limited to members sixteen (16) years of age or older.
  B. Nonresident - Nonresident membership applies to missionaries, students, members of the armed services and relocated members who have been received as regular members and are away from the church area but return for periods of time. The full privileges of this type of membership are granted to such members during their stay in this area. Any relocated member who has not supported or communicated with the church for one year will be placed on inactive status.
  C. Inactive - The membership rolls of the church shall be reviewed at least annually under the direction of the Elders. Following such review, any member determined to be absent from, and not participating in, the church fellowship for a period of six months shall have his or her name placed on inactive status, provided (i) the Senior Pastor or the Board of Elders has communicated with the absent member, and (ii) no explanation of the absence satisfactory to the Elders has been given. Inactive members will be considered nonvoting members and shall be ineligible to hold any elected office.

SECTION 3. TERMINATION
A member may have his or her name removed from the

church rolls by joining another church and so notifying this church, by disciplinary action of the membership or by making written request of the Board of Elders. In addition, any member placed on inactive status, at the conclusion of one year will be dropped from the church membership rolls, unless he or she has communicated to the Board of Elders reasons satisfactory to the Elders as to why he or she should not be dropped. On the Board of Elders' approval of such reasons, the inactive member will be allowed to continue his or her inactive status, but only for one additional year. Any members removed from the church membership rolls, except for those removed by disciplinary action, must go through the procedure outlined above (Article V, Section 1) to be reinstated as a member. Any members removed from the church rolls by disciplinary action must follow the procedure outlined in Article VI, Section 5(B) to be reinstated as members.

SECTION 4.   RESPONSIBILITIES
1. To walk together in Christian love.
2. To exercise Christian care and watchfulness over one another.
3. To pray with and for one another, sharing our burdens, sorrows and joys.
4. To be thoughtful and courteous to one another, slow to take offense, quick to forgive and quick to seek forgiveness.
5. To guard the spiritual and scriptural purity, peace and prosperity of the church and its growth in scriptural knowledge and godliness.
6. To assist, as the Lord enables, in the work of the church and to promote its usefulness as a witness to the saving grace of God in Christ Jesus.

7. To contribute, as the Lord directs, to the financial support of the church.
8. To engage regularly in personal Bible reading and prayer.
9. To bring up such children as may be entrusted to our care in the nurture and admonition of the Lord.
10. To live an exemplary Christian life in accordance with biblical principles.
11. To endeavor to bring others to an acceptance of Jesus Christ as Savior and Lord.

ARTICLE VI — DISCIPLINE

SECTION 1. POLICY

This church believes that the discipline of members is a biblically taught responsibility. Members who espouse doctrines contrary to Scripture or contrary to those outlined in the Statement of Faith (Article II) and members who are found to be living lives inconsistent with clearly defined biblical standards shall be subject to disciplinary action.

SECTION 2. PURPOSE

The primary purpose of discipline is the loving restoration of the erring member, through his/her repentance, to the end that the erring member experiences the full forgiveness of Christ and His body. It is this experience of repentance and forgiveness that will free the erring member to renewed spiritual growth and will maintain or restore unity within the church. While restoration is the primary purpose for discipline, there are several other reasons why discipline is an important expression of Christ's life in His Church. Disciplinary action conveys to the church the attitude that sin is not to be taken lightly and is a reminder that the follower of Christ must be careful to maintain a life of spiritual purity. Discipline is also a means by which the church can preserve a pure presentation of Christ to those who are watching from without. Finally, discipline is a means of maintaining effective ministry through the preservation of order and harmony.

SECTION 3.   RESPONSIBILITY

The responsibility for all disciplinary actions shall rest with the Board of Elders. At its discretion, the Board of Elders may select representatives to handle such actions.

SECTION 4.   PROCEDURE
  A. Any official disciplinary action shall take place only after personal, private attempts to resolve the problem.
  B. Any cause for discipline shall be presented, in writing, to either the Senior Pastor or the Chairman of the Board of Elders.
  C. The Board of Elders or its representatives shall examine the grievance to determine its accuracy. If there is no verification of the grievance, it shall be dismissed, and written notice given to the person bringing the grievance.
  D. If there is verification of the grievance, the Board of Elders or its representatives shall meet with the accused and encourage him/her to repent.
  E. If the erring member refuses to repent, the findings shall be presented to the Board of Elders, which may then call a special church business meeting to revoke that person's membership. Upon a two-thirds favorable vote of those members present and voting at the meeting, membership will be revoked.

Such a vote shall be taken by secret ballot. If the accused member is not present at the meeting, a written record of the proceedings shall be mailed to him/her.

SECTION 5. RESTORATION

A. If the accused member repents at any time prior to the deprivation of his/her membership, an immediate plan for the restoration of that member shall be implemented under the guidance of the Senior Pastor and Board of Elders.

B. Any member who has been excluded from membership for disciplinary reasons may be restored only upon the recommendation of the Board of Elders and a two-thirds favorable vote of the members present and voting at a regularly scheduled or specially called business meeting of the church. It is the duty of the church to forgive and fully accept members who are thus restored.

ARTICLE VII — BOARD OF ELDERS

SECTION 1. COMPOSITION

The government of the church shall be vested in a Board of Elders. The Board of Elders shall consist of at least seven (7) members. The Board of Elders shall consist of the Elder elected to serve as Chairman of the Board, the Senior Pastor and at least five (5) other persons elected to the office of Elder. Any increase or decrease in the number of Elder positions shall be submitted to the congregation for approval at a regularly called business meeting of the church pursuant to Article XII of this Constitution (or at a special congregational meeting called for that purpose in accordance with the provisions of this Constitution). Elders shall serve for a term of one year, beginning on July 1 of each year and continuing through June 30 of the year following, or until their successor has been duly elected. The maximum number of successive one-year terms for each Elder, other than the Senior Pastor, shall be four (4), after which they shall be ineligible to serve as an Elder for a period of one year. The Senior Pastor shall continue as a member of the Board of Elders during his service as Senior Pastor.

SECTION 2. ELECTION

Elections for the office of Elder shall be conducted annually at a regularly called business meeting of the church pursuant to Article XII of this Constitution (or at a special congregational meeting called for that purpose in accordance with the provisions of this Constitution). Any vacancy occurring on the Board of Elders during the church's ministry year shall be filled following the same procedure. Nominees for the office of elder shall be submitted to the congregation for vote individually, by written ballot.

SECTION 3. QUALIFICATION
- A. All Elders must be regular members of the church in good standing and must show evidence of established Christian character (Article V, Section 4). They shall be godly men of mature Christian experience and knowledge who exemplify the standards of this office as detailed in 1 Tim. 3:1-7.

B. Before nomination each candidate for the office of Elder shall assent, as attested to by signature, to the following statements:

1. I have publicly confessed Christ as my personal Savior and have experienced the new birth as set forth in John 3: 3-6.
2. I reaffirm my agreement with this Constitution.
3. My life is consistent with the expectations for office outlined in Acts 6:3 and 1 Timothy 3.
4. I agree to serve in the capacity of Elder, if elected, for the term for which I am elected

SECTION 4. DUTIES

A. The Board of Elders shall monitor the overall spiritual life and ministry of the church. They shall also be responsible, in conjunction with the Senior Pastor and pastoral staff, for establishing personnel and other policies, for conducting evaluations of the Senior Pastor and for reviewing staff reviews conducted by the Senior Pastor or his designee. Members of the Board of Elders shall also be responsible for interviewing candidates for membership and recommending to the church those candidates found to meet the requirements established by this Constitution. The Board of Elders shall have responsibility for overseeing the spiritual life and pastoral care of the members of the church, including the handling disciplinary actions in accordance with Article VI.
B. The Board of Elders shall have oversight over all church operations and transactions with power to act. It shall not encumber the church with any

transfer, sale, purchase or loan of any real estate, except by authorization conveyed through a majority vote of the church membership present at a constitutionally called business meeting. The Board of Elders shall have authority to approve the appointment of all salaried personnel except as otherwise stated in this Constitution. The Board of Elders shall handle and consider suggestions, recommendations and grievances from or against any member or group affiliated with the church. The actions of the Board of Elders shall be subject to review by the membership at any constitutionally called business meeting.

C. The Board of Elders shall also appoint a Nominating Committee, which shall recommend to the church for election one or more qualified persons: (i) to fill each position on the Board of Elders which is or will be vacant, , and (ii) to serve on the Pulpit Committee as set forth in Article XI, in accordance with this Constitution. Nominees for the Nominating Committee and any such position shall be regular members of the church, in good standing at the time of their nomination and election.

ARTICLE VIII   STAFF

SECTION 1.   SENIOR PASTOR

A. Selection - To be called as Senior Pastor, a candidate must be presented to the membership by the Pulpit Committee (Article XI) and must receive three-fourths of the written ballots cast in person or by absentee ballot at a constitutionally called business meeting of the church. Public notice of this meeting and its purpose shall have been made on two successive Sundays prior to the meeting. The Senior Pastor shall serve for an indefinite term or for such a term as the church may decide.

B. Qualifications - The Senior Pastor shall be an ordained minister of good reputation, conservative in theology and willing to serve a nondenominational church without attempting to promote any denominational interest. He shall assent, by signature, to this Constitution.

C. Duties
   1. The Senior Pastor shall have general spiritual oversight of the entire program of the church and shall perform all duties necessary to such leadership.
   2. The Senior Pastor, or his designee, shall have charge of all staff and shall assign to them such specific duties and responsibilities as deemed necessary and appropriate from time to time.

D. Termination - If the Senior Pastor desires to resign, or if a three-fourths vote by secret ballot of the regular membership present and voting desires the termination of his ministry, a written notice must be given by either party thirty days in advance of the terminating date, unless waived by mutual consent.

Section 2.   Staff
   A. Selection - Staff shall be appointed by the Senior Pastor or his designee with prior approval of the Board of Elders and as provided for in the annual budget.
   B. Duties - The duties and responsibilities of staff members shall be assigned by the Senior Pastor or his designee from time to time as deemed necessary and appropriate.

Article IX   - Corporate Officers
Section 1. Officers - The officers of the Glen Ellyn Bible Church, as recognized by the State of Illinois, shall be the Chairman of the Board of Elders (who shall function as the President of the Corporation), Secretary, and Treasurer. Officers shall serve for a term of one year beginning on July 1 of each year and continuing through June 30, or for such other term as stated in this Article IX., or until their successor has been duly elected or appointed. Unless otherwise stated in this Constitution, the maximum number of successive one-year terms for any person to fill any office, shall be four (4), after which they shall be ineligible to serve as an officer in that office for a period of one year.

Section 2   President
   A. Election - The Elder elected to serve as Chairman of the Board of Elders shall, by virtue of this office, serve as the President of the Corporation. Elections for the office of Chairman of the Board of Elders shall be conducted each year at a regularly called business meeting of the church pursuant to Article XII of this Constitution (or at a special

congregational meeting called for that purpose in accordance with the provisions of this Constitution).

B. Duties - The Chairman (as president of the Corporation) shall preside at Board of Elders meetings and shall have authority to call special Board of Elders meetings, appoint <u>ad hoc</u> committees and conduct other business as the church directs. The Chairman or, in his absence, another member of the Board of Elders designated by the Chairman, shall also act as the moderator of all church business meetings.

SECTION 3 SECRETARY

A. Election - The Board of Elders shall appoint an elder to the position of Secretary at their first meeting following the annual election of Elders.

B. Duties - The Secretary shall, either directly or through his designee, keep an accurate record of the proceedings and decisions of all Board of Elders and church business meetings and shall perform any other necessary duties as the Board of Elders directs.

SECTION 4 TREASURER

A. Appointment - The Treasurer shall be appointed from time to time by the Elders with such oversight by the Elders as is deemed by them to be reasonable and appropriate. The Treasurer may be an Elder or other member of the congregation, or a staff member hired in accordance with the provisions of this Constitution. In the event that a staff member is designated as the Treasurer, their term as Treasurer shall continue for such time as they remain a member of the staff and no term limit pursuant to Section 1 of this Article IX shall apply.

B. Duties - The Treasurer shall be responsible for reporting monies donated to the church and reporting disbursements in accordance with the annual budget and the special decisions of the church. The Treasurer shall provide such information to the Elders as is deemed necessary, reasonable, and appropriate by the Elders from time to time. The book of accounts shall be closed at the end of each calendar year, and a detailed report of all receipts and disbursements shall be presented.

ARTICLE X   FINANCIAL REVIEW COMMITTEE

SECTION 1.

A. Appointment - The Board of Elders shall appoint annually, from the membership of the church, a Financial Review Committee of at least three members. The Committee shall consist of persons who have not been members of the Elder Board or members of the staff (a) during the period to be reviewed and (b) who are not currently serving on the Board of Elders or staff.

B. Duties - The Financial Review Committee shall, at the direction of the Board of Elders, either perform an annual review of the church books and financial records for the church fiscal year preceding its appointment, or shall, in the event deemed by the Committee to be reasonably necessary and appropriate, engage an outside auditor to perform an audit. This audit or review shall be made after the end of the church fiscal year or at such other times as are deemed necessary and appropriate by the Board of Elders. Any audits shall be conducted in accordance with generally accepted auditing standards. An auditors' written opinion or, in the case of a review, a written discussion of procedure and findings, shall be submitted to the Board of Elders and made available to the congregation within six months or by a mutually agreed upon date after the close of the period being audited.

ARTICLE XI — PULPIT COMMITTEE

SECTION 1. COMPOSITION - A Pulpit Committee shall be formed when there is a vacancy in the office of Senior Pastor. This committee shall consist of a chairman and six members.

SECTION 2. ELECTION - The Chairman and members of the Pulpit Committee shall be elected by the membership from candidates properly nominated by the Nominating Committee (pursuant to Article VII, Section 4(C) of this Constitution, at a constitutionally called church business meeting. Any vacancy occurring while the Committee is in place shall be filled following the same procedure.

SECTION 3. QUALIFICATIONS - The Chairman and members of the Pulpit Committee shall be regular members of the church in good standing.

SECTION 4. DUTIES - The Pulpit Committee shall seek out and investigate qualified individuals who could be considered as candidates for the position of Senior Pastor. Upon selection of a candidate and the consent of the Board of Elders, the committee shall present the individual at a constitutionally called church business meeting. Only one candidate shall be presented at a time.

Section 5. Termination - The Pulpit Committee's duties end upon the acceptance of a call by a candidate or, prior to the call of a candidate, by two-thirds vote of members at a constitutionally called church business meeting.

ARTICLE XII   MEETINGS

SECTION 1. ANNUAL MEETING AND SPECIAL MEETINGS - The annual church business meeting shall generally be held in November. A church business meeting shall also generally be held in May of each year for the purpose of electing the Chairman of the Board of Elders and Elders pursuant to Articles VII and IX. Special business meetings may be called by the Board of Elders or when twenty (20) percent of the regular members make a written request to the Board of Elders for such a meeting. Public notice of every such meeting and its purpose shall be given on two successive Sundays prior to the date of the meeting.

SECTION 2. PROCEDURE - The Chairman of the Board of Elders (or, in his absence, another member of the Board of Elders designated by the Chairman) shall preside at all business meetings.

SECTION 3. VOTING - The right to vote at a Meeting is restricted to those regular members of the church who are sixteen (16) years of age or older, and in attendance at such meeting or pursuant to absentee balloting procedures established by the Elders from time to time. In connection with the elections, nominations for candidates shall be presented by the Elders, and there shall be no nominations accepted from the floor at such meeting.

SECTION 4. QUORUM - Twenty-five percent of the regular members constitute a quorum. All resolutions, except as otherwise provided in this Constitution, are valid if a majority of the members present and voting, are in favor.

ARTICLE XIII   ORDINATION

SECTION 1. COMPOSITION - It shall be within the power of the Board of Elders to call and conduct an ordination council.

SECTION 2. DUTIES - The ordination council shall thoroughly examine the applicant's call to the Christian ministry, education, Christian experience, reputation, character, doctrinal belief and demonstrated effectiveness in Christian service.

SECTION 3. REVOCATION - It shall be within the province of the Board of Elders to discipline, even to the extent of revoking the ordination credentials, any minister ordained under this Constitution, if said minister fails to adhere to those doctrines outlined in the Statement of Faith (Article II) or is living a life inconsistent with clearly defined biblical standards. Such disciplinary action shall be taken only after an impartial hearing conducted in the spirit of 1Corinthians 13. The minister shall have the privilege of appealing his case to the congregation within sixty days after the decision of the Board of Elders.

Article XIV   Property

Section 1. The title to all real property of the corporation shall be in the name of the corporation, and no member or group of members shall have any individual property rights in the assets of the corporation.

Section 2. In the event that this corporation is dissolved, the properties shall be sold, and all proceeds and residual monies, above liabilities, shall be divided among those mission organizations which the church has supported, including those organizations represented by individuals supported by the missions budget for at least five consecutive years during the ten-year period immediately prior to the date of dissolution. This division shall be proportioned on the basis of the relative support levels among those eligible mission organizations as averaged over the aforementioned ten-year period. Those mission organizations which no longer exist as legally recognized nonprofit organizations at the time of dissolution shall be considered ineligible to receive any of these funds, even though they may have received support from the church in the past.

Section 3. By incorporation, the church has legal standing before the courts of the State.

Article XV   Limitations of Corporate Authority
  A. The Church, being organized exclusively for religious purposes, may make distributions to organizations that qualify as exempt organizations under Section 501(c)(3) of the Code. No part of the net earnings of Church shall inure to the benefit of, or be distributable to its members, directors, officers, or other private persons, except that the Church shall be authorized and empowered to pay reasonable compensation for services rendered and to make payments and distributions in furtherance of the purposes set forth in Article 4 above.

ARTICLE XVI   AMENDMENTS
This Constitution may be amended at any business meeting of the church, properly called for that purpose, provided that he proposed amendment(s) be made available in writing to the members at least two weeks prior to such meeting, and if two-thirds of the voting members are in favor of such amendment(s).

FOLLOWING JESUS
Defining Discipleship in the 21ˢᵗ Century

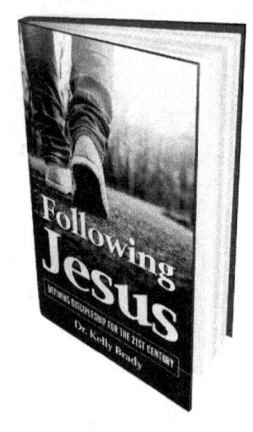

Whether you are a non-Christian, wanting to understand Christianity better, or a Christian wanting to succinct definition of discipleship, *Following Jesus* is for you.

In that first-century world disciples were those who detached themselves from their own way of life and reattached themselves to a *rabbi* (teacher), committing themselves to his service and to becoming like him in every way.

When following a rabbi, first-century disciples would pay attention to every word he spoke and every move he made, sometimes even trying to mimic his mannerisms. So complete was a disciple's commitment to the rabbi that it became the defining element of their character, and the nature of what it means to be a disciple has not changed in over 2000 years.

Following Jesus is aimed at defining discipleship in order to help those following after Jesus better understand his call upon their lives.

WAIT...WHAT?
Biblical Teachings Worth Repeating

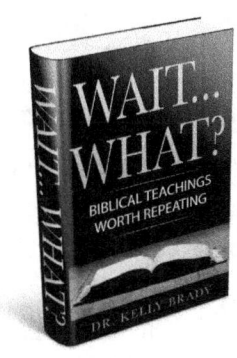

Jesus described himself as the Good Shepherd and those who follow after him as his sheep (John 10:11). Being compared to sheep is not flattering, as there are stories of sheep walking into an open fire. There are also stories of sheep stuck on their back and unable to right themselves. It's called being "cast." The short of it is that sheep can be too weak to care for themselves and too stubborn to change course, a deadly combination. Yet, I must be honest. I certainly find within myself a lot of sheep-like tendencies.

Jesus is the Good Shepherd, but he also gifts some to help him in his work (Ephesians 4:11-12). That's my passion. I love helping other sheep follow the Good Shepherd. Toward that end, this book is a collection of sermon excerpts from the last couple decades. The title, "Wait...What?" came from my teenage children, who daily remind me of the value of repeating important messages. The chapters are short, which can be read in under 12 minutes.

DRIVE THRU THEOLOGY
A guide to the Bible's teaching for those on the go

People have lots of questions about what the Bible teaches. Offering concise theological statements on a broad range of topics, this book is meant to be a quick reference guide. Sprinkled throughout are also short answers to commonly asked questions about Christian faith. Questions like: "How much faith is needed to receive healing?" and "Why might our prayers go unanswered?"

As a pastor, I am reminded daily that shepherds do not grow the grass. Shepherds simply point to where they can find the grass. This means anytime we are caring for others spiritually, our job is to simply point to the truth found in Scripture. Our job is not to try and create food, but rather direct them to the nourishment of Scripture. Ultimately, it is only the truth of God's Word that sustains God's people.

It is tempting to offer our own wisdom when guiding others spiritually, or the popular psychology of the day. But the greatest need we have is to hear the truth of God's Word, because it is the Scripture that is "God-breathed" (2 Timothy 3:16).

RESTORE
Experiencing The Power of a Healing Fellowship

The Apostle Paul wrote of those entangled in sin that "You who live by the Spirit should **RESTORE** that person gently (Galatians 6:1). The Greek word translated as "restore" has in mind the work of repairing what has been damaged. Sin damages us. It leaves us in need of repair, and by God's design, we are to play an active role in restoring one another.

RESTORE is a gathering for those who want to heal from their wounds caused by sin, whether their own sin or someone else's sin, as well as gain freedom from the sinful behaviors those wounds have fueled in their life. RESTORE is a gathering for those who want to talk about experiences that cause feelings of shame, anger, fear, and anxiety. RESTORE is a time and place to share our stories of trauma, temptations, and unwanted sinful behaviors, as well as our hope for increased freedom and joy in life. RESTORE is a gathering for those who want to act courageously by sharing with and listening to one another, and by persevering in prayer for God's healing.

www.ingramcontent.com/pod-product-compliance
Lightning Source LLC
Chambersburg PA
CBHW070818250426
43672CB00031B/2765